THE VICTORIAN SOLDIER

STUDIES IN THE HISTORY OF THE BRITISH ARMY

1816-1914

NATIONAL ARMY MUSEUM
CHELSEA

THE VICTORIAN SOLDIER

STUDIES IN THE HISTORY OF THE BRITISH ARMY

1816-1914

Edited by Marion Harding

First published 1993
Copyright © National Army Museum, London 1993

ISBN 0-901721-28-X

Designed by Amy Bridgman

Photography by Ian Jones and Nigel Armstrong

Cover Picture:
The Battle of Isandhlwana by Charles Edwin Fripp (detail)
NAM. 6011-83

Printed in Great Britain by Sterling Press Limited

CONTENTS

FOREWORD

T he opening of the Permanent Gallery 'The Victorian Soldier' on 25 November 1993 by General Sir Peter Inge GCB ADC Gen, Chief of the General Staff, is an important milestone in the history of the National Army Museum. Third in a sequence of Permanent Gallery Refurbishments which began with 'The Road to Waterloo' in 1990, to be followed, in 1992, by 'The Forgotten War: The British Army in the Far East, 1941-1945', it marks a return to the very heartland of the Museum's Collections and to an historical period when, in the opinion of many, the British and Indian Armies attained their zenith.

Visitors to the Museum today who can still recall the earliest period of its existence in the Old Riding School at the Royal Military Academy, Sandhurst or, more recently, the 'Story of the Army' Gallery in what was for a time known as 'the New Military Museum in Chelsea', will find many old favourites restored to public view and, in addition, a multitude of objects never previously seen, assembled and re-interpreted from the Museum's Study Collections, as well as a veritable cascade of acquisitions - by gift, bequest or purchase for the Nation - from recent years. Appropriately, in offering the present volume to the public to accompany the new Gallery, the Museum has taken the opportunity to restore to general circulation many of the most interesting contributions made over the years by staff and guest authors to our published *Annual Reports* and their successor publication *Army Museum*, all of them revised and comprehensively re-illustrated, nearly all for the first time in colour, together with articles written by the latest generation of Museum staff.

Biographical details of the authors may be found towards the end of this volume: all of them have, at some time or another, worked at the National Army Museum as staff members or volunteers, or have contributed to the work of the Museum in other ways. It is a particular pleasure for me to acknowledge the assistance of Mr William Reid CBE, Director of the National Army Museum from 1970 to 1987 and author of two articles in this collection; also Mr Aubrey Bowden of Messrs Christies, Mr David Harding, Regimental Archivist of the 10th Princess Mary's Gurkha Rifles and authority on the armaments of the East India Company, Mr John Harding of the Ministry of Defence, Ms Jane Insley of the Science Museum and Mr Stephen Wood, Keeper of the Scottish United Services Museum. On behalf of these guest contributors, I also acknowledge the help and advice provided to them at various times by Dr D J Gerhard, Mr Michael Hibberd, Lieutenant-Colonel Charles Holland, Mr Mark Jones, Dr Sue MacLaughlin-Black, Dr Anita McConnell, Ms Helen McCorry, Professor Jack Pike and Major Sedley Sweeny. (Miss Elizabeth Talbot Rice and Dr Alan Guy were the editors of the first versions of these papers as published by the National Army Museum between 1975 and 1987).

The term 'The Victorian Soldier', with its echoes of Kipling's 'Soldiers Three', the doomed riders in the Charge of the Light Brigade or the red-coated defenders of Rorke's Drift immortalized on screen in the influential film 'Zulu', has been used by us to span the entire period from the aftermath of the Battle of Waterloo to the outbreak of the Great War in 1914, a century during which the legacy of Wellington and his Peninsular Generals - many of them young men in 1816 with years of service on the Imperial frontiers ahead of them - finally passed to Wolseley, Roberts, Kitchener, French and Haig. This was an heroic age which has been visited often by the National Army Museum, notably in the Special Exhibitions and accompanying publications *Lady Butler, Battle Artist* (1987), *Butterflies and Bayonets: The Soldier as Collector* (1989), *Artist on the March: Paintings of India, Abyssinia and Kashmir by Colonel Cornelius Francis James, 1838-1889* (1989), *Tommy Atkins' Letters: The History of the British Army Postal Service from 1795* (1990) and *Portraits for a King: The British Military Paintings of A J Dubois Drahonet (1791-1834)* (1990). Students of the Indian Army, who may lament the relative absence of Indian material from this volume, can also look forward to 1997, when the fiftieth anniversary of the end of the British Raj will be commemorated by a Special Exhibition and publication devoted to the history of Britain's military involvement in the sub-Continent, while the approaching millenium will see an Exhibition and publication commemorating the South African War (or 'Anglo-Boer War') of 1899-1902, for which the National Army Museum is one of the most important research centres in the World. Meanwhile, readers looking for a general overview of the period 1816-1914 may consult the National Army Museum publication, *The Armies of Britain* (1980) by Michael Barthorp, which provides a worthy accompaniment to many of the more specialist topics addressed in the present volume.

As with the Permanent Gallery itself, so this publication demands that credit be given to the production team, notably the editor, Mrs Marion Harding of the Department of Archives, Photographs, Film and Sound; the designer, Miss Amy Bridgman, Head of the Department of Design; Mr Ian Jones, Head of the Department of Photography and all the contributors not already mentioned. The index was prepared by Dr Linda Washington, Head of the Department of Printed Books. Editorial assistance was provided by Dr Alan Guy, Assistant Director (Collections) and the manuscript was typed by Miss June Hicks, Miss Kate Plowman and Mrs Liz Carpenter.

Ian G Robertson
Director

National Army Museum
November 1993

plate 1   **Major-General Sir James Kempt**

Oil on canvas, artist unknown, c1824

NAM. 5911-278

SOLDIERS, DECORATIONS AND THE DICTATES OF FASHION

STEPHEN WOOD

Much of the documentary evidence affecting decorations comes from diaries or memoirs; that from the pens of civilians like Horace Walpole tends to be technically inaccurate but amusing, whereas the thoughts of soldiers such as Lord George Paget vary from the blasé to the acerbic. Information from the last half of the nineteenth century is more reliable, but proportionately less diverting, as the unwritten rules of fashion gradually submit,

with the increase of professionalism in the Army, to the written ones of *Queen's* and *Dress Regulations*. Much of the evidence for documenting the changes in style of wearing decorations is illustrative, at first from paintings and later from posed photographs. However, since portraits, cabinet photographs and *cartes de visite* were usually produced as records of the social position of the subjects it should naturally follow that the dress in which the subjects are portrayed need not always reflect the dress which they habitually wore. Dr Mark Girouard has implied[1] that because the Duke of Newcastle was portrayed by Francis Wheatley in country clothes and Garter star he always wore the star when shooting at Clumber and, by extension, when involved in other country pursuits. What is more likely is that the 'props' of country clothes and Garter star were adopted for the portrait because the Duke wished posterity to realise that he had been a country landowner and a Knight Companion of the Order of the Garter and thus influential in the country and at court, invaluable assets for the eighteenth-century politician.

plate 2   **Lieutenant-General Sir Joseph Thackwell**
Oil on canvas, artist unknown, c1840
NAM. 5604-40

plate 3   *Colour-Sergeant John Paul, Royal Sappers and Miners, 1856.*

Photograph from 'Crimean Heroes' by J Cundall and R Howlett
NAM. neg no 23539

Before the beginning of the nineteenth century such problems as were presented by the wearing of decorations were fewer simply because the number available for award were fewer. During the preceding two centuries British Orders had increased from one, the Garter, to four by the institution or revival of the Orders of the Thistle (1687), of St Patrick (1783) and of the Bath (1725). By 1700 the conflict about the correct wear of the riband with badge appendant seems to have been resolved, and it was worn across the shoulder and under the arm rather than round the neck, which had been common practice during the previous century. A general award of campaign medals was unknown before their institution by the East India Company in 1784 and these and any other medals awarded seem to have been intended for wear round the neck, assuming that they were supposed to be worn at all. The insignia of Orders tended to be worn singly, rather than in clusters, since few, with the notable exception of Royal Princes, were knights of more than one Order at a time, the practice being to resign from a lesser Order upon promotion to a greater, rather as one might progress from club to club. Since the robes and collar of an Order could only be worn on specified occasions, the riband, badge and star became essential everyday wear, at least in London, and James Risk identifies two instances which indicate that this was the case.[2] Stars seem, generally, to have been of the embroidered type which were sewn on the outer garment and replaced as they wore out. Ribands were worn either inside or outside the coat, the distinction perhaps depending upon the quality of the badge pendant from the riband. With the scarcity of decorations the taste of the eighteenth-century gentleman seems to have been reflected in the quality of the insignia worn. Nabobs like Robert Clive were noted, as the Prince Regent was later to be, for the magnificence of their badges and stars, but the global conflict which drew the eighteenth century into the nineteenth was partially to redress the balance so that, for some people at least, quantity would be equated with quality.

Britain's Great War against France which began in 1793 resulted in a flood of decorations which were distributed and despised as much, and for the same reasons, as those instituted during the First World War. The extension of the Order of the Bath from one class to three in 1815 produced as many curled lips as did the lavish award of the various grades of the new Order of the British Empire after 1917; the Order which the ever-perspicacious wit of the music-hall dubbed the 'Order of Britain's Everybody'. The unprecedented quantity of decorations (many of them awarded by Britain's Allies) accumulated by senior officers during the Napoleonic Wars presented problems of a practical and sartorial nature, some of which are illustrated in plates 1 and 2. As 'the Maecenas of the Age ... an Adonis in loveliness',[3] George, the Prince Regent was expected to lead the way in style of dress, but his posturing in military uniform, however elegant it might be, was unlikely to convince anyone who had been at the sharp end of the war in the Peninsula or at Waterloo. The Prince Regent's interest and taste in military dress were undoubtedly affected by his contact with his peers on the continent of Europe and toward the end of the War much exchanging of decorations had taken place between the Allies as grateful monarchs rewarded eminent foreign soldiers and each other.

The Prince Regent may have been among the first in this country to wear the insignia of his Orders in miniature, as shown in the distinctive copy at Knole, Kent, of Sir Thomas Lawrence's original 1815 portrait of the Prince

plate 4   *Colonel William Drysdale CB, 9th (Queen's Royal) Lancers c1864.*

Carte-de-visite *photograph*

NAM. neg no 45969

Regent in the uniform of a Field Marshal. As well as the embroidered stars of the Orders of the Garter, the Holy Ghost of France, the Black Eagle of Prussia and Christ of Portugal he wears a bar of miniatures, hanging vertically beneath his badge of the Golden Fleece. In addition to the miniature ribands of the Orders already mentioned, the bar carries the Orders of the Bath, Maria Theresa of Austria and St George of Russia and tiny stars of each of the Orders fixed on a gold bar above the appropriate ribands. As an exercise in restraint, elegance and discretion, it is admirable and rather in contrast to that displayed by Sir James Kempt (plate 1) who, in order to demonstrate the full extent of his decorations, commits the sin of wearing his Grand Cross badge of the Royal Hanoverian Guelphic Order as a neck decoration beside the lesser grade badges of the Orders of Maria Theresa of Austria and William of the Netherlands. The true reason for this lapse is not clear since it was quite common practice, as shown in Sir Thomas Lawrence's portrait of the Duke of Wellington in the Waterloo

Gallery at Windsor Castle, to wear the ribands of two Orders at the same time. Wellington is depicted wearing the ribands of the Orders of the Garter and Maria Theresa 'bandolier' fashion, crossed over his chest. The officer depicted in plate 2 represents a fashion that was to be current from the late 1820s until well after the Crimean War - that is a cluster of decorations arranged in a tight overlapping group. Plates 3 and 4 show that this practice was continued into the era of portrait photography but it is known that many elderly and senior soldiers, notably Hugh, first Viscount Gough, continued until the 1860s to wear their decorations 'necklace' fashion, strung from one side of their collars to the other, a style that was anachronistic by 1840.

Aside from sartorial problems the practical difficulties produced by the deluge of decorations involved methods, rather than styles, of wear. Although the statutes governing the four British Orders were specific about the way in which the insignia were to be worn, little consideration was given to the actual attachment or supply of the everyday pieces, probably because this was felt to be a matter for discussion between the knight and his tailor or jeweller. Before 1856 no metal stars were given to British knights at their investiture, embroidered or 'tinsel' stars being given instead. Replacements for these embroidered stars were sold by most tailors and lacemakers, but the practice gradually arose after the beginning of the nineteenth century of having metal stars privately made. The advantage of the metal stars, apart from the improved aesthetic effect of faceted silver or twinkling precious stones, was one of pure practicality; they lasted longer and could be easily unpinned and re-pinned as one changed clothes. Privately made stars decreased in number after the introduction of metal investment stars but have continued to be made, especially for members of the Royal Family, as being more comfortable for wear on evening clothes.

plate 5   Medal 'pockets' in the tunic of a
captain, Cavan Militia, c1855
NAM. 5305-100

The institution of the Navy Gold Medals in 1794 gave rise to the same sort of problem but at a marginally less exalted level. These were ordered to be worn, depending upon the rank of the recipient, either round the neck or at the buttonhole of the coatee. Generally speaking this seems to have caused few problems for those sailors distinguished enough to receive the Gold Medals; these really only arose when the same style was ordered to be adopted by recipients of the Army Gold Medals after their institution in 1810. The Duke of Wellington sourly observed that a medal worn on a long ribbon round the neck of an admiral would cause him little discomfort on the quarterdeck but give considerable annoyance when riding and requested that the authorities at Horse Guards might see fit to alter the regulations so that his officers and their medals might not cause each other serious damage. As a result it was

plate 6   Nineteenth and early twentieth century miniature decorations with a full-size
medal to indicate scale

Left to right, top row: Field Marshal Lord Combermere *(1773-1865), NAM. 9205-12;*
Major-General T S St Clair, *late 5th Caçadores, Portuguese Army, c1840, NAM. 6907-30-10*
Middle row: Full-size Military General Service Medal 1793-1814 *to Lieutenant J D'Arcy, 88th (Connaught*
Rangers), NAM. 6405-66; **General Sir Arthur M Becher,** *Indian Army Staff c1873, NAM. 5409-16-2*
Bottom row: *Unidentified* **Ghuznee and Cabul Medal** *1842 and* **Sutlej Campaign Medal** *1845-46,*
NAM. 6411-52-3; **Field Marshal Lord Roberts** *(1832-1914), NAM. 6310-73-26*

decided that officers could wear just the ribbon at the buttonhole in undress, an instruction which gradually led to a style of wearing decorations that persists today. 'At the buttonhole' really meant that the medal ribbon should be passed through the buttonhole in the lapel and fastened to a button underneath; Sir James Kempt wears his Waterloo Medal in this fashion in plate 1. Although some medals are still found with buttonholes sewn into their ribbons, most seem to have had buckles attached after 1815 as a result of two factors, firstly the alteration in style of the coatee which removed open lapels and, secondly the adoption of a buckle as part of the decoration on the ribands of the Companion's badge of the Order of the Bath. Buckles remained an essential part of medal ribbons until at least 1875 when mention of them in this connection in *Queen's Regulations* ceases, but they remained an integral part of Companions' badges until 1917.

Few people familiar with military photographic portraiture of the third quarter of the nineteenth century will have failed to realise that considerable leeway seems to have been exercised in matters of appearance; for example, unpressed trousers, badly fitting tunics, scuffed shoes and an abundance of badly-trimmed hair were common among the officers. The same casual approach seems to have applied to medals; groups of officers are photographed, some with ribbons, some with miniatures and some with full-size medals on a variety of tunics and jackets. Little positive guidance appears to have been given from above and so it is probable that most soldiers knew what not to wear but not necessarily how not to wear it. The medal 'pockets' shown in plate 5 are often encountered in coatees during the period 1845-1855 and in tunics from 1855 until 1880 and seem, by their deliberately functional and yet also ornate nature, perfectly to encapsulate the attitudes of the time.

Miniature decorations have been mentioned thus far only *en passant* since theirs is a sub-culture that is difficult to categorise and define. Plate 6 shows a few of the National Army Museum's many examples of miniature decorations, from those manufactured with exquisite care and perfection in the early nineteenth century to the miniaturised miniatures rather crudely made for Lord Roberts VC at the end of his long career. Miniatures have always been essentially private items. The early ones were more in the nature of pieces of personal jewellery intended for wear in plain clothes or at other times when the full-size items would be out of place. Although later and modern ones were, and are, carefully governed by regulations their provision is still the responsibility of the individual.

A brief study such as this can, by reason of its wide-ranging nature, touch only a few of the facets of the subject and it will have left many questions unanswered, many myths unexploded. Individuals have worn decorations since before the first laurel wreath touched a Roman brow and it is quite probable that there have always been pedants ready to criticise, analyse and misinterpret. Since, fortunately, all soldiers are subject to human frailties, it is no more than natural that the manner in which they wear their decorations, ill-gotten or hard-earned, should reflect their sartorial attitudes and the dictates of fashion.

THE HIGHER COMMAND
OF THE INDIAN ARMY,
1816-1914

PETER BOYDEN

In 1911 Messrs Adam and Charles Black published in London a volume entitled *The Armies of India*. It contained reproductions of 72 watercolours by Major A C Lovett, described by Major G F MacMunn, and a foreword by Field Marshal Lord Roberts. Many of the regiments of the Indian Army were illustrated in the plates; men wearing brightly-coloured clothing and headdresses, derived from a mixture of British military uniform and indigenous Indian costume. The romance of the Indian Army, comprised of men born and bred thousands of miles away, loyal to the King Emperor, commanded by a small number of British officers, was a powerful one in Britain in the years that preceded the First World War.

The uniforms of the Indian Army during this period have been the subject of many books and articles, but the organisation that lay behind the men and the clothes that they wore has received less attention from historians. This paper seeks to redress the balance by beginning to explore the position of the Army in the overall administration of India, the evolution of the constitutional relationship between the Viceroys and the Commanders-in-Chief and the changes in the higher command that occurred between 1816 and 1914.

THE POSITION OF THE ARMY IN THE ADMINISTRATION OF INDIA

The origins of what was to become Britain's Indian Empire lay in the Royal Charter granted in 1600 by Queen Elizabeth I to a group of City traders who described themselves as 'The Company of Merchants of London trading to the East Indies'. The Charter created a monopoly of British trade in the east, and the Company's representatives were able to obtain permission from the Mogul emperors to establish 'factories' in the Indian sub-Continent. These factories were protected by small groups of European and native guards, in whom lay the origins of the Company's Army. The original Company of 1600 prospered, but in 1691 a new, rival, East India Company was granted a Charter, which was extended in 1698. Inevitably, the existence of the two rival Companies led to conflict, but this was short-lived as in 1709 the two Companies merged to form the 'United Company of Merchants of England trading in the East Indies'. One of the first actions of the new Company was to divide its possessions and areas of operations into three distinct 'Presidencies', each under the control of a President, who also commanded the military forces within it. The Presidents were equal to

Francis Rawdon, first Marquess Hastings and second Earl of Moira *(1754-1826)*

Oil on canvas, by Sir Martin Archer Shee (1769-1850)

After a distinguished military career stretching back to the Battle of Bunker Hill in 1775, General Francis Rawdon Hastings, second Earl of Moira, was appointed Governor-General of Bengal and Commander-in-Chief in India in 1813. He was created Marquess Hastings after the successful conclusion of the war against Nepal 1814-16.

This portrait, which shows him in general officer's uniform, pre-dates his Indian appointments.

and independent of each other, being responsible only to the Company's Directors at home.

During the 1740s and 50s the military forces of the Company were re-organized along European lines, a process aided by the appointment in 1748 of Major (later Major-General) Stringer Lawrence (1699-1775) as commander of the troops in all three Presidencies, with his headquarters at Fort St David in the Madras Presidency. The next two decades saw, as a result of the defeat of the French, considerable areas of India brought under the control of the Company, and the amassing of substantial sums of money by Robert Clive (Baron Clive, 1725-74), and other Company employees during the course of a few years' service in the sub-Continent. This produced complaints from owners of East India Company stock (who demanded, and got, increased dividends), and also aroused the interest of Parliament, which from the 1760s played a steadily increasing role in the affairs of the Honourable East India Company and its activities in India. This first manifested itself in legislative form in the 1773 Regulating Act, which created a Government for the expanded Presidency of Bengal, headed by a Council comprising a Governor-General and four Councillors appointed by the Crown in consultation with the East India Company Directors. The Governor-General was also responsible for the foreign affairs of the Presidencies of Madras and Bombay, thereby beginning their subordination to Bengal.

The British Government's control of the Company's operations was strengthened by the East India Act of 1784, which although it left untouched the Company's trading enterprises, reduced its political activities by the establishment in London of a Board of Control, which acted in practice as a Government department, chaired by a President, the first of whom was Lord Sydney (1733-1800). Royal approval was required for the appointment of the Governor-General, the Governors of the other Presidencies, and Members of Council, although the Commander-in-Chief of all the troops in India was appointed exclusively by the Crown. Although the Company's Charter was periodically renewed, its trading monopoly became unenforceable and was abolished in 1822. The Company's role in the government of India was ended by the India Act of 1858, by which the Court of Directors and Board of Control were

James Andrew Broun Ramsay, tenth Earl and first Marquess Dalhousie *(1812-60)*

Although his father had been Commander-in-Chief in India (1830-32), Dalhousie, Governor-General of India 1848-56, did not make life easy for the three Commanders-in-Chief who served under him.

NAM. neg no 12834

Sir Hugh Gough, first Viscount Gough *(1779-1869)*

Steel engraving by H B Hall after J R Jackson, c1850
General Sir Hugh Gough, Bt., commanded the troops in India 1843-49 under three Governors-General - Lord Ellenborough, Sir Henry Hardinge, and Lord Dalhousie, whose complaints about him, particularly concerning the high casualty rate at the Battle of Chillianwallah in 1849, led to his recall.
This portrait probably commemorates his period of command in India.

NAM. 6012-321-17

General Sir Charles James Napier *(1782-1853)*
Napier, the second of Dalhousie's Commanders-in-Chief, as depicted in one of the earliest photographs in the National Army Museum's Collections. It was taken c1850 by Surgeon John McCosh of the Bengal Medical Establishment.

NAM. neg no 6261

Field Marshal Sir William Maynard Gomm *(1784-1875)*
General Gomm was Dalhousie's third, and final, Commander-in-Chief, 1850-56. He is here shown in the dress of Colonel, Coldstream Guards, c1863.
From F C Carr-Gomm, Letters and Journals of Field Marshal Sir William Maynard Gomm GCB, *London (1881)*

NAM. neg no 54047

Field Marshal Horatio Herbert Kitchener, first Earl Kitchener of Khartoum and of Broome (1850-1916)
It was General Kitchener who, as Commander-in-Chief, India, was instrumental in the resignation of the Viceroy, Lord Curzon. The photograph, which shows him in full dress, was taken c1905.

NAM. neg no 10285

George Nathaniel Curzon; Marquess Curzon of Kedleston (1859-1925)
'A very superior person' - Marquess Curzon of Kedleston in the robes of a Knight Grand Commander of the Most Exalted Order of the Star of India. The photograph was taken in 1903 at the time of the Delhi Durbar.

NAM. neg no 504

replaced by a Secretary of State and a Council of fifteen members.

Notwithstanding the prominence given to it by some later military historians, it is clear from contemporary information that the Army did not occupy a pre-eminent place in the government of India, either before or after its transfer to the Crown. In 1816 the 'Board of Commissioners for the Affairs of India' - as the Board of Control was described in the *East India Register and Directory*, contained eleven Privy Councillors among its thirteen members, including Lord Bathurst (1762-1834), Secretary of State for War and the Colonies, while its Chairman was the Earl of Buckinghamshire (1760-1816), a former occupant of that position. In India itself, the Governor-General, the Earl of Moira, (Marquess Hastings from February 1817) also held the position of Commander-in-Chief and had three civilians as his fellow Members of Council, while in Madras and Bombay the only members of their four-man Councils with any military experience were the respective Presidency Commanders-in-Chief. Things had changed little by 1914. Only two of the fourteen members of the Secretary of State's Council held Army rank, one, Lieutenant-

Colonel Sir David Barr (1846-1916), whose career had chiefly been spent in the political service, the other, General (later Field Marshal) Sir Charles Egerton (1848-1921), who had commanded the Somaliland Field Force of 1903-04. There was only one military member of the Viceroy's Council, the Commander-in-Chief, General Sir Beauchamp Duff (1855-1918), who was in fact an 'Extraordinary Member' to his six civilian colleagues.

Not only was the Army's influence in policy-making limited, both in London and India, but Army officers, even at the highest level, were subordinate to their civilian counterparts. Historically this can be traced back to the early eighteenth century, when the Presidents commanded the troops under their jurisdiction themselves, so that the dependent nature of Commanders-in-Chief, when they were appointed, was obvious. A royal appointment gave no right to lord it over the Company's officials, as Colonel John Adlercron (d1766) had discovered when he commanded the 39th Regiment of Foot in India 1754-58[1]. In addition to his administrative work, an important element in the Commander-in-Chief's *raison d'être* was to act as adviser on military matters to the Governor-General. A Governor-General with extensive military experience of his own could hold both positions himself simultaneously, as did the Earl of Moira (already noted) and Lord William Cavendish Bentinck, who also felt able to combine the two positions, in the former case for nine years. Their ability to do this may also reflect the demands made upon a Commander-in-Chief in early nineteenth-century India.

The increasing importance that the security of the North-West Frontier of India had to the strategic military considerations of the British Government during the last third of the nineteenth century led to a brief enhancement of the position of the Commander-in-Chief, particularly during the years (1885-93) that Sir Frederick (later Field Marshal Lord) Roberts held the position. However, after Lord Kitchener vacated it in 1909, and partly as a result of his activities while occupying it, it suffered a loss of prestige that was not to be recovered until the 1920s.

COMMANDERS-IN-CHIEF AND THE GOVERNORS-GENERAL OF INDIA

The relationship between the Commander-in-Chief and the Governor-General changed considerably between 1816 and 1914, in a way which gave the military supremo a freer hand than he had enjoyed in the past. All three of the Commanders-in-Chief who held office during the 1840s resigned or were superseded - Sir Jasper Nicolls in 1843 as a result of a series of disagreements with Lord Ellenborough, whose 'somewhat despotic disposition deprived the Commander-in-Chief of the power of influencing affairs'.[2] His successor, Sir Hugh (later Lord) Gough was suspended in 1849 as a result of complaints made about him to the authorities in England by the Governor-General, Lord Dalhousie. His successor, Sir Charles Napier, resigned in 1850 as a result of a reprimand that he received from Dalhousie, to be succeeded by the more placid General (later Field Marshal) Sir William Maynard Gomm, to whom the Governor-General wrote the following letter on 29 October 1850;

> 'My Dear Sir William
> No official intimation of your appointment has reached me but the tenor of my
> private letters leaves no doubt in my mind that you will arrive at Calcutta, to

assume the Command of this army, early in November. I pray you to accept the welcome wh[ich] I offer you, and to be assured of the satisfaction with which I learnt that an old acquaintance was to be my new colleague. We shall stand together in a relation closer and more important than others of our colleagues; and I am, therefore, anxious to convey to you in the first hour of your Command the assurance of my desire, as the head of this government, to afford you full and cordial support in the position you occupy, and to enter on the transaction of public affairs with you in a spirit of frankness and confidence.

This is the more necessary for me to address you thus at the present time, because I perceive that strenuous efforts are being made by your predecessor, Sir Charles Napier, to persuade the public and the service, that he has not received from this Government the support that was due to him, and that his rights and powers have been so curtailed as to compel him to resign his high appointment.

You and I have now been acquainted for a good many years, and you have had opportunities of ascertaining what is my natural disposition, and what the nature of my conduct and bearing as a public man. I feel confident that you have never heard of me as arrogant - as exacting or inclined to grasp all power to myself - or as seeking, while I grasped all powers, to throw the responsibility on those who served under me - to refuse them countenance or to give it grudgingly.

I received Sir C Napier on his arrival in India with good will. I have given him from first to last a steady and prompt support. I have treated him with the utmost confidence: and notwithstanding the provocation I received, I have loyally maintained his authority in the eyes of the army he commanded, and have readily assented to almost every important suggestion he has made. Consult the records - refer to the staff: and I am very confident you will thereafter rely on the sincerity of the desire I express, to conduct the business of the state in cordial cooperation with you; and on the correctness of my statements as to the spirit in which I have sought to conduct it with your predecessor.

The position of the Commander in Chief will very probably appear to you, as it has appeared to many others, less independent and less powerful than it should be. But this is not my doing: it is the constitution of this government; it is a portion of the system wh[ich] I am charged to administer, and it is my duty to administer it. While, therefore, I am bound to exercise the power of the Supreme Government according to the best of my judgement, I hope that in assuming the command of the Indian Army, you will do so with the conviction, that you will receive at my hands full support and confidence in the exercise of the authority which belongs to you.

I will not say more than this opening word now. Bye and bye when I know your plans you will be troubled with me often enough; for the line which H E Sir C Napier has lately thought proper to take has necessarily compelled me to suspend many questions on wh[ich] decisions were much required.

Lady Gomm, I take for granted, accompanies you. Pray offer her my kindest regards, and believe me, my dear Sir William

Yours very sincerely

Dalhousie[3]

Dalhousie was quite correct in his perception that Sir Charles would attempt to place his account of his resignation before the public, which duly appeared the year after Napier's death in the form of a 119-page booklet entitled *Minutes on the Resignation of the Late General Sir Charles Napier of the Command of the Army in India*, and which reprinted a series of verbose memoranda that had passed between Napier and Dalhousie over the fact that the Commander-in-Chief's action had led to the expenditure of an additional £9.10s.6d;[4] but Lord Dalhousie was more interested in principles than pence. In order to prevent the outbreak of a mutiny among the troops at Wazirabad Napier had agreed to the suspension of a regulation and thereby enabled the Indian soldiers to be paid an additional allowance to cover the

'Types of the Indian Native Army, Madras'

Chromolithograph after Richard Simkin, from the series Military Types, *1901.*

Although the Madras Army had, with its Commander-in-Chief, ceased to exist in 1895, it was not until 1903, two years after this print was published, that Presidency designations were removed from the titles of regiments of the Indian Army.

NAM. 5812-153-4

increased cost of their food. The absence from Calcutta of the Governor-General and the other members of the Council led Napier to take this step on his own authority, although he informed Dalhousie of his action as soon as he could. He resigned on the receipt of a severe reprimand for exercising powers that belonged to the Council.

The Commander-in-Chief was regarded as the Governor-General's principal military adviser, although as the following extract from a letter from Dalhousie to Gomm shows, he was himself very well-informed in this, as in all other aspects of the government of India;

'A third Dragoon reg[imen]t in Bengal is in excess of the establishment. It was bought up, I think, from Bombay in 1846 on the occurrence of the war, and has been continued ever since.

It is an enormous expense. Each Eur[opea]n Cav[alr]y corps costing one way & another not less than eight lacs [of rupees] annually [approx £80,000].

It is not only enormously costly, but it is comparatively speaking of very little use. In making that observation I do not by any means intend to disparage the Cavalry: for if in the last campaign one corps did misbehave, their catalogue of glorious services in India is more than sufficient to write out that failure. But what I mean is that European Cavalry are not fitted to be generally useful in Indian warfare, & more than a certain proportion is a needless expense. A certain proportion of Eur[opean] Cavalry, sufficient to form a backbone for a cavalry division in the event of a great campaign, sh[oul]d certainly be retained: and I submit that two regiments are sufficient now, as they were formerly, for that purpose.

For any other object they are of no use. They do no duties in peace. You c[oul]d not see them with any effect in sudden insurrections; for it is useless to deny that singly or in small bodies they are no match for the native light horse man. They have not the same command either of their horses or of their weapons as he has - & however stout their hearts may be they are beaten by difference of habit & inferiority of training.[5]

This knowledge was not necessarily a bad thing, as some of the Commanders-in-Chief had little recent experience of India - Kitchener, for example, had never set foot in the sub-Continent until 1902 when he took over command of its Army. General (later Field Marshal) Lord Combermere, the first of three Commanders-in-Chief appointed on the recommendation of the Duke of Wellington, had last been in India 25 years previously when he arrived in 1825 to command its Army, and in due course to capture Bhurtpore (1826). However, during the middle years of the nineteenth century, the tendency developed, as part of the creation of a career path for senior Army officers, for commanders of one or the other Presidency armies to succeed to the chief command in India. Of the thirteen Commanders-in-Chief who held office between 1839 and 1893, six had previously commanded the Madras Army and three that of Bombay, while of the other four only Gomm had not previously commanded troops in India at a senior level.

The increasing complexity of the government and administration of India tended to reduce the ability of later Governors-General and Viceroys to influence the *minutiae* of military affairs in the way that Dalhousie had done. The relationship between the Viceroy and the Commander-in-Chief was also very dependent on the personalities of the two men. The following letter, from Lord Dufferin, to General Sir Frederick (later Field Marshal Lord) Roberts is the complete opposite of anything that Dalhousie might have sent to Napier;

'My dear Roberts

I have read with very great pleasure your second note on the military situation in Burmah. It is a most creditable record of the successful exertions of yourself and of the officers under your command for the restoration of order, and I have given directions to the Military Department that due recognition of what has been done should be embodied in the covering despatch.

Ever yours sincerely
Dufferin[6]

The generally good relationship that existed between successive Viceroys and Commanders-in-Chief during the latter part of the nineteenth century came to an abrupt end in 1904 when a serious disagreement erupted between Lord Curzon and General Lord Kitchener, who had been 'head-hunted' by the Viceroy to succeed General Sir Arthur Palmer as Commander-in-Chief in 1902. During the seven years that he held the appointment Kitchener carried out many important reforms and improvements to the organisation, administration and general condition of the Indian Army, which were described in the 651 page *Record of Lord Kitchener's Administration of the Army in India 1902-1909*, produced at the end of his period of command. The first 74 pages of this volume deal with 'Military Administration', an account, including extensive quotations from relevant memoranda, of the eventual abolition of the Military Department.

In 1854 Lord Dalhousie had succeeded in abolishing the Military Board, which under the Commandant of Artillery, the Chief Engineer and the Commissary-General, was responsible for the Ordnance and supply aspects of the Army in India, the command and discipline of the men being the concern of the Commander-in-Chief. In 1861, on the reorganization of the Indian Government after its transfer to the Crown, one of the seats on the Governor-General's Council was reserved for an Army officer, known as 'the Military Member', who was responsible for the Military Department,

Edward Robert Bulwer Lytton, second Baron and first Earl of Lytton (1813-91)

Lytton was Viceroy and Governor-General of India 1876-80. The photograph is taken from an album compiled by Major-General Sir Frederick (later Field Marshal Lord) Roberts, whose military success in Afghanistan in 1878-80, helped to achieve the Viceroy's policy aims towards that country.

NAM. neg no 23968

which handled many of the functions of the former Military Board, as the following diagram demonstrates;

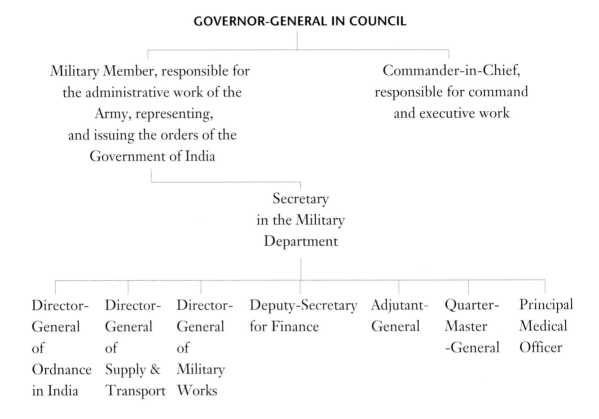

GOVERNOR-GENERAL IN COUNCIL

Military Member, responsible for the administrative work of the Army, representing, and issuing the orders of the Government of India

Commander-in-Chief, responsible for command and executive work

Secretary in the Military Department

| Director-General of Ordnance in India | Director-General of Supply & Transport | Director-General of Military Works | Deputy-Secretary for Finance | Adjutant-General | Quarter-Master -General | Principal Medical Officer |

Although the Military Member was junior in rank to the Commander-in-Chief, he was, unlike the latter, one of the permanent Members of the Council and not an 'Extra-ordinary Member', as was the Commander-in-Chief, whom he could theoretically out-vote, even though in the Warrant of Precedence in India the Commander-in-Chief ranked at number five and the Military Member at number nine. For a Commander-in-Chief who was prepared to work within the existing framework and a Viceroy with a flexible approach this system had worked, and might have continued to do so had opportunity allowed. However, a man with Kitchener's personality found such an arrangement irksome, and he wished to have all of the responsibilities of the Military Department transferred to the Commander-in-Chief. This would have resulted in the abolition of the Military Department and the Military Member of Council, leaving the Commander-in-Chief as the sole military representative on the Viceroy's Council. Lord Curzon disliked this proposal, and after a great deal of lobbying by the supporters of both, a compromise was agreed, whereby the role of the Military Department was curtailed to deal only with stores and supplies, all other Army matters coming under the Army Department headed by the Commander-in-Chief, who was to be a full Member of Council. However, the 'Military Supply Member', who now replaced the 'Military Member', was a serving General, and Kitchener insisted upon the right to nominate him. Curzon objected to this, as it deprived him of independent military advice from a Council source other than the Commander-in-Chief, and threatened to resign if he were to lose the right of nominating him. To his disgust his resignation was accepted, and in 1909, on the eve of his departure from India, Kitchener succeeded in obtaining the abolition of the Military Supply

Member, thus concentrating the whole of the responsibility for the Army in India into the Commander-in-Chief's - i.e. his own - hands. Someone with Kitchener's drive and energy was capable of undertaking the heavy work-load that he had placed on the Commander-in-Chief's shoulders, but the same cannot be said of either of his immediate successors, General Sir O'Moore Creagh, Commander-in-Chief 1909-13, and General Sir Beauchamp Duff, who held the position 1914-16. Duff had the misfortune to be Commander-in-Chief at the time when it was necessary to plan and carry out the operations in Mesopotamia during the First World War, including the unsuccessful attempt to relieve Kut. The organisation of the Indian Army, as left by Kitchener, proved to be quite unequal to these demands, and as a result Duff was worn down by mental strain and died in 1918, having been unfairly assigned a large share of the blame for the reverses suffered in 1916-17.

Kitchener's tour of duty as Commander-in-Chief undoubtedly resulted in many improvements, but it had also compromised the authority of the Viceroy at the expense of boosting his own standing, and created an administrative structure which was found to be unworkable in practice.

THE PRESIDENCY ARMIES AND THEIR SUCCESSORS

We now descend from the highest levels of the administration of India to the next tier, that of the Presidencies of Madras and Bombay. The Commander-in-Chief in India was also the Commander of the Bengal Army; the other Presidencies of Madras and Bombay also had their own Commanders-in-Chief, Governors and Councils, which mirrored, on a smaller scale, the arrangements in Bengal. From the January 1875 edition of *The Indian Army and Civil Service List* it is possible to build up a picture of the senior military personnel in the other Presidencies. Each was commanded by a lieutenant-general, under whom were a number of major-generals and brigadier-generals commanding respectively divisions and brigades. Each of the Presidency armies also had their Adjutant-Generals, Quarter-Master Generals and Judge Advocate-Generals; Barrack, Military Finance, Pay, Commissariat and Ordnance Departments. This arrangement had evolved from the simpler organisation of the earlier Presidency armies. In addition, there was a separate military body, the Punjab Frontier Force under

Robert Cornelis Napier, first Baron Napier of Magdala (1810-90)

General Baron Napier of Magdala, Commander-in-Chief, India, 1870-76, photographed c1872. Napier served as Military Member of the Governor-General's Council 1861-65, and commanded the troops on the Abyssinian Expedition 1867-68.

NAM. neg no 36010

Commanders three

A revealing photograph of c1885 from an album compiled by General Sir Frederick Roberts. Roberts, Commander-in-Chief, Madras, stands in the centre with, to his left, General Sir Donald Stewart, whom Roberts was about to succeed as Commander-in-Chief, India, and, on his right, the out-going Commander-in-Chief, Bombay, General the Hon Sir Arthur Edward Hardinge, shortly to become Governor of Gibraltar.

NAM. neg no 23975

the control of the Lieutenant-Governor of the Punjab, who was responsible to the Government of India in the Foreign Department.

The concept of Presidency armies became increasingly irrelevant to contemporary conditions as the nineteenth century wore on, while the independence from the control of the Commander-in-Chief of the Punjab Frontier Force had caused difficulties during active service. Sir John Malcolm (1769-1833) had advocated the abolition of the Presidencies in the 1830s, and Sir Charles Napier had complained about the existence of the separate Punjab Frontier Force. In 1879 the Viceroy and Governor-General, Lord Lytton, set up a commission under the chairmanship of Sir Ashley Eden (1831-87), Lieutenant-Governor of Bengal, to investigate the organisation and administration of the Army in India. This advocated the replacement of the three Presidency armies by four geographic Army corps, the placing of the Punjab Frontier Force under the command of the Commander-in-Chief and other changes, designed both to reduce the cost to the Indian revenue of the Army and to improve its efficiency.[7]

Many of the reforms advocated were carried out piecemeal during the next sixteen years - among them the amalgamation in 1884 of the three Ordnance Departments, the transfer of the Punjab Frontier Force from the control of the Government of the Punjab to that of the

Commander-in-Chief in India in 1886, and finally, in April 1895, the abolition of the Presidency armies and their replacement by four Commands - Punjab, Bengal, Madras and Bombay. Each of these was commanded by a lieutenant-general who was responsible to the Commander-in-Chief. The change in command structure was in reality less revolutionary than it appeared to be, for the regiments retained their former 'Presidency' titles - for example, 1st Regiment of Bombay Infantry (Grenadiers); while the Punjab Frontier Force remained as a distinct entity in the form of a District at Abbottabad. Although the officers of the three Presidency Staff Corps had been brought together into the India Staff Corps in 1891, further action was required to amalgamate the vestiges of the three independent Presidency armies into a unified Indian Army. This took place in 1903 when, as part of Kitchener's reform of the Indian Army, the regiments of cavalry and infantry were re-numbered in two continuous sequences and all mention of their Presidency origins omitted. Thus, the 1st Regiment of Bombay Infantry (Grenadiers) was retitled the 101st Grenadiers. Further changes were made in the higher command structure which was reduced in 1905 to three Commands - Northern, Western and Eastern, and again in 1908 to two Armies - Northern and Southern, each divided into divisions and brigades in readiness for active service.

The abolition of the Presidency Commanders-in-Chief removed from the list of military appointments two posts which had been available to be filled by either senior officers who were coming to the end of their careers, or by up-and-coming 'high fliers' who were having their suitability for a more senior post confirmed by holding a Presidency command. An example of the former category would be General Sir Charles Staveley (1817-96), Commander-in-Chief Bombay 1874-78, and of the latter, Lieutenant-General Sir Robert Napier, later Lord Napier of Magdala and Commander-in-Chief of India, who had held the same position 1865-68. By 1914, with the Army organised for active service, there was a greater requirement (which was not always met) for active senior officers than had been the case in earlier decades.

CONCLUSION

Even the limited compass of this paper will have demonstrated the changes which occurred in the higher command structure of the Army in India between 1816 and 1914 - many of these during the last twenty years of the period. There had also been changes in the size and shape of the Army at regimental level - the numbers of native cavalry regiments had more than doubled during the 98 years from sixteen to 39, with the infantry regiments showing a similar increase from 63 to 130. In the re-organization that accompanied the transfer of the administration of India to the Crown in 1858 the East India Company's European regiments had been transferred to the British Army, while officers of the Royal Artillery and Royal Engineers served on attachment with the Indian Artillery and the Corps of Sappers and Miners.

In conclusion, it is probably true to say that the higher command structure and organisation of the very different Indian Armies of 1816 and 1914 reflected the thinking and requirements of their respective ages. The need to adapt rapidly to changing circumstances, both military and political, was to become an important element in the post-1914 history of the Indian Army, and one to which it responded with considerable success.

APPENDIX A

GOVERNORS-GENERAL OF FORT WILLIAM IN BENGAL

Assumed charge of office

The Earl of Moira (subsequently Marquess Hastings) (1754-1826)	4 Oct 1813	Also Commander-in-Chief
Lord Amherst (1773-1857)	1 Aug 1823	
Lord William Cavendish Bentinck (1774-1839)	4 Jul 1828	Also Commander-in-Chief from 16 May 1833

GOVERNORS-GENERAL OF INDIA

Lord William Cavendish Bentinck (1774-1839)	14 Nov 1834	Also Commander-in-Chief from 16 May 1833
Lord Auckland (1784-1849)	4 March 1836	
Lord Ellenborough (1790-1871)	28 Feb 1842	
The Right Hon Sir Henry Hardinge (1785-1856)	23 July 1844	
The Earl of Dalhousie (1812-60)	12 Jan 1848	
Viscount Canning (1812-62)	29 Feb 1856	

VICEROYS AND GOVERNORS-GENERAL

Viscount Canning (1812-62)	1 Nov 1858
The Earl of Elgin and Kincardine (1811-63)	12 March 1862
The Right Hon Sir John Lawrence, Bart (1811-79)	12 Jan 1864
The Earl of Mayo (1822-72)	12 Jan 1869
Lord Northbrook (1826-1904)	3 May 1872
Lord Lytton (1831-91)	12 April 1876
The Marquess of Ripon (1827-1909)	8 June 1880
The Earl of Dufferin (1826-1902)	13 Dec 1884
The Marquess of Lansdowne (1845-1927)	10 Dec 1888
The Earl of Elgin and Kincardine (1849-1917)	27 Jan 1894
Baron Curzon of Kedleston (1859-1925)	6 Jan 1899
The Earl of Minto (1845-1914)	18 Jan 1905
Baron Hardinge of Penshurst (1858-1944)	23 Nov 1910

APPENDIX B

COMMANDERS-IN-CHIEF IN INDIA

Assumed charge of office

General the Earl of Moira (subsequently Marquess Hastings) (1754-1826)	4 Oct 1813	Also Governor-General
Lieutenant-General the Hon Sir Edward Paget (1775-1849)	13 Jan 1823	
General Lord Combermere (1773-1865)	7 Oct 1825	
Lieutenant-General the Earl of Dalhousie (1770-1838)	1 Jan 1830	
Lieutenant-General Sir Edward Barnes (1776-1838)	10 Jan 1832	
General Lord William Bentinck (1774-1839)	16 May 1833	Also Governor-General
Lieutenant-General Sir Henry Fane (1778-1840)	5 Sept 1835	
General Sir Jasper Nicolls (1778-1849)	7 Dec 1839	
General Sir Hugh Gough (1779-1869)	11 Aug 1843	
General Sir Charles Napier (1782-1853)	7 May 1849	
General Sir William Gomm (1784-1875)	6 Dec 1850	
General the Hon George Anson (1779-1857)	23 Jan 1856	
Lieutenant-General Sir Colin Campbell (1797-1863)	13 Aug 1857	
General Sir Hugh Rose (1801-85)	4 June 1860	
General Sir William Mansfield (1819-76)	23 March 1865	
General Lord Napier of Magdala (1810-90)	9 April 1870	
General Sir Frederick Haines (1820-1910)	10 April 1876	
General Sir Donald Stewart (1824-1900)	8 April 1881	
General Sir Frederick Roberts (1832-1914)	28 Nov 1885	
General Sir George White (1835-1912)	8 April 1893	
General Sir William Lockhart (1841-1900)	4 Nov 1898	
General Sir Arthur Palmer (1840-1902)	19 March 1900	
General Viscount Kitchener of Khartoum (1850-1916)	28 Nov 1902	
General Sir O'Moore Creagh (1848-1923)	10 Sept 1909	
General Sir Beauchamp Duff (1858-1918)	8 March 1914	

FROM 'CRUEL AND PREPOSTEROUS' TO 'COOL AND COMFORTABLY CLAD'

THE BRITISH ARMY'S JACKET FROM 'UNDRESS' TO 'SERVICE DRESS'

SYLVIA HOPKINS

On the subject of military clothing worn in India, Lord Dalhousie[1] wrote in 1852 'from the 15 April to 15th October the Government prohibits drill as dangerous to the men, especially in the cruel and preposterous dress which we obstinately and stupidly insist on their wearing in this climate as on Salisbury Plain'.[2]

'UNDRESS' UNIFORM

The 'cruel and preposterous dress' was the full dress uniform worn by the other ranks for almost all duties except fatigues. Immediately after Waterloo, undress and working uniform were made from the cast-off full dress. Little of this type of uniform has survived, and this is not to be wondered at in view of the often inferior textiles employed and the doubtful talents of some regimental tailors.

Officers fared a little better. Staff officers, and those of the Household Cavalry and the Foot Guards, had an undress or frock uniform. This was a coatee, similar to that worn in full dress but with less lace or with the lace replaced by twist loops. Military uniform was designed to identify and attract or repel, depending on whether the observer were friend or foe. The tight-fitting coatees, with heavy, impeding embellishments such as epaulettes or wings, were hardly a sensible approach to a garment worn for work of a grim, grimy and energetic nature.

The lessons of camouflage and practicality learnt during the warfare in North America from the 1750s until 1783 had been quickly forgotten. The legacy, such as it was, was a dark green uniform for Rifle units and short tails on the coatees of the Light Infantry. Dark green may have afforded camouflage protection in forest conditions, but was as stark as scarlet, blue and white against the scenery of the North-West Frontier. During the Peninsular War the coatee tails were shortened, almost to vanishing point in the case of the cavalry, although for heavy cavalry, staff, corps and infantry the tails progressively lengthened again, reaching just above mid-knee by 1855.

The earliest moves towards a comfortable form of undress was the stable jacket or shell jacket. Both were tail-less, single-breasted garments, almost devoid of ornament. The stable jacket was worn by the cavalry and the shell jacket by the infantry. For the purposes of this brief article the term 'shell jacket' will be used. In practice, the shell jacket had scant advantage over the coatee. It was tight fitting, and the raising of the arms resulted in a most un-soldierly gap between jacket and netherwear. The shell jacket was made up in light-weight[3] fabric by officers' tailors for hot-weather wear or in white cotton or linen.[4] The other ranks wore a similar pattern in inferior fabric.[5] The shell jacket made its official appearance in the 1831 *Dress Regulations*; it proved to be a garment which had come to stay. It passed through many minor changes and subsequently evolved into the mess jacket. Its demise as an undress and working dress, albeit slow, was accelerated by the Crimean War of 1854-56.

The privations experienced in South Russia by officers and men alike partly as a result of their 'cruel and preposterous' uniform, woefully inadequate for the harsh conditions of the Crimean winter, inaugurated the quest for the perfect fighting uniform which continues even today. The time-honoured coatee and the cavalryman's 'bum-freezer' jacket were replaced by the double-breasted tunic, still resplendent in lace, but with the added protection of a skirt which extended from the waist to mid-thigh.

The tunic was based on the blue frock coat, a garment worn by civilians and unofficially by officers, certainly from the beginning of the nineteenth century. The Duke of Wellington was painted by Andrew Morton wearing a plain civilian frock coat. This garment gradually became a feature of undress uniform for all arms in the *Officers' Dress Regulations*. For the infantry[6] it was plain and serviceable but for the cavalry[7] Royal Artillery, Royal Engineers and corps it was bedecked with black braid and lace. It was worn on campaign and variants in thick fabric with astrakhan collars were worn in Canada. The frock coat, like the shell jacket, moved on to higher things and today is worn by certain ranks and appointments as part of their ceremonial dress.

In 1856[8] the shell jacket was abolished in favour of the white frock for use in hot climates. In January 1857[9] provision was made for the addition of regimental facings. White was considered the proper hot-weather colour, regardless of its stark appearance against most terrain. Officers tended to embellish and add pockets to their white frocks.[10] According to the 1891 *Officers' Dress Regulations* white clothing was worn for China, Straits Settlements, Ceylon, Mauritius, West Indies and Malta (off parade only at the last-named station, and then at the option of the wearer). The 1891 *Dress Regulations, India* also described the white frock in terms basically the same as those contained in the British Regulations - 'a plain white drill jacket (blue patrol jacket shape), without braid, of sufficient length to just clear the saddle when the officer is mounted; fastened by five small buttons ...; cuffs pointed; one inside breast pocket; shoulder straps of same material as the coat'.[11] The version described in the British *Dress Regulations* has the addition of 'velvet or silk' shoulder straps in a number of colour variations. An other ranks' universal pattern white duck frock for use in tropical climates was sealed in 1865. It was known as the 'Miscellaneous Service Frock', and became obsolete in November 1891.[12] By now, the days of the white frock as undress were numbered. The 1891 *Dress Regulations, India* ends its description of the white frock with 'khaki is worn by British corps, staff and departments, at musketry, fatigues etc'. The white frock, as with other undress garments, is worn today as part of tropical ceremonial dress.

Left to right: Company officer's, light-weight, hot-weather shell jacket c1864, worn by Major F Fawkes when serving with the 71st (Highland) (Light Infantry), 1855-65. NAM. 7707-32-4; *White hot-weather shell jacket, c1839*, worn by an officer of the 70th (Surrey) Regiment when in Barbados, 1838-41. NAM. 8403-38; *Other ranks' shell jacket, c1848*, 13th (1st Somersetshire) or Prince Albert's Regiment of Light Infantry. NAM. 7905-24

In more temperate climes the undress wear for officers and men alike was a frock coat in either scarlet or blue. An order of 1873 gives some idea of when and why the scarlet frock was worn; 'The scarlet patrol jacket will be worn by officers whenever the regiment is on parade in brigade. The blue patrol jacket may be worn for all regimental duties except on parade when the men wears shakos'.[13] The blue frock or patrol jacket was heavily adorned with black lace and braid and in the case of hussars, with astrakhan. In 1886 a more simple pattern in dark green was introduced for the Rifle Regiments. It had roomy pockets, a concession to the idea that the frock was a working garment, not a jacket just slightly below the status of full dress.[14]

Ten years later, a Universal Pattern blue serge frock was introduced, incorporating breast and skirt pockets. It was re-sealed as 'Frock Serge A' in 1913.[15] From 1913-28 an open-necked, step-pattern collar blue serge frock, known as the 'Frock Serge B' was offered as an alternative to the Frock Serge A.[16] The Frock Serge A evolved into Number 1 Dress having played its part as an undress, working and indeed fighting garment for officers.

Unembellished, inferior quality blue frocks of a shape similar to those worn by the officers were issued to other ranks. Officers also experimented with this garment on their own account. One of them was Surgeon James Peterkin who, when serving with the 16th Madras Native Infantry as a surgeon during 1859-63, wore a double-breasted, scarlet tunic of padded serge for protection against the harsher features of the Indian climate.[17]

The scarlet serge or cloth 'patrol jacket' was officially introduced for officers in 1872.[18] It was abolished, two years later[19] in favour of a tunic, in all respects similar to the full dress tunic, but made in a light-weight fabric. In 1876[20] the patrol jacket in scarlet serge was re-introduced for service in India. This loose fitting garment, without a waist seam, was less elaborate than the blue frock, but the rank of the wearer was indicated by the quantity of Russia braid. This

Field Marshal Arthur Wellesley, Marquess of Wellington, *c1814*

Watercolour over pencil by Thomas Heaphy, 1819

Wellington habitually wore civilian costume on campaign in the Peninsula; Heaphy's post-war image depicts
him in a civilian frock coat.

NAM. 9304-6

Left to right: Civilian frock coat, 1845, worn by Field Marshal the Duke of Wellington on the occasion of his portrait being painted by the artist Andrew Morton. NAM. 9212-29; *Lieutenant-Colonel's frock coat, c1855,* worn by Major-General G B Payne, Royal Marine Light Infantry. NAM. 5909-11; *Officer's frock coat, c1855,* worn by Colonel G R Edwards, 2nd Regiment of Light Cavalry, Madras. NAM. 9104-203-4

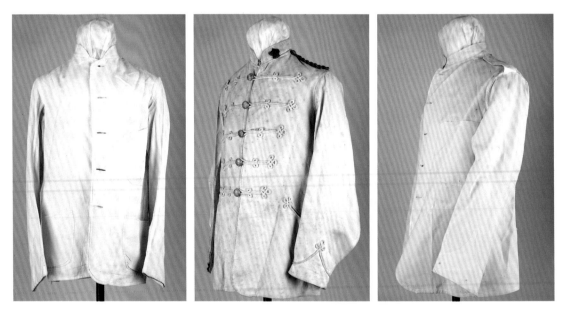

Left to right: Officer's white drill frock, c1860, worn by Lieutenant J R Lee, 30th Bengal Native Infantry. NAM. 6612-36-8; *Officer's white patrol jacket, c1858,* worn by Surgeon Major James Peterkin, 20th Madras Native Infantry. NAM. 9111-35-2; *Officer's white drill frock, c1881,* worn by Brigade Surgeon E Hoile, Army Medical Department. NAM. 6612-24-20

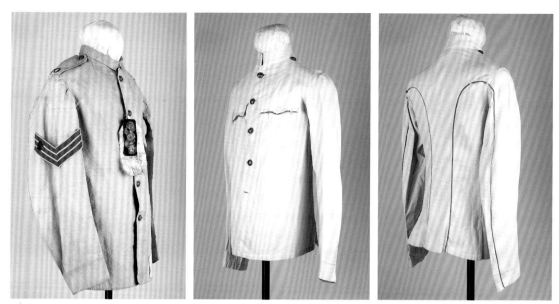

*Left to right: **Miscellaneous Service Frock, Tropical Climates, other ranks'**, sealed pattern 1865-91. NAM. 7402-52; **Other rank's white drill frock, c1898**, worn by Trooper W A Wilkins, 9th (Queen's Royal Lancers). NAM. 8309-66-1*

*Left to right: **Officers' sealed pattern frock, 1886**, Rifle Brigade (the Prince Consort's Own). NAM. 7403-96; **Officers' sealed pattern blue serge frock, 1896**, Universal Pattern except for the Household Cavalry, Foot Guards and Royal Malta Artillery. NAM. 8006-115; **Officer's Frock Serge B, c1913**, worn by Lieutenant-Colonel R Crerar, 8th (Territorial) Bn, Duke of Cambridge's Own (Middlesex Regiment). NAM. 9009-66*

*Left to right: **India pattern frock, 1876-81**, 17th (Leicestershire) Regiment. NAM. 8906-5; **Officers' scarlet serge, sealed pattern frock, 1896**, infantry of the line. NAM. 7402-61; **Unofficial pattern padded tunic, c1861**, worn by Surgeon Major James Peterkin when a surgeon with the 16th Madras Native Infantry. NAM. 9111-35-1*

*Left to right: **Other ranks' experimental frock**, 17th Bengal Native Infantry. Manufactured by the Army Clothing Factory Calcutta for the International Health Exhibition at South Kensington, 1884. NAM. 7802-59; **Other ranks' blue serge frock, c1902**, 6th Dragoon Guards (Carabiniers). NAM. 7807-70; **Sergeants' and other ranks' scarlet serge frock, sealed pattern, 1913**. NAM. 7512-68-3*

pattern was known as the 'India Pattern'.[21]

The 1891 *Dress Regulations, India* describe a scarlet serge patrol jacket, with a pleat down each front rather in the manner of a Norfolk jacket, and a flapped pocket on each breast. A footnote states that 'The Scarlet Serge Patrol Jackets of the India pattern may continue to be worn until required to be replaced'. In 1896 a scarlet serge frock[22] of the pattern similar to that of the blue Frock Serge A was introduced. With the 1904 *Dress Regulations* the scarlet serge frock, unlike the shell jacket, frock coat and blue serge frock, vanished from the Orders of Dress.

Other ranks also wore an inferior version of the India pattern frock and it was worn, with minor changes, into the early twentieth century. The 1896 Officer Pattern was adopted, again in a cheaper fabric, by some warrant officers and senior non-commissioned officers.

A noteworthy addition in 1891[23] to the other ranks' scarlet frock was a shoulder pad, 'In order to protect the scarlet frocks from stains caused by the magazine rifle'. This pad was required to last for two years and one penny was allowed for fitting the pad to the frock.

The other ranks of the Indian Army also wore the scarlet frock, a doubtful privilege in view of the number of campaigns which took place against the light-coloured terrain of India throughout the nineteenth century. A scarlet serge frock,[24] worn on an experimental basis by the 17th Bengal Native Infantry was considered so beneficial to the health of the soldier that it was put on display, with considerable acclaim, at an International Health Exhibition at South Kensington from 8 May to 30 October 1884. Its label proudly proclaimed that it was 'machine made ... from the Army Clothing Factory, Calcutta 1884'.

THE TRIUMPH OF *KHAKI*

It is somewhat extraordinary that in 1884 the Indian Army should bother with a scarlet frock, for it was in India that the most positive moves towards a universal camouflage garment were made. In 1846, Sir Henry Lawrence, at that time the Governor-General's agent for foreign relations in the Punjab and the North-West Frontier, ordered a young lieutenant, Harry Lumsden[25] to raise a native Corps of Guides, consisting of both infantry and cavalry. Lawrence stipulated that their dress should be workmanlike and, 'that to get the best work out of the troops and to enable them to undertake great exertions, it was necessary that the soldier should be loosely, comfortably and suitably clad'.[26] It is to Harry Lumsden that credit must go for providing, at last, a comfortable, camouflage uniform for the fighting man. It is related that he purchased all the white cotton fabric he could find and caused it to be dyed with river mud. The result was a drab, sandy colour which blended with the local scenery. The fabric was made-up into loose blouses, probably based on the native *alkalic* or *kurta*. The Hindi word for dust was *khaki* and was adopted as the name for this innovative colour for military uniforms. In 1848 Major William Hodson,[27] second-in-command of the Corps of Guides, informed his brother that drab khaki was the colour most likely 'to make (soldiers) invisible in a land of dust'.[28] Lumsden recorded that he and another officer rode '24 miles to Nowshera to make my bow to the Old Gentleman [the Commander-in-Chief India, Sir Charles Napier]. He looked at us both for a minute and then remarked "Yes, it's not a bad colour for

*Left to right: **Colonel's khaki drill tunic, c1886**, worn by General T T Turton, 5th Infantry, Hyderabad Contingent. NAM. 6208-6; **Captains' full dress tunic, c1865**, Somersetshire Rifle Volunteers. NAM. 8604-109; **Brown corduroy frock, c1860-90**, probably a trial pattern. NAM. 9111-39*

work'".[29] Napier told Hodson that the Guides were 'the only properly dressed light troops' he had seen in the sub-Continent.[30]

The utility of khaki quickly became apparent to both British and Indian regiments. During the Indian Mutiny, 1857-59, the 3rd Bombay Europeans (later the 2nd Battalion, the Leinster Regiment) managed to obtain large supplies of stone-coloured cotton, which were made-up into blouses and trousers. They also wore turbans or *pugris* dyed to match their uniforms.[31]

Two British regiments, the 52nd and the 61st, also adopted khaki during the Mutiny. As the commanding officer of the 52nd, Colonel George Campbell, recalled in 1859;

> 'I had a suit per man of white clothing dyed at Sealkote immediately I arrived at Lucknow ... My reason at the time for adopting it was the ulterior view of diminishing the Indian kit but, on account of the difficulty of getting white trousers and jackets washed quickly, the men were obliged to have five pairs of trousers, whereas with khaki two were sufficient. Moreover, I thought it would be a good colour for service.[32]

Bugler Johnson of the 52nd Foot recalled that almost all his comrades dyed their clothing khaki, including their flannel shirts. The shirts were worn outside the trousers and belted with a 'waist turban'. 'I have seen many paintings in which officers and men are portrayed as wearing European clothing at Delhi', recalled Johnson, yet 'which is totally at variance with the facts'.[33]

In spite of the obvious advantages of khaki clothing it was not until May 1885 that it was adopted as the universal service dress by the Indian Army.[34] The 1891 *Dress Regulations, India* note that the summer clothing for the 5th, 7th, 8th and 12th Bengal Cavalry and the Bhopal

Battalion was to be khaki and a description is given which draws attention to the presence of pockets on the breast and skirt, an attached waistband and a shoulder yoke at the back. The sleeve had three-pleats into the pointed cuff. The shoulder straps were the same colour as the garment, which could be made of cotton drill or serge. Until the appearance of these regulations, it would appear that officers tended to design their own hot-weather garments, or that there were regimental patterns of khaki tunic.[35]

Khaki clothing did have its opponents. The once white uniforms of one regiment were returned from the dyers in such an unsatisfactory condition that the soldiers refused to walk out of barracks, preferring to spend their leisure time in the canteen. The resulting increase in drunkenness necessitated a quick return of the white uniform.[36] In the British Army, khaki tended to fall into disfavour after the Indian Mutiny, although it was revived for the Abyssinian Expedition of 1868.[37] The Second Afghan War 1878-80 saw the Indian Army efficiently dressed in khaki. Meanwhile, the 17th Lancers, who had worn khaki during the Mutiny with back and sleeve seams piped in blue, and the 92nd Foot, had to resort to the time-honoured technique of dying their white uniforms with river mud.

In Britain, as in India, military minds were slowly beginning to appreciate the value of some form of camouflage garment. The main incentive for change came from an originally civilian source. In the late 1850s and early 1860s a number of auxiliary Rifle Volunteer units were formed in response to fears of a French invasion. These part-time enthusiasts generally wore a uniform in grey or brown, of a loose cut, based on the country gentleman's shooting apparel. Military embellishments on the cuff and collar were used to denote rank, following the practise of the regular Rifle Regiments. One such tunic, of the 1st Somersetshire Rifle Volunteers, was even made in the local West Country tweed.[38]

Left to right: Other ranks' 'invisible grey' experimental, sealed pattern frock, c1901. NAM. 7402-62; Other ranks', experimental issue, sealed pattern khaki serge frock, 1884, infantry. NAM. 7402-63; All ranks' khaki serge, experimental issue, sealed pattern waistcoat, 1884-1920. NAM. 7403-85

These browns and greys produced a reasonable camouflage effect in the British countryside and various trials of similar 'invisible' colour uniforms were made for regular troops. In 1873 Major-General Sir Garnet Wolseley[39] ordered that his entire command for the Second Ashanti War should be dressed in grey.[40] The Royal Marine Artillery and Light Infantry are credited with the wearing of tunics and trousers of a greyish smoke-colour with dust-colour helmets.[41]

The Egyptian Expedition of 1881-82 is usually regarded as the first campaign where some form of field or service dress was worn by the majority of British troops present. Two United States Navy officers, Lieutenant-Commander C F Goodrich and Ensign Charles Rogers, observed that, 'towards the end of September a grey serge tunic was issued for trial to the troops in Egypt. It looked much cooler than the garment it replaced, and it would certainly stand the wear and tear of campaign'. Goodrich also remarked on the cool appearance of the Indian Contingent in their khaki compared with the scarlet worn by some of the British infantry.[42] Rogers noted that '30,000 suits of grey serge clothing in addition to the red and blue serge were sent out'.[43]

The colour grey did not appear to satisfy the authorities, so experiments continued. A trial pattern frock[44] of a drab heather mixture, described 'invisible grey', was sealed in 1888 and was still on trial as late as 1904. A khaki experimental issue frock,[45] probably sealed in the late 1880s, was not reckoned as obsolete until 1907. Another khaki experimental frock, incorporating cartridge holders sewn to the front and wings embroidered with the regimental title 'Derbyshire', was approved in 1884 and declared obsolete in 1907.[46] A brown corduroy frock was also experimented with between the late 1860s and about 1890.[47] Trials in khaki extended beyond the frock. An experimental sleeved waistcoat of khaki serge was issued on 30 January 1884 and was declared obsolete as late as 21 June 1920.[48]

The main objection to khaki was its fugitiveness as a dye. This problem was overcome by a chemist, Mr Frederick Albert Gatty, who patented a mineral khaki dye in 1884. Trials of this dye proved successful, but even in 1893 only troops employed in Egypt, India, and parts of Africa were allowed a khaki drill suit. In 1896 khaki drill was introduced for all stations abroad.[49]

The South African War of 1899-1902 finally resulted in the seal of approval being applied to a universal khaki field service uniform. This was made of khaki cotton drill cloth, which proved insufficiently warm, so a similar uniform in khaki serge was introduced in April 1900. For the officers and other ranks the shape of the khaki drill tunic was that of the scarlet frock, with breast pockets. The pattern was repeated in serge for the other ranks. The Officers' Pattern serge tunic bore a close resemblance to the pattern described in the 1891 *Dress Regulations, India*. By 1904 the back yoke had been removed and there was a box pleat down the centre back of the tunic.

The universal khaki uniform for wear at home and abroad, 'designed with a view to furnishing a comfortable uniform, light enough to be worn on service abroad, and in warm weather at home, and also, with the addition of warm underclothing, for wear in winter at home' was introduced in 1902.[50] The tunic was of a drab khaki woollen mixture, weighing eighteen to twenty ounces per yard. To identify each regiment, the other ranks wore an embroidered shoulder title on a curved coloured ground on the upper sleeve, one inch from

Left to right: Captains' service dress tunic, c1897-c1902, Lancashire Fusiliers; NAM. 7704-24; Lieutenants' service dress tunic, 1902-13, Royal Munster Fusiliers; NAM. 7410-148; Major's service dress tunic, 1913-17, worn by Major O T R Crawshay, Duke of Wellington's 3rd Reserve Bn (West Riding Regiment). NAM. 7303-8-11

the arm seam. A separate patch, bearing the battalion number, was ordered to be worn below the shoulder title in December 1902.[51] The officers' service dress tunic introduced in 1913 resembled the Frock Serge A in shape.

Thus, the British Army entered the Great War wearing a reasonably comfortable, camouflaged service tunic that, at the time, was probably envisaged as the ultimate in fighting dress.

THE BRITISH LANCERS'
CHAPKA

AUBREY BOWDEN

Few sights on the battlefield could have been more impressive than the deployment of lancers *en masse*. The lance, dubbed the 'Queen of Weapons' by the seventeenth century general and military writer Raimondo Montecuccoli, had been a most important weapon in its heyday, but in Great Britain it had nevertheless long since disappeared when the regular Army was born in the second half of the seventeenth century.

But the renaissance of the lance in Western Europe was yet to come, and it came from Poland: almost inseparably linked with it came a distinctive style of uniform with a unique Polish headdress of antique origin. The style of uniform - and particularly the headdress - became so firmly implanted that even after 100 years of small modifications a visitor from another planet might well have picked out the lancers of several nations in the belief that they belonged to one army, whereas the hussar style had already developed very diversely in most armies.

Lancers were established in the British Army in 1816 but, as often happens in such cases, there were a few earlier contacts with the lance and the chapka. In the Hanoverian Army, the *Frei Korps von Scheiter* (c1760) incorporated an Uhlan or Bosnian lancer unit with crimson and white clothing of broadly hussar character, but with a fur-trimmed red cloth cap not unlike a *konfederatka*, the four-sided, flat-topped peasant cap worn by the men of Krakow, Poland.

In the wake of the French Revolution a large number of *emigré* regiments was raised, each being formed by a proprietary colonel under contract to the British Government. Prince Lubomirski unsuccessfully attempted to raise one such unit dressed and armed in the Polish fashion. In November 1793, the Comte de Bouillé raised a force which became the nucleus of the *Uhlans* (or *Hulans*) *Britanniques de St Dominique*. The soldiers of this regiment wore a fairly stiff white-topped *konfederatka* with yellow piping, black fur trimming, red plume and yellow cap lines. It is believed that the officers' headdress acquired a peak soon afterwards.

Although it is essentially true to say that no British soldiers except lancers ever wore any form of chapka, there are a few exceptions even to this rule. The latitude allowed to auxiliary forces in matters of bandsmen's dress was almost unlimited, even in the case of infantry units, and an illustration exists showing a boy musician of the St George's Volunteers c1795 playing a triangle and wearing a headdress very like that of the *Uhlans Britanniques*. A very exotic variant of the chapka was also worn by the kettledrummer of the 2nd Life Guards in the 1830s, but in this case with a round stiff top and a peak. It is even more astonishing to find that in India in 1846 the 28th Bengal Native Infantry had bandsmen wearing a conventional chapka.

Battle experience in the Peninsular War, particularly at the Battle of Albuera in May 1811,

Mounted Lancer, 1811

Coloured aquatint from Captain J B Drouville On the Formation of British Lancers ... *1811*

convinced some British officers of the immense value of lancers (which they at first called 'pikemen') and on 5 November that year Captain J B Drouville submitted a proposition to the Commander-in-Chief, the Duke of York, that a corps of British Lancers be formed. Conscious of the great enthusiasm in high places for fine uniforms, he included in his published proposal full uniform details and coloured plates. The intended uniform was green, with a wide-topped shako.

In May 1814 Lieutenant-Colonel R H de Montmorency submitted another paper to the Duke of York at a levée at the Horse Guards. This officer had recently spent three years as a prisoner in France and there had studied closely the 'celebrated Polish Lancers'. He now praised their virtues eloquently, proposing regulations for a lance exercise based on that of *Maréchal* Prince Joseph Poniatowski and advocating a trial of the weapon. As a result, in April 1815, 50 men from de Montmorency's former regiment, the 9th Light Dragoons, undertook lance training at Pimlico, where they were armed with lances fifteen feet in length.

In January 1816 the Prince Regent's decision to convert four light dragoon regiments into regiments of lancers was announced - the 12th, 16th and 23rd being selected in addition to the 9th. The post-War Army was, however, contracting; the 23rd were disbanded a year later and the 19th were converted to lancers to take their place until they too were disbanded in 1821, to be similarly replaced by the 17th.

In an age of romantic elegance and ostentation most armies took a keen interest in military fashion, but the enthusiasm of George, the Prince Regent in this field was unparalleled. It is no surprise that the man for whom the exotic Royal Pavilion at Brighton was built should be an ardent advocate of hussars and their costume. Equally, faced with a sound military case for introducing lancers, reinforced by events in the Waterloo campaign, he ensured that the opportunity to introduce the chapka with them was not missed. One of his brothers, the Duke of York, was Commander-in-Chief of the Army; another, the Duke of Cumberland, constantly sent him examples of foreign uniforms acquired on his travels while a third, the Duke of Clarence, was later to show an interest in uniforms, albeit a rather misguided one.

Between them they presided over the fundamental uniform changes made in 1812 which included the introduction to the light dragoons of a uniform in which Polish as well as French and Austrian features could be discerned. The hectic pace of changes in military fashion was further accelerated by the period of competitive contact with other Allied armies in France following Napoleon's final defeat.

Although the basic uniform of the light dragoon regiments converted to lancers remained as in 1812, the appearance was greatly altered by the adoption of the chapka, an aiguillette and the loose style of trousers known as 'Cossacks'. One lancer officer of the time, Lieutenant-Colonel John Luard, later commented thus on the decision to dress the lancers like Poles;

> 'why they were to be so dressed merely because they were to carry lances is difficult to understand ... the lancer cap is nearly the worst that ever was invented, has the same objection (as the heavy cavalry helmet) on account of its height and plume, and does not in the least protect the back of the head from a blow of the sabre.

Apart from regimental differences of colour of top and devices on the plate there was at first a surprising degree of variation between regiments in other details of the chapka. The shape, particularly that of the waist, varied considerably from one regiment to another and it was not until c1856 that a great degree of uniformity was established. Even then one regiment, the 9th Lancers, continued to eschew lace altogether in favour of elaborate gilt metal ornaments and a plain metal-edged peak: the regiment adopted this form of ornamentation in 1832 and never conformed thereafter to normal patterns except in shape and size of chapka. The general rule was that the top matched the facings of the uniform. Thus the 9th originally had crimson tops as did the 23rd, the 16th red, the 19th yellow and the 17th, whose facings had been white ever since they were raised in 1759, had a white top. The 12th briefly had yellow and then changed to red. The lace for officers conformed with that on the uniform but when in 1831 silver lace was abolished in the regular Army, gold became the universal colour for lace, while yellow braid replaced white for the men.

Early dress regulations for officers can be misleading as they frequently give details which are valid only for the senior regiment in each category but some useful details can be gleaned: the typical chapka of the early 1820s was eleven inches high and had a 'trencher top' (that is to say like a square platter or a student's 'mortar-board') ten inches square. The bottom edge of the skull was straight and there was a large peak at the back permanently turned up and trimmed with lace, the decoration being in much the same style as that on the front peak.

This decoration is often described as being of simple French lace, which also ringed the black leather skull, but many examples are to be found with fine embroidery deliberately designed to look like ordinary lace and, in the case of the early chapka of the 16th Lancers, there is evidence that there was ornate embroidery of scroll design on the front peak. The lower part of the fluted cloth top of the chapka was encircled with bands of broad lace of distinctive pattern. The corners of the top were trimmed with vertical cord, which normally crossed the top of the chapka and the left front section of the top bore an elaborate boss of wire-work with a coloured centre bearing the Royal cypher in wire embroidery, but even these details varied from regiment to regiment. From the boss protruded a plume, always of the drooping type, which early regulations describe as being crimson and white, twelve inches long, at first of cock's-tail and later swan's feathers; they were in reality much larger and by 1831 all regiments had enormous black feather plumes which drooped sixteen inches at the front. The men's plumes were of horsehair and from an early date officers were also permitted similar plumes for use in India. Massive chin-scales with lion's head bosses also adorned the early chapka.

The large, early, chapka plates matched the lace in colour and were normally of rayed design with angular ends to the rays and bore a small inner plate with the Hanoverian Royal Arms and devices such as the elephant of the 19th Lancers. The 9th Lancers, independent as ever, had a plate without rays that was decorated with lines of small bead-like protrusions and an interesting miniature portrait of an officer of the 12th Lancers c1816 shows a large rayed

The 16th Lancers breaking the square of Sikh infantry at the Battle of Aliwal, *18 January 1846*

Watercolour by Michael Angelo Hayes, c1850

The Battle was fought during the First Anglo-Sikh War (1845-46) between a force of 10,000 British and Indian troops under the command of General Sir Harry Smith and a 15,000-strong Sikh army led by Ranjur Singh. The Sikh forces occupied an entrenched position between the villages of Aliwal and Bhundri, close to the river Sutlej. Smith drove the Sikhs out of Aliwal with his infantry and then rolled up their line with cavalry and artillery support. The 16th Lancers charged several times during the action, breaking a number of Sikh infantry squares and overrunning a battery of Sikh artillery.

The Lancers are shown wearing over their chapkas the white cotton cover which had been adopted for service in the tropics.

NAM. 7912-1

19th Regiment of (Light) Dragoons (Lancers)

Officer's chapka worn by Major William Moray Stirling who served with the regiment 1819-21

NAM. 5912-112

plate devoid of any device which suggests that their chapka may have been worn even before such details were settled.

The private men's chapka was always considerably simpler, having only worsted braid, cord and boss, plain black leather peaks and crown and a die-struck plate, whereas sergeants had their headdress embellished with lace and there was later a more elaborate chapka of superior quality for higher non-commissioned grades.

By 1828 official moves were being made to enforce a standard and more economical pattern of chapka for officers, which was to be lower and less lavishly decorated, but there seems to have been some resistance, as *Dress Regulations* of 1831 show that the main changes were confined to a small reduction in height, the discarding of the broadest lace band and the replacement of the chin-scales with a chin-chain. The new plate had rounded rays and a plain panel at the bottom, which bore a regimental number or motto below the Royal Arms. In some cases, battle honours and regimental devices also adorned the plates, which remained very elaborate.

An interesting feature at this time was the special chapka for regimental staff - apparently worn in both dress and undress by these officers. This is described as plain black with black silk lace, but it is believed that no actual example survives. In 1834 and 1846 this chapka was simply described as being without gold ornaments and by 1856 it had been discontinued.

A new pattern chapka was adopted shortly before the 1846 edition of *Dress Regulations* was published. These prescribed a slightly smaller top and a more shapely skull which extended down at the back and the rayed plate no longer had the plain panel.

In the aftermath of the Crimean War the uniforms of the British Army underwent revolutionary changes which included the introduction of the tunic and the abolition of the pelisse, coatee and epaulette. After much discussion the lancers managed to emerge with a uniform which retained essential features, notably a plastron front and piping to the tunic and, of course, the chapka itself.

The new pattern chapka for officers was officially sealed in July 1856. Like most other headdress introduced at that time, this was smaller and simpler than previous models, being only seven inches high at the side and with a seven-and-a-quarter inch square top. The lace at the waist was narrow and the back peak had gone to reveal narrow French lace trim all round the skull. The front peak bore simple embroidery except in the 9th Lancers. This pattern of chapka was henceforward to remain virtually unchanged, future developments being mainly confined to details on the plate. Coloured plumes were now reintroduced, but for some years the horsehair version was worn by officers on most occasions even in Britain, the feather plumes, now smaller, being reserved for levées. Musicians and trumpeters in several cases had previously had special plates and red plumes. In the 9th Lancers trumpeters at one time had even worn a chapka with a scarlet top, although in that regiment the men, like the officers, at the time had a black surface to their chapka-tops, with blue sides and a distinctive waist band and boss of pressed metal made to resemble cord. In some regiments, the men crimped their plumes by dampening them and binding them between wooden shapes and, remarkably, in the 16th Lancers they even crimped the lance pennons in memory of the soaking in blood these had received at the Battle of Aliwal in 1846.

9th (The Queen's Royal) Light Dragoons (Lancers)
Officer's chapka, c1850

In view of the pressing need for more cavalry experienced during the Indian Mutiny (1857-59) two more mounted regiments were raised, one of which was a lancer regiment and took the number 5, which had been vacant since its predecessor's disbandment in 1799. The 5th Royal Irish (Light) Dragoons (Lancers) wore a scarlet-topped chapka with a green plume. Soon afterwards, three regiments of British hussars were formed from European light cavalry of the East India Company and one of these, the 21st Hussars, was converted to a lancer regiment in honour of Queen Victoria's Diamond Jubilee in 1897.

The lance was then in the ascendant, spreading rapidly through the cavalry of the Indian Army and, remarkably, even being carried for a short while by the front ranks of British cavalry other than lancers. At first, scarlet facings and a scarlet-topped chapka were to be worn by the 21st, but the colour was soon changed to French grey, the attractive pale blue colour long associated with Indian cavalry. The officers must have been put to great expense, as they also acquired the first of several new plates that followed one another in quick succession when the regiment was honoured with the title 'Empress of India's'. A small feature of heraldic interest was the use of the Imperial Crown, normally confined to India, and of the Imperial Cypher of Queen Victoria on the boss, which was retained even after her death, whereas for other regiments the boss cypher changed with the Sovereign. While other regular lancers had gradually added battle honours to their chapka plates, this young regiment was very conscious of having none, but, having taken a conspicuous part in the Battle of Omdurman (2 September

1898), the 21st were awarded the battle honour KHARTOUM, which was promptly displayed on their chapka plates, the central device of which was for a while a cypher instead of the usual Royal Arms. The Royal Arms were however soon restored to the plate and were also the central feature of the plate intended for an obscure new regiment, whose existence was brief: Her Majesty's Reserve Regiment of Lancers, 1900-01, whose prescribed facings, chapka-top and plume were all red.

The only other regular British lancer regiments it remains for us to consider are the 24th Lancers and 27th Lancers which were raised in 1940-41 and disbanded in 1948. Although at that time the modern Polish chapka, worn by Polish servicemen, was frequently seen in London, these two War-time regiments never wore a chapka and their only real connection with the lance was confined to their titles and badges. Meanwhile, in the contraction that usually follows a war, the 5th Lancers had been amalgamated with the 16th and the 21st with the 17th in 1922, the uniforms adopted being in each case that of the senior partner. In 1959 the 12th similarly amalgamated with the 9th.

Naturally, in the field, concessions were made in dress even in the earliest days and a black oilskin cover, which already existed for other headdress before lancers were introduced, was supplied for the men's chapkas and was worn with the usual lines but no plume. For the officers the more elegant equivalent item by 1826 was an actual undress chapka, described by *Dress Regulations* as being of oiled silk of the same shape and size as the full dress headdress, but with a chin-chain. Later these were made to resemble a cover of glossy American cloth, complete with buttons. Soon a few special features appeared, such as the death's head chain-bosses of the 17th Lancers. The 'foul weather cap', as it was called, was widely worn in the field until after the Crimean War and lingered until late in the nineteenth century. Similarly, a white cotton cover for the men (later worn over a special form of chapka) and the equivalent white headdress for officers were worn with neck-curtains in tropical climates in the same period. These were seen on many battlefields in India and were even worn at Varna during the Crimean War.

17th Lancers

Officer's foul-weather chapka c1872 worn by Brigade Surgeon E Hoile

NAM. 6806-25-1

Before 1826, the lancer officers' normal undress headdress had taken the form of a somewhat simplified low chapka with a boss and a small horsehair plume and no plate, but this item varied a great deal from regiment to regiment. An extremely interesting example of a 23rd Lancers officer's undress cap c1816 is preserved in the Manx Museum, Douglas, Isle of Man. This is very similar in shape to the modern Polish headdress and has a very low square crimson crown with pleated sides (reflecting the cane-reinforced 'fluted' sides of a genuine chapka), a broad silver lace band and a tooled leather peak of French style. This cap seems to resemble an evolutionary link with the ordinary peaked forage cap and even the forage caps of lancer regiments today have quarter-welts to represent the square top once worn. Indeed, at most times before the advent in 1902-05 of the modern shape, the various forage caps had crossed lines of Russia braid right across the crown.

British lancer dress has been remarkably consistent and it is sad from the point of view of the uniform enthusiast that the great extension of lancer uniforms to remote corners of the Empire occurred after the chapka had vanished from tropical climates. From about 1860 other forms of headdress, notably the white tropical helmet, had displaced normal European headdress for service overseas and yet in India from c1874 onwards numerous native cavalry regiments were progressively armed (or in some cases rearmed) with the lance, while lancer regiments were even created in Australia. With the lance came uniform features to delight the purist, such as the special forage cap, plastron, seam-piping, girdle and lines but, alas, the crowning glory of the chapka was withheld.

One Indian Army regiment, however, became a lancer unit in time to wear the chapka: the 1st Regiment of Bombay Light Cavalry was a lancer regiment from 1842 until 1861 and all ranks wore a chapka with scarlet top and black plume. For the officers the chapka lace was gold and the plate device was of unusual design, consisting of the letters BLC on a black velvet ground within a garter surrounded by roses, thistles and shamrocks. They had both feather and horsehair plumes and, of course, they also had the undress chapka and the distinctive lancer forage cap.

21st (Empress of India's) Lancers

Officer's chapka, c1910

In addition, one obscure volunteer unit in India, whose members were local European citizens, is alleged to have adopted the chapka. The Calcutta Volunteer Lancers only existed from 1872 until 1877 and the regimental history admits that recruits joined mainly to acquire a fine lancer uniform and to escort the Viceroy on ceremonial occasions. An officer's chapka preserved for many years in the Calcutta Light Horse Club had attached to its front a rayed plate, bearing the initials CVL on crossed lances beneath a crown, but this may have been a trial pattern as surviving photographs only show the unit in lancer uniforms with just tropical helmets or pillbox caps.

It may well be that the lengthy, rigorous training demanded by the lance discouraged even the more dedicated auxiliary units from adopting it. In Britain, the ubiquitous mass of small auxiliary cavalry units comprising the Yeomanry wore very varied uniforms, mainly of light dragoon or Hussar character. Many auxiliary cavalry units had been raised in the 1790s and so many individual troops were raised in the troubled 1830s that in many cases nothing is known about them. In Buckinghamshire, the Taplow Troop was a lancer unit and in Suffolk in 1850 the Long Melford Troop (Lancers) wore a gold-laced, scarlet-topped chapka with a white plume, while the West Essex Yeomanry had men in chapkas but did not bother with the lance. By the end of the century, however, the only Yeomanry unit with a lancer uniform was the Lanarkshire Yeomanry, who wore a spiked helmet of infantry style.

But the dearth of lancer uniforms within the Yeomanry was soon to be remedied, the inspiration coming from a surprising quarter: the impression created by the Australian and other lancers attending the Diamond Jubilee celebrations shortly before the raising of a large force of Imperial Yeomanry in 1900 for the South African War seems to have been the cause of several of the sixteen new Yeomanry regiments adopting lancer uniforms. The Surrey Yeomanry, whose lancer uniform was khaki and scarlet, instead of the chapka wore the Australian slouch hat with a green feather plume for officers but several other regiments over the next few years adopted the proper headdress, even though the lance itself now went out of favour for a time. The Bedfordshire Yeomanry wore a chapka of 9th Lancer pattern and colouring with a silver eagle on the plate and the officers of the East Riding of Yorkshire Yeomanry wore a rather similar metal-trimmed chapka with pale blue top and a pale blue and white plume with their maroon uniform. The device on the gilt plate beneath the cypher was a silver fox, reflecting the County's devotion to hunting. For the City of London Yeomanry (Rough Riders) the chapka was of the normal pattern with gold lace but the top was bright blue to match their uniforms rather than their facings, which were purple. Their plate bore the arms of the City of London whereas those of the City of Lincoln in silver were borne by the Lincolnshire Yeomanry, which had green uniforms. Their chapka, which had a white top and green plume, had the rare distinction of silver lace trimming. Somewhat belatedly the Lanarkshire Yeomanry followed the trend and finally purchased a small number of chapkas of 9th Lancer pattern for King George V's Coronation in 1911.

Although the lance was finally abolished as a weapon of war in the British Army in 1927 it did not vanish altogether: thirty years later the 17th/21st Lancers procured enough of these weapons to arm every man on parade with this symbol of their lancer traditions. In dress, too, the lancer tradition survives modestly in the form of piped back seams (mainly in mess dress); and, in the case of the forage cap, quarter-welts survive to remind us of the chapka.

Even the British chapka itself lives on, regular lancer regiments being permitted at their own expense to dress their lance-bearing orderlies and their bands in the traditional full dress; in the case of the 16th/5th Lancers modern technology has helped the headdress to survive, the regiment having recently procured fibreglass versions. Chapkas have gladdened the hearts of uniform enthusiasts on many occasions since the Second World War and provide a remarkable example of continuity, having undergone but little change since lancers first appeared in the British Army one and a half centuries ago.

'THE LITTLE ONE WAS A SHARP ONE'

SOME UNIFORMS OF GENERAL F R CHESNEY (1789-1872)

WILLIAM REID

In May 1798 an Irish child trudged barefoot and alone for twenty miles to Newry from his home near Kinkeel. Nine-year old Francis Rawdon Chesney was marching to join his regiment, for he held the rank of sub-lieutenant in the Mourne Company of the Down Volunteers. At Newry friends of Alexander, his father, delighted Francis by giving him the nickname 'Suvaroff', and may even have salved the pain he felt on hearing the great Cornwallis describe him at a review as 'very small'. But small he was, even for an 'officer', whose father, a Scots-Irish veteran of the American Revolution, thought that some military rank would be a valuable first step towards a cadetship at the Royal Military Academy at Woolwich. Years later the young man wrote that his early association with adult soldiers 'confirmed the confident disposition which would not be if I continued at my books as became one of my age'.

There can be little doubt that his assessment of the effect of this absurdly premature introduction to military affairs was not overstated. For 'confident' one might even read 'irrepressible', as he revelled in physical discomfort, conflict and challenge throughout his life, never seeming to consider any simple project worthy of his attention. Francis Chesney was of the stuff of heroes, his innate courage tempered in the fire of severe discipline, first undergone at the hands of a strict father and later self-

General F R Chesney (1789-1872) in the uniform of a Major-General 1863. From S Lane-Poole ed., The Life of the Late General F R Chesney ... by His Wife and Daughter, *London (1885)*

NAM. neg no 49504

imposed. His self-mastery is best exemplified by the way that he, who so hated the cold, drove himself to swim in winter seas and to walk and climb among ice-covered mountain tops. This harsh regime stood him in good stead as he remained capable of long, strenuous hill-walks until he was in his eighties.[1]

Capt Chesney's Raft in 1830. Descending the Euphrates towards Hadisah

From F R Chesney, Narrative of the Euphrates expedition ... during the years 1835, 1836 and 1837, *London (1868)*

His skill as a swimmer and his courage were both tested in the most practical way while home on leave in Ireland in 1814. On 10 January he swam to the rescue of a local fisherman called Hugh Purdy in a storm which drowned 40 others. For the first time in his life, and almost certainly for the last, his courage was perpetuated in a poem, *The New Sorrowful Lamentation of the Mourne Fisherman Drowned on the 10th January, 1814.* Written by some local McGonagall to be sung to the tune of the Highland dirge 'Lochaber no more', one stanza runs;

> Great praise is due to Captain Chesney's son:
> In the middle of all danger to the quay he did run,
> And swam o'er the waves like Leander of old,
> And of young Hughey Purdy he quickly took hold,
> He saved him from drowning, relief being near,
> Wherein different forms grim death did appear,

And brought him to land by the help of an oar,
Or he ne'er would have seen Mourne shore.

A day later, before the storm blew itself out, Chesney was instrumental in getting a line to the *Leda* that enabled her master and crew to reach the safety of the shore. The first incident earned him an Honorary Certificate from The Royal Humane Society, the second the medal of the *Société Française de Naufrage*; a not inconsiderable double for a landsman.

As well as his 'service' with the Mourne Volunteers, the boy had other early connections with the profession of arms. His name was a reminder of his father's military career, as he was called after Francis Rawdon Hastings, first Marquess of Hastings and second Earl Moira, with whom Alexander served in South Carolina at Fort Ninety-Six and King's Mountain before returning in 1783, ill and impoverished, to the post of tide-waiter at Waterford. His Customs duties required him to carry arms and his pistol was among the first toys Francis played with. On an outing to Dublin in 1796, Lord Moira, already the child's patron, gave him a wooden gun and a drum, but then proposed that the boy should be educated for the Church; perhaps the first suggestion that the rigours of military life might prove too much for one of such slight physique.

A year later, the Master-General of the Ordnance acknowledged Alexander Chesney's application for the long-cherished cadetship at the Royal Military Academy Woolwich, but added that Francis could not be considered until his fourteenth birthday. He continued with his schooling in Ireland and England until, at the appointed time, he appeared before Major Phipps, Inspector of Cadets at Woolwich, and the Examining Master, Mr Evans. But he was still very small for his age; well below the cadet's height standard of four foot nine inches. In the summer of 1803, when he was seen again by Major Phipps, he took the advice of another officer who suggested that a pair of cork heels worn inside his stockings might just lift him above the entrance height. They did so, but by a mere quarter-inch.

Life at Woolwich was neither especially pleasant nor easy for the son of an unmoneyed Customs official. He held out, despite pecuniary difficulties that were to plague him for most of his life, to be gazetted into the Royal Artillery on 9 November 1804. He was then fifteen years and eight months old, on the threshold of a career of extraordinary distinction, albeit devoid of active service. What one might have expected to have been his most productive years as a soldier were spent on routine regimental duties at Portsmouth, Guernsey, Leith, Dublin and Gibraltar. During that professionally uneventful period, and subsequently, he volunteered without success for every British military expedition from the Waterloo campaign to the invasion of the Crimea in 1854-55.

Chesney always had friends in high places. Among those whose counsel he took in his early years was Sir Robert Gordon, British Ambassador in Constantinople. Their conversations inspired Chesney, already a skilled surveyor, to embark on explorations in 1830-31 that resulted in a report on the feasibility of a canal at Suez, and detailed maps of the Euphrates Valley.[2] His views on the former encouraged Ferdinand de Lesseps, who was later to pay tribute to Chesney as 'the father of the Canal', to undertake the task that altered the face of travel to the Orient. The Euphrates adventure led in turn to an almost incredible journey in 1834.

After some two years of continually lobbying men of influence, from William IV to the diplomatist, Sir Stratford Canning and Lord Ripon, who, as Viscount Goderich, was Secretary of State for War and the Colonies 1830-33, Chesney was authorised to lead an expedition to test his theory that the Euphrates was navigable from the point nearest to the Bay of Antioch, on the eastern shore of the Mediterranean, to the Persian Gulf. Then a captain employed in the rank of colonel, he commanded thirteen other Royal Navy and Army officers and a mixed company of engineers, gunners and seamen who carried two armed, iron steam launches 140 miles overland from Samandag on the coast of Turkey to Birecik on the upper Euphrates. On the downstream voyage the *Tigris* sank with the loss of twenty lives. The other launch, the *Euphrates* reached the Persian Gulf port of Bushire in the summer of 1836. The Chesney route was proved.

The expedition leader had already accepted the accolades of the Royal Society and the Royal Geographical Society, receiving fellowships from both in 1833. On his return to London in the middle of 1837 Chesney began to compose the report that was to earn him the Gold Medal of the latter society, only to have his work interrupted by orders to take command of the artillery at the Hong Kong station where he was involved in excitements and controversy from 1843 to 1847. Three years after his return the first two volumes of *The Expedition for the Survey of the Rivers Euphrates and Tigris* were published.[3] The final volume, under the title *Narrative of the Euphrates Expedition*[4] was not to see the light of day for another eighteen years, by which time General Chesney had been honoured by the *Gesellschaft für Erdkunde zu Berlin*, and by the University of Oxford, which awarded him an Hon DCL in June 1851. Between the publication of the first two report volumes and the third Chesney produced two other important works, *Observations on the Past and Present State of Firearms*[5] and *The Russo-Turkish Campaigns of 1828 and 1829*.[6] These were to confirm his position as a military thinker and reporter of some consequence but brought him neither title nor decorations.

Statements to the effect that Chesney refused all honours from the Crown are not supported by the evidence of his journal. As early as 1833 he shows signs of having been sorely disappointed that the King merely shook his hand at a levée when he expected to be decorated. Towards the end of his life the authorities may have had some thought of conferring a KCB, but Chesney's Toryism often clashed with the philosophies of his political masters. A supplementary cause may have been Chesney's abrasiveness; he was as capable of the inadvertent cutting remark as many others whose formative years were spent in the coarser strata of society. After one verbal indiscretion his hostess was heard to remark 'the little one was a sharp one'. A tendency to ridicule, albeit gently, stayed with him to the end of his days. One also senses that the impassioned and persistent advocacy of his causes, and repeated importuning of the highest in the land in support of his schemes were unlikely to endear him to other soldiers, politicians or civil servants. They were not inclined to propose him for honours, but members of his personal circle were prepared to give him, in his own words, 'a lift'. For example , 'General Anderson, amongst the rest, proposed me as a member of the

Athenæum of his own accord'. One wonders what the man from the bare, bleak shores of Mourne made of Decimus Burton's palace, built a decade earlier for men like Humphrey Davy, Thomas Lawrence and Walter Scott. He was duly elected in March 1838, not as an ordinary member but under Rule II, one of eight distinguished men invited by the club's general council to join that year. Before Chesney's death the up-and-coming Wolseley and Roberts were among the members of his profession who joined under the same honorific rule.[7]

When his *Observations* and *The Russo-Turkish Campaigns* appeared, Chesney was on half-pay at his family home, Packolet, Ballyardle, County Down, but his service to the Crown was by no means finished. In 1855, soon after his promotion to major-general, only a change in the Cabinet prevented his being given the task of leading a foreign legion to the Crimea.

The possibility of opening up a route to India through 'his' Euphrates valley took him to the Middle East again in 1856 at the age of 65. Plans to build a railway were dropped by an apprehensive British Government in the face of opposition from Napoleon III both then and in 1862 when, at the age of 72, Chesney won fresh concessions from the Ottoman authorities in Constantinople. For ten more years this tough little man, still fit and energetic, continued to battle for his dream of a direct route to India with a pertinacity approaching fanaticism. In his 82nd year he could still hold his own with a House of Commons committee although he did not live to see its favourable, if ineffectual report. On 30 January 1872 he died at Packolet, aged 83. He was survived by his third wife Louisa, née Fletcher, whom he married on 30 March 1848. She and Jane, his daughter by his first wife, Georgette Forster, collaborated in a loving biography.

In March 1979 some of this remarkable soldier's uniforms were found, piled on a scrap-merchant's floor, and purchased by the National Army Museum.[8] Like many other men of action, Chesney had a sentimental attachment to articles of clothing he had worn on special, though not always auspicious occasions. Indeed, he had a lifelong feeling not only for uniform, but for all male and female costume. Writing to his father from the Royal Military College, Great Marlow, on 21 September 1803 he described his newly-issued uniform;

> 'The dress is red with blue facings, and pantaloons, red waistcoat, black gaiters,
> silver lace; there is no blue on the breast of the coat; our head-dress is a cap with
> a silver plate on the front, with the "Royal Military College." The officers
> intended for the Line and for Woolwich wear all the same dress.

He was to wear a red coat again in 1811. In a letter to his mother telling her of his appointment as acting ADC to General Sir Albert Gledstanes he wrote 'I put on a scarlet coat yesterday (for the first time since Great Marlow College)'.

His biographers record that he not only kept his uniforms carefully until the end of his life, but he even expressed the wish that they be buried with him. This romantic element in Chesney's character bubbled to the surface when, on 30 April 1839, he married for the second time. He had fallen in love with Everilda Fraser when her father was second-in-command in

Royal Regiment of Artillery; single-breasted coatee*, worn by Francis Rawdon Chesney on the occasion of his marriage to his first wife in 1822 and to his second wife, Everilda, in 1839. The coatee was placed over the body of Everilda Chesney in her coffin in 1841. The collar was placed across the breast, the remainder extending to just below knee level.*

NAM. 9307-21-1

Royal Regiment of Artillery; pair of company officer's epaulettes, c1830; pair of unofficial pattern ankle boots and a peaked forage cap, 1822-41. The epaulettes were placed, with the crescents towards the head, one on each upper breast within Everilda Chesney's coffin. The rolled forage cap was at the left of the upper part of the skull. The boots, which rested at her feet, had been worn by Francis Rawdon Chesney during his Euphrates Expedition.

NAM. 9307-21-4, -5, -6

Guernsey during Chesney's time there between 1808 and 1814. His ardent proposals of marriage were all rejected until, after many years of separation, the widowed colonel of 50 again met his still charming, but desperately ill 'Evé' in 1838. His journal describes the wedding-day, which took place under the dark cloud of the bride's fatal illness; she was to live less than eighteen months more. After calling on his future father-and mother-in-law he changed into;

> 'the old single-breasted uniform coatee and gold-lace blue trousers, both first worn 11th May 1822, when I was united to my affectionate G., then changed to uniform and became my full-dress whilst she lived. In these I followed her to the grave, with the sash now worn. I had kept them expressly for this union, and my dress was completed by adding the old shoes worn when the Tigris went down. I had the forage cap which, like these clothes, had made the tour of the Euphrates, and went also on my first journey. I also wore the brooch with poor G's hair, and one of the two wedding shirts she made, the other being around her, poor soul.

The description is a shade ambiguous at more than one point, as Mercer records that the uniform of battalion officers of the Royal Artillery included at one period, up to five different jackets and that their coats were probably long-skirted for full dress, with either short skirts or none for undress or service wear.[9] Campbell notes that 'It is difficult to differentiate between the uses of some of these garments or to date them accurately before about 1831'.[10] The Chesney account suggests that for him, if not for all Gunner officers, his 'best', i.e. newest, uniform was worn as full-dress in the absence of a strictly observed dress regulation. There is, however, a possibility that he married Miss Forster in a civilian suit of dark blue that was subsequently altered for wear as military full-dress. The closing sentences of the account of his second wedding-day confirm Chesney's sentimental nature almost as much as does the constancy of his love for Evé. It lasted through three decades that covered his short and companionable, if unromantic, marriage to Georgette, who died in January 1825, and his many thrilling foreign excursions.

By an extraordinary coincidence, four coffins unearthed in July 1991 by workmen repairing the crypt of St Barnabas' Church, West Kensington, confirm the depth of Chesney's feeling for his second wife and his strange, almost eerie obsession with military uniform. Everilda Chesney's name is engraved on one lead coffin-plate, the others being those of her parents, General Sir John and Lady Fraser and her sister. Arranged around his beloved Evé was her husband's uniform, probably the one he wore at his weddings to Georgette Forster and to Everilda, comprising a peaked forage cap, a coatee with epaulettes of the pattern worn from c1822 to 1827, overalls and ankle boots.[11]

The garments bought in 1979 included two coatees of the pattern introduced in 1838 and abolished by the dress regulation of 1855. One of them, now in the Royal Artillery Regimental Museum, shows much wear and careful repairs that suggest that Chesney had worn it long and hard, possibly on those expeditions where he was not forced by circumstance into native dress. The other is in such near-pristine state that it could have had almost no wear before the Royal Artillery officer's pattern tunic of 1855 was taken into service.

A Royal Warrant announcing the retirement of many officers of the Royal Engineers and Royal Artillery, brought Chesney's name to the top of the list of colonels and hence, in January 1855, to the rank of major-general. In his new rank he would not have worn his artillery coatee, but the scarlet tunic of a general officer. One such with a general's rank badges of a crown and star formed part of the batch of uniform bought for the National Army Museum. It may date from soon after his promotion to major-general although the badges it bears are those of his last rank, to which he was promoted in 1868.

In the light of the understandable deceit that carried him into Woolwich and his biographers' statement that 'He was a small wiry man with very small hands and feet' it is worth mentioning that the two coatees, the general officer's tunic and a frock coat that accompanied them were made for a boyish figure of no more than five foot one.

The balance of the Chesney wardrobe preserved in the National Army Museum consists of the uniform of a major-general worn in the 1863 photograph that forms the frontispiece of his biography. It shows the sitter, as do almost all portrait photographs of the day, in rather stiff repose. His widow and daughter record that this was far from being his usual expression, which they remembered as intelligent and genial, not handsome but 'so instinct with life and humour that it never failed to make a pleasant impression'. Chesney is wearing a major-general's frock coat of blue cloth with blue velvet facings; crimson and gold sash; and holds white kid gloves and the cocked hat with a white-over-red plume of swan's feathers, that he would more properly have worn with his scarlet tunic. The waistbelt and sword are no longer with the uniform.

When Francis Rawdon Chesney's turn came to embark on the last journey, it is a safe bet that he went in something more dramatic than a common shroud as he asked that the 'articles of dress used on special occasions' should be buried with him. He was a fascinating personality, distinguished even by the standards of Royal Artillery general officers, whose relics in the collections of the Royal Artillery Regimental Museum and the National Army Museum will help to remind future generations of the debt we owe to one of those rare men of moral stature whose strength of will, courage, and sheer toughness helped to open up the modern world. Chesney was in the first rank as an explorer; as an expedition leader he has rarely been excelled. Yet his journals show that he retained to the end a tender romanticism, at once a weakness and a strength.

THE LINEAGE OF
A COUNTY REGIMENT

THE HAMPSHIRE REGIMENT

IAN MAINE

Apart from the huge administrative, technological and social change that occurred in the British Army during the years 1815 to 1914 there were also important changes in the organisation at the heart of the Army at that time - the Regimental System. The Hampshire Regiment has been chosen to illustrate some of these developments as it displays many of the changes typical of those affecting regiments around the country.

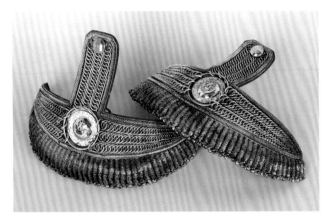

North Hampshire Militia, light company officer's wings, c1831

In 1831 silver lace was adopted by the North Hampshire Militia. During this year they were embodied for 28 days' training, although it was not until 1853 that the Regiment was embodied again. Wings such as these were worn by officers of flank companies of infantry. The strung bugle-horn indicates the light company.

NAM. 7107-20

REGULAR ARMY

In 1816 Hampshire was represented by two Foot Regiments, the 37th (or the North Hampshire) and the 67th (or the South Hampshire). Radical change did not occur to the numbered system until Edward Cardwell, the Secretary of State for War, 1868-74, undertook a whole series of reforms which altered service conditions and organisation of the Army. In 1873 sub-districts were formed under the 'localisation scheme', which enabled home service to be more co-ordinated. Each sub-district consisted of a brigade depot, two battalions of line infantry as well as Militia and Volunteer units. As a conclusion to this policy, under Cardwell's successor, Hugh Eardley Childers, 'territorialisation' was undertaken in 1881. This abolished the system of numbered regiments and replaced them with County titles. Two numbered regiments of infantry were normally paired, to form 1st and 2nd battalions of the new territorial regiment. In Hampshire, the 37th and 67th Foot became the 1st and 2nd Battalions, the Hampshire Regiment.

The territorialisation scheme was designed to harmonise components of the Army with a specific locality, so that a regiment would not only bear the County name, but would also recruit and retain its depot within the county boundary. This system remained unchanged until after the end of the period examined here.

THE MILITIA

At the end of the Napoleonic Wars the Militia was disembodied. In Hampshire, there were two Militia infantry units - the North and South Hampshire Militias. The Militia had provided a steady supply of volunteers into the regular Army. Militia units were embodied occasionally after 1816. During 1853 the North and South Hampshire Militia were amalgamated. A critical shortage of soldiers for home defence resulted in them being embodied throughout the Crimean War and, following the end of the War, annually until 1908.

In 1881, as part of the territorialisation scheme, Militia battalions became part of their regular Army regiment. In the case of Hampshire, the single Militia battalion became the 3rd Battalion, Hampshire Regiment.

R B Haldane, Secretary of State for War from 1907, framed the Territorial and Reserve Forces Act of 1907, which created a new auxiliary force, the Territorial Force. The Militia regiments were offered the choice of becoming part of either the new Territorial Force or the regular Army. Most refused. As a result, Militia regiments were either disbanded or replaced with the Special Reserve, which was abolished in 1921.

2nd Volunteer Battalion, Hampshire Regiment, officer's pouch c1890

This Battalion recruited in the Southampton area. The pouch shows silver lace instead of gold. Volunteer officers' dress had silver lace to distinguish them from the regular Army which wore gold.

NAM. 7404-1

Isle of Wight Volunteers, officer's helmet, c1880

All the Isle of Wight Rifle Volunteers adopted Rifle Green uniform. This distinction was retained when the unit became the 5th Volunteer Battalion Hampshire Regiment, in contrast to the Hampshire Rifle Volunteer units who had all adopted scarlet by 1880.

NAM. 8004-92

THE HAMPSHIRE REGIMENT

OUTLINE LINEAGE

REGULAR   AUXILLIARY

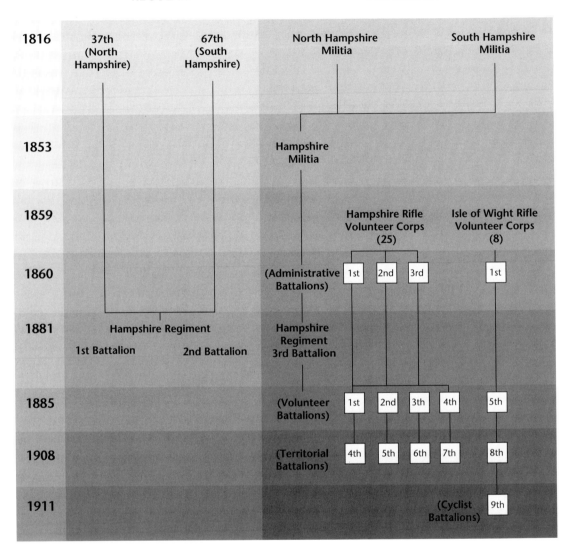

	REGULAR		AUXILLIARY	
1816	37th (North Hampshire)	67th (South Hampshire)	North Hampshire Militia	South Hampshire Militia
1853			Hampshire Militia	
1859			Hampshire Rifle Volunteer Corps (25)	Isle of Wight Rifle Volunteer Corps (8)
1860			(Administrative Battalions) 1st 2nd 3rd	1st
1881	Hampshire Regiment 1st Battalion	2nd Battalion	Hampshire Regiment 3rd Battalion	
1885			(Volunteer Battalions) 1st 2nd 3th 4th	5th
1908			(Territorial Battalions) 4th 5th 6th 7th	8th
1911			(Cyclist Battalions)	9th

THE VOLUNTEERS

The infantry and artillery Volunteers of the French Revolutionary and Napoleonic Wars were all disbanded soon after 1815. With a few exceptions, the Volunteers did not exist until 1859 when the culmination of French invasion scares and public pressure led the War Office to issue a circular on 12 May 1859 empowering Lords Lieutenant of Counties to raise Volunteer corps of artillery and infantry under the provisions of the consolidated Volunteer Act of 1803.

Initially, on account of the fact that Volunteer units were locally raised and organised on a small scale, they were relatively autonomous, each corps having its own set of rules, different uniform and standards. Very quickly, however, they were formed into 'Administrative Battalions'. Hampshire raised 25 Rifle Volunteer corps and the Isle of Wight raised eight. These were grouped into four Administrative Battalions during December 1860.

In 1881, the Administrative Battalions were linked to the County regular Regiment under the 'territorialisation' scheme. In Hampshire, another Administrative Battalion was formed in 1885 and during that year the battalions were re-titled, forming the 1st to 5th Volunteer Battalions, the 5th being the Isle of Wight Battalion. On conversion to the Territorial Force in 1908, the Volunteer battalions became the 4th to 8th Battalions, Territorial Force.

CYCLISTS

As Marion Harding relates later in this book, by the end of the nineteenth century, many Volunteer battalions incorporated cyclist units. In most cases these formed part of Volunteer battalions, although in some cases they were of sufficient numbers to be formed into battalions themselves. In Hampshire, a cyclist battalion, the 9th (Cyclist) Battalion, Hampshire Regiment, was raised in 1911.

CONCLUSION

The Lineage Outline which accompanies this article illustrates the changes over eighty years or so as they affected the Hampshire Regiment, and stands as a model for other historic regiments of infantry.

THE ART OF WAR

THE EVOLUTION OF MILITARY PAINTING IN VICTORIAN BRITAIN

JENNY SPENCER-SMITH

As Richard Caton Woodville regretfully observed in his memoirs;

> 'It is a curious thing how little the English public care for military pictures; there are hardly any in our public or private galleries. And as for the Army, they would much rather hang the latest Gaiety actress in their mess than the finest episode of their regimental history.[1]

This generalization seems to reflect an unspoken tradition in this country, for in the two-and-a-half centuries since the establishment of a standing Army in Britain until the outbreak of the Great War, also the year in which Caton Woodville's statement appeared in print, the depiction of contemporary military events was not especially popular here. Indeed, even in the present day, much interest in military painting of the last century and earlier has been centred on those works of art that can be read as a factual record of some aspect of the development of costume, and there has been little recognition of a 'military genre' by the fine art world. Nor is this because some of our finest artists have failed to contribute military paintings for posterity - they have, and there is an abundance of pictures which are also important documents of social history or mirrors of public taste.

The reason may lie partly in the general unpopularity of the Army in times past, since it was both an instrument of state power and because it was composed of the humblest in society, notoriously prone to the temptations of strong drink and sometimes even criminal.[2] Irrespective of the fervent patriotism to which the Nation is quickly aroused in time of war, there has long existed a general attitude of anti-militarism in Britain, which has engendered a sense of moral ascendancy over other states (especially the French). It has been pointed out that, contrary to the evidence of their military activity overseas during the reign of Queen Victoria, the British people (as typified by the military historians of the time) did not regard themselves as a military nation, but rather believed that they fought when forced to do so from a sense of duty and public-spiritedness.[3] This discouraged the representatives of the state from patronizing battle painting of an overtly triumphant nature, the very opposite of the situation in France, where it had been adopted as royal and imperial propaganda. Queen Victoria and Prince Albert themselves, despite being passionately interested both in art and military matters, had rather conservative aesthetic tastes and so did little to patronize new developments in art or to encourage artists by commissioning much new work: instead they bought what was already available.[4]

In comparison, France had enjoyed a rich genre of battle painting since the reign of Louis XIV which, ultimately, was concerned with the glorification of the head of state. This reinforcement of the monarch's absolute power was redefined at the beginning of the nineteenth century in a contemporary idiom to enhance the imperial image of Napoleon, for example Antoine-Jean Gros' *Napoleon on the field at Eylau, 1807* (1808; *Musée du Louvre*) and Jacques-Louis David's *Napoleon crossing the Alps* (1800; *Musée National du Chateau de Malmaison*).[5] In Britain, such glorification had been political anathema since the late seventeenth century, and there was no exact equivalent in British military painting. It could be said that the nearest approach was the hero-worship expressed in the theme of heroic sacrifice, which reached its apogee in Benjamin West's *Death of Wolfe* (1770; National Gallery of Canada, Ottawa) or John Singleton Copley's *Death of Major Peirson* (1784; Tate Gallery).[6] In fact, these pictures and one or two others of this era were very popular, being applauded as much for their freshness and innovation as for their sentiment, and they constitute one of a few exceptions which can be claimed against Caton Woodville's accusation.[7]

However, part of the problem in analysing the history of military painting as a discrete genre is that it does not stand up to scrutiny either as a legacy of academic 'history painting'

The Recruit

Oil on canvas by Henry Liverseege (1803-32), c1830

NAM. 6402-42

nor, despite Britain's active imperial history, have we inherited a continuous tradition of battle painting. In fact, formal, academic notions of battle painting as a type of history painting belong to eighteenth-century aesthetics, in which the various genres of painting, portraiture, landscape and so on, were stratified in terms of worthiness; the highest form being that which embodied a didactic lesson in good conduct (which, by example, 'improved' the spectator), and this was understood to be history painting. 'History' in this context originally was strictly that of the ancient Greeks, although the subject matter became more 'modern' after a time.[8] The staginess of the 'heroic sacrifice', in which the actual battle merely forms a background to a hero's death, became translated in the early nineteenth century into a grander theatricality, but one which, despite the intense fervour aroused by the victory at Waterloo, failed to arouse much public enthusiasm. That this may have been a consequence of a dearth of talent and direction is suggested by the comment of a *Times* reviewer with regard to the work produced for the competition announced by the British Institution in 1815 to commemorate the Napoleonic Wars in painting; 'There are unquestionably a few good pictures, but the collection, considered on average, betrays a poverty of intellect and imagination of native artists'.[9] The first prize was won by James Ward's elaborate allegory of Waterloo (1821; Royal Hospital Chelsea, since destroyed), which was accompanied by a discouragingly lengthy exegesis on its iconography, and the second by George Jones for his view of the battle (1820; Royal Hospital Chelsea).

Ward may have been too academic for popular taste but Jones' grand Waterloo painting made his reputation, for he had successfully balanced the components to create an appropriate spectacle. Taking a slightly elevated viewpoint, with intense fighting visible in the middle to far-distance, Wellington can be identified in the centre middle-distance of the painting (that is, relegated from the foreground as the all-consuming point of interest) making an eloquent gesture against a cloud of smoke, while a number of small narrative incidents unfold nearer the spectator. During a long career in which he exhibited over 200 paintings at the Royal Academy, Jones covered all the principal contemporary military campaigns up to the Abyssinian Expedition of 1868. However, few of these captured the 'balance' of his first military work, and his output became formularized, respected but not widely popular. It is significant, too, that, while Jones was the leading exponent of battle painting until the 1840s, military pictures constituted but a fraction of his total production, which was a mixture of classical and historical subjects, themes from the Old Testament, and contemporary subjects.[10]

While Jones' theatrical works satisfied a desire to see recent victorious actions formally commemorated, public interest was gratified by the vogue for depicting these events in panoramic form (some of which also take an elevated viewpoint or 'bird's-eye view') which were exhibited publicly in such arenas as Henry Aston Barker's Leicester Square Panorama Theatre. While these were primarily of interest for their curiosity value in purporting to convey an illusion whereby the spectator became an eye-witness of the event, they had an influence on easel paintings for a while, exemplified by Sir William Allan's panoramic paintings of the Battle of Waterloo (...*from the French side*, 1843; Wellington Museum, Apsley House [Victoria and Albert Museum] and ...*from the English side*, 1847; the Sandhurst Museum, Royal Military Academy Sandhurst). Allan was praised for the way in which he arranged an accurately represented contemporary army into a pleasing battlefield composition, a combination which 'elevated' war reportage into the academic aesthetic. However, he was unsuccessful with his 'Waterloo' entry for the Westminster Palace competition in 1847, where, in a grand scheme intended to glorify British history which would rival the enormous battle paintings at Versailles, public sponsorship attempted to retain the last vestiges of history painting as construed by Sir Joshua Reynolds. The only battle painting to be accepted by the competition's committee of judges was by the French-trained artist, Edward Armitage, whose enormous canvas of *The Battle of Meeanee* (Royal Collection) constituted a very dramatic interpretation of the recent Sikh Wars, and showed an entanglement of groups engaged in hand-to-hand fighting, including two British soldiers bayoneting fallen Sikhs in the centre foreground. However, it so appealed to Queen Victoria that it was ceded to her instead.[11]

The immediate reaction to Armitage's work showed the confusion which had developed about academic concepts of art; on the one hand, it was applauded as a history painting, but it also received criticism for reproducing mere fact, that is it could not elevate the mind as history painting should. In general, however, these theories had become outmoded and during the first half of the nineteenth century, the era of the 'Long Peace', popular taste moved away from history painting; now genre painting, showing soldiers in domestic or other civilian settings, constituted the most significant military art. These changes have been ascribed both to the rise of the bourgeoisie as an economic force in post-Industrial Revolution society, and to the gradual improvement in the civilian perception of the Army, a view which was partly engendered by the fashion for all things gothic, including romantic notions of chivalry. However, the common soldier was more likely to be the butt of humour than a paradigm of honour, such as in Henry Liverseege's *A Recruit* (1830; National Army Museum 6402-42). Pictures on themes such as recruiting, departing for war, the veteran's reminiscences, or even news of the war were the very opposite of the grand theatrical spectacle of panoramic battle paintings. One such, Sir David Wilkie's *Chelsea Pensioners receiving the London Gazette Extraordinary of 22nd June 1815, announcing the Battle of Waterloo* (Wellington Museum, Apsley House [Victoria and Albert Museum]), commissioned by the Duke of Wellington himself, was so well received at the Royal Academy in 1822 that it had to be protected from the crush of onlookers by a barrier, the first time that this had ever occurred. It was admired for setting a strong narrative action into a recognisable London location, and for its mixture of characterization and emotion, and carefully-balanced but apparently artless composition.

The first major European campaign since 1815, the Crimean War (1854-56), generated an intense public interest in the Army and the conduct of war. It was also the first time that a major conflict was reported and illustrated by 'special' journalists and artists present at 'the seat of the war'. Public awareness was also marked by an increase in the number of canvases exhibited of Crimean subjects, as many artists were moved to depart from their usual subject-matter to tackle war-related themes, but, lacking any particular tradition, or artistic or military training which would have assisted in approaching such subjects, very few of their works were battle paintings. Some artists who had been out to the Crimea, such as the watercolourist William Simpson, depicted scenes of conflict, but no important battle painting was produced at this time, in contrast to the considerable number of such works the War generated in France. Instead, the most popular pictures were those

A Welcome Arrival

Oil on canvas by John D'Albiac Luard (1830-60), 1857
Luard visited the Crimea in the winter of 1855-56 to see his
brother, Captain Richard Amherst Luard of the 77th Regiment,
who is believed to be the central figure in the painting. The
officer on the left is Deputy-Assistant-Commissary William
Gair. The third sitter has never been positively identified, but
may be a self-portrait of the artist.

NAM. 5808-18

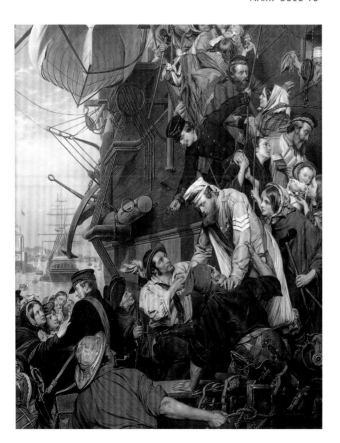

that continued in the vein of domestic genre, now showing the effect of war upon the families of those involved. Representations of the lower classes were now treated with all seriousness, as for instance in Joseph Noel Paton's *Home* (1856; location unknown, & 1859; Royal Collection), which shows a corporal of the Scots Fusilier Guards returned home, having lost an arm.

A further type of picture relating to the Crimean War which excited public interest was that which commemorated an official occasion, usually involving Queen Victoria (who represented both the British state and a proper concern for the welfare of the troops). These comprised large-scale group portraits of those present, from the highest to the lowest. Probably the most important of these are Jerry Barrett's *The Queen's First Visit to her Wounded Soldiers* and its companion, *The Mission of Mercy* (1858 & 1859; both in the National Portrait Gallery), the latter showing Florence Nightingale receiving Crimean

Home Again

Oil on canvas by Henry Nelson O'Neil (1817-80), 1860
The picture shows soldiers returning from the Indian
Mutiny of 1857-59 being greeted by their families.
Among the figures are (from left to right) a junior
officer of a line infantry regiment being greeted by his
mother and sister in the tender; an In-Pensioner of the
Royal Hospital Chelsea, a young rifleman of 60th
(King's Royal Rifles), anachronistically proffering his
Victoria Cross; a wounded NCO and his anxious wife.
Descending from the troopship, a young woman peers
over the shoulder of a bearded infantry corporal whose
wife has just given him their child for the first time.
Below them, an infantryman holds hands with his
sweetheart, while a highlander of 93rd (Highlanders)
looks away in distress from a letter in which the words
'deceive ... wife ... who loved you' can just be traced.

NAM. 8806-49

wounded at the hospital set up in the old barracks at Scutari. Both of these paintings function primarily as group portraits with an humanitarian sub-plot, and are quite remote from the conflict.

A unique variation on the domestic theme was John D'Albiac Luard's *A Welcome Arrival*

Patient Heroes: *a Royal Horse Artillery gun team in action, c1882*

Oil on canvas by Elizabeth Butler, later Lady Butler (1846-1933), 1882

Although the uniforms and equipment of the gun team are carefully observed, the scene of the action has not been positively identified. As the work was painted in 1882, the scene is most likely to be the Egyptian War of that year. The painting was reproduced as a supplement to the Summer Number of The Graphic *in 1889.*

NAM. 9305-232

The Battle of Isandhlwana

Oil on canvas by Charles Edwin Fripp (1854-1906), 1885

Originally exhibited at the Royal Academy in 1885 under the title of The last stand at Isandhula, *this illustrates one of the worst disasters suffered by the British Army in the second half of the nineteenth century. On 22 January 1879, while guarding the base camp of Lord Chelmsford's force near the distinctive hill of Isandhlwana, six companies of the 24th (2nd Warwickshire) Regiment [later the South Wales Borderers] were attacked by a large Zulu army and all but annihilated. Although the artist was present in Zululand as the 'special artist' for* The Graphic, *he reconstructed the event as rather more heroic than the shambles that it must have been.*

NAM. 6011-82

(1857; NAM.5808-18), which, although set in the Crimea, shows the interior of an officers' hut. The setting is spartan, but the occupants have made it more comfortable by pinning up engravings cut from the illustrated press, and they are in the process of examining a number of items just received from home, not least of which is a tea-chest full of groceries from the Army and Navy Stores. The picture was well received by reviewers of the 1857 Royal Academy exhibition and no comparison was made between it and the conditions in which the troops themselves were quartered in that severe second winter in the Crimea. The popularity for didactic and often moralising themes encouraged a vogue for pictures with pendants, when an artist would follow up a successful work with a companion piece shortly after. Luard had painted *Call to Duty* (1855; private collection) showing an officer summoned by his regiment taking leave of his family, before travelling to the Crimea in October 1855 which resulted in *A Welcome Arrival*, and in 1858 he also exhibited a third work. Entitled *Nearing Home* (1858; location unknown), it shows a wounded officer lying on the deck of a ship, comforted by his wife. Similarly, the pictures of the Indian Mutiny (1857-59) which aroused immediate public admiration were genre works, of which the best-known are Henry Nelson O'Neil's pair of didactic paintings (of which he painted two sets) *Eastward Ho!* (1858; Elton Hall and 1860; private collection) and *Home Again* (1859; private collection and 1860; NAM.8806-49). These quayside scenes of troops departing for and returning from service in India are to be read as stories of 'before' and 'after', appealing for their narrative qualities rather than being accurate records of actual events. However, in 1859 there was a bid to revive battle painting when the British-born French artist Louis Desanges exhibited 24 oils of action scenes entitled *The Victoria Cross Gallery* at the Egyptian Hall in Piccadilly. Intended to enhance the prestige of the newly-constituted gallantry medal, which was open to all ranks, each depicted an individual incident for which the medal was awarded, and the completed set of 50 pictures went on to be exhibited at the Crystal Palace from 1862 until 1880 (now in the National Army Museum, regimental and naval collections). The series had popular appeal as illustrations of tales of derring-do, but did not attract a sponsor, reflecting both Desanges' lack of technique and the failure of the pictures to marry the demands of academic art with the journalistic subject matter and thereby qualify as 'serious' painting.[12]

In the 1870s there occurred another exception to Caton Woodville's 'rule', one which, although not mentioned in his memoirs, must have been an inspiration to his own career, for battle painting in Britain enjoyed a brief resurgence in popularity largely as a result of the tremendous impact made by Elizabeth Thompson's (Lady Butler) *The Roll Call* (Royal Collection) at the Royal Academy in 1874. Her extraordinary success was due to a judicious combination of factors at a certain moment; the planimetric composition (the Guardsmen are disposed in a line across the picture plane) and contrasting palette of black-grey and white tones produced a shockingly dramatic effect, while the depiction of the stoicism of ordinary soldiers after an horrific battle coincided not only with the prevailing national taste for the notion of 'heroism in adversity', but also with the current fashion for social realism; the other great 'hit' that year was Luke Fildes' grim workhouse scene, *Application for Admission to a casual ward* (Royal Holloway and Bedford New College, University of London). Another factor was the choice of the Crimean War, then Britain's most recent European conflict but which, after twenty years, provided a suitably weighty context, yet was also sufficiently in the past to have become historic. Thompson avoided glorifying war by her novel representation of the common soldier in the midst of adversity on campaign, thereby making him a national hero, and, as this also averted attention from the ostensible organizational incompetences which had originally caused such a public outcry, it was freely admired by all classes of spectator. Unlike the previous generation of artists who produced military paintings, such as Edward Armitage and Thomas Jones Barker, Thompson saw herself as a battle artist and continued a long career as such until the final stages of the Great War. Her work was widely reproduced as engravings and chromolithographs, and some of her most famous and evocative images also depict the effect of war on animals, most notably *Scotland for Ever!* (1881; Leeds City Art Gallery), and *Patient Heroes* (1882; NAM.9305-232).

For a while, battle painting in Britain found a mode of presentation with popular appeal which encouraged artists to become specialists in this *métier*. Thompson had not been the only painter working in this field at the time, but the exceptional acclaim which she received at the outset of her career heralded a more general revival in military paintings. Of her immediate contemporaries only Ernest Crofts had begun to exhibit pictures of war before *The Roll Call* appeared, although he too only displayed his first painting at the Royal Academy in 1874, *A retreat: episode in the German-French war* (location unknown). Among those who exploited this new market were Richard Caton Woodville, whose first Royal Academy work, *Before Leuthen, Dec 3rd, 1757* (private collection) appeared in 1879; Robert Gibb, who switched to military themes in 1878 with *Comrades* (private collection, USA? and a copy by the artist at the Black Watch Museum, Balhousie Castle), and William Barnes Wollen, whose second Royal Academy picture, *The Rescue of Private J Andrews by Captain Garnet Wolseley ... at the storming of the Motee Mahal, Lucknow* (location unknown) was shown in 1881. By the 1880s, these painters were successfully challenging Elizabeth Thompson's (now Mrs Butler) leadership in the field.[13]

As battle artists, they were still concerned with presenting a complex and far-ranging spectacle by means of a two-dimensional painted surface, which involved the linking of a multiplicity of figures within certain defined rules of composition. Following Butler's example, for the first time in British painting they successfully combined the serious representation of events from past military history with a sense of the awareness of individuals as presented in contemporary genre scenes, although not generally tempered with the humanitarian concern of Butler's pictures. The unsentimental realism of the French artists of the Franco-Prussian War (1870-71), such as Edouard Detaille and Alphonse de Neuville, also had a profound influence upon the character of British battle painting. Equally, there were other influences affecting its development in the last quarter of the nineteenth century, arising from British involvement in a series of colonial wars.

Since the founding of *The Illustrated London News* in 1842, the public was accustomed to seeing pictures of contemporary conflicts published in a matter of weeks after the event. The Crimean War was the first major British campaign to be reported in this way, and in those early days the lively sketches of the *Illustrated*'s special artist, Joseph Archer Crowe (NAM.6806-310 to -320 *et al*), lost much of their immediacy when translated by the journal's engravers. However, contributions to the illustrated press by artists present at the front, some of them

The Battle of Tamaai, Soudan Campaign, 1884

Oil on canvas by Godfrey Douglas Giles (1857-1923), 1885
During the First Sudan War (1884-85), a British force of 4,000
was almost defeated by a Dervish army under Osman Digna at
Tamaai. The British fought in two brigade squares, one of
which was temporarily broken by the Dervishes. The situation
was only retrieved when the second square moved up in
support after a desperate hand-to-hand struggle.

NAM. 6311-5

officers, and the development of photography generated a new, realistic military art which had nothing to do with formal notions of painting. By the 1870s, the work of the best 'specials', such as Melton Prior for *The Illustrated London News*, and the Academy-trained artist, Frederick Villiers in *The Graphic*, had reached a very high standard, covering all aspects of the campaigns in which they often took an active part. Their work remained journalistic, but it encouraged the public to expect a more accurate depiction of war,[14] and this, in turn, also had a direct bearing upon academic painting. Several of the battle painters exhibiting at the Royal Academy and other venues were also known for their contributions to the illustrated press. Richard Caton Woodville provided imaginative 'reconstructions' of contemporary actions for *The Illustrated London News* when sketches from the correspondent at the front failed to arrive in time for publication; and Charles Edwin Fripp, whose picture, *The Battle of Isandhlwana*, (1885; NAM.6011-82) became one of the best known images of the Zulu War (1879), worked as a 'special' for *The Graphic* and its daily edition from 1879 to 1900.

Another exhibitor at the Royal Academy, Godfrey Douglas Giles, depicted the First Sudan War (1884-85) in which he had served as an Indian Army officer on attachment to the Egyptian Police (for example, *The Battle of Tamaai, Soudan Campaign, 1884*, 1885; NAM.6311-5). He went on to represent *The Graphic* in the South African War, (1899-1902), producing several canvases, such as *Cronje's Laager, seen from Kitchener's Hill, Paardeberg, 18 February 1900* (1900; NAM.6705-67) and *The Advance to relieve Kimberley, 13 February 1900* (1901; NAM.6705-68). These, in their depiction of the wide-open *veldt*, recall the earlier 'bird's-eye views' of the post-Napoleonic era, but they have evolved into distantly-peopled landscapes, a result of the changes wrought by technological developments upon the nature of war.

Although battle painting continued to be recognised as a serious category of art far removed from the instant journalism of '... those newly invented curses to armies',[15] it did not remain generally as popular among the art-loving public after the 1870s. The reception given to *The Roll Call* and Butler's succeeding pictures was unusual and, although subsequently there were a few individual works which were highly popular, notably Robert Gibb's *The Thin Red Line* (1881; John Dewar & Sons Limited) and de Neuville's *Defence of Rorke's Drift* (1879; Sydney Art Gallery, Australia), no other military pictures caught the public imagination in quite the same way from the moment when they were first exhibited, until the Great War. Public interest in receiving a visible record of contemporary wars was now provided by the 'special'

CHAPTER
72
SEVEN

journalists, while the popular love of narrative illustration was fed by an enormous increase in the production and sales of prints, which coincided with the development of cheap colour printing or chromolithography. Such pictures, often of a sentimental or melodramatic character and, from a military point of view, highly inaccurate, were often taken from oils or watercolours specifically made for reproduction in this way, never intended as serious art. The number of 'academic' artists who also worked as 'specials' or illustrators (as Caton Woodville himself did) in the latter part of the nineteenth century may be seen as an indication that it was difficult to earn a livelihood from military painting. In contrast to the admiration battle paintings received in France, the status of the genre in Britain was reflected in the scant attention paid to it by the journals that extensively reviewed Royal Academy and other

The Charge of the Light Brigade

Oil on canvas by Richard Caton Woodville (1856-1927), 1897

Perhaps the most famous image of the charge of 25 October 1854, this painting was reproduced as a chromolithograph supplement to Holly Leaves, The Illustrated Sporting and Dramatic News, *Christmas Number, 1897*

NAM. 8901-1

art exhibitions, often glossing over these pictures with a paragraph in the second or third notice. During the South African War (1899-1902) there was a brief upsurge in the numbers and prestige of battle paintings, though no canvas received particular acclaim. Instead, the War resulted in an unprecedented quantity of pictures on paper; drawings, prints and photographs, instant images reproduced for immediate and widespread public consumption in newspapers and illustrated histories. Among art collectors and patrons there was little demand for large-scale battle paintings.

With the revival of interest in Victorian painting since the 1960s, some of the canvases depicting famous incidents from British military history, such as Caton Woodville's *The Charge of the Light Brigade* (1897; NAM.8901-1) and Fripp's *The Battle of Isandhlwana* (see above) have attracted much interest, attaining popularity long after they were painted. It could be taken to suggest that those military works with which the British people have most empathy are those depicting a fallen hero, a last stand, an heroic but foolhardy cavalry charge, or the human consequences of war - the return of the survivors from the battlefield.

A RECIPE
FOR DISCONTENT

THE VICTORIAN SOLDIER'S CUISINE

DAVID SMURTHWAITE

'Buttered toast, buttered toast' was reputedly the cry with which the Duke of Wellington greeted his native land as he came ashore at Dover in 1814. The Duke, usually indifferent to the character of his daily fare,[1] had obviously found that six years of campaigning on army food could try even his ascetic resolve. Of the fact that it drove the European officers attached to Wellington's Army to despair there can be little doubt. The Spanish liaison officer, General Miguel de Alava, was haunted by the customary answer to his nightly enquiry as to the Staff's hour of departure and the next day's menu: 'I became disgusted', he complained, 'with the two words "daylight" and "cold meat."'[2]

The first attempt to provide a regular and consistent ration for the British soldier was made during the last quarter of the sixteenth century when the Crown, under the pressure of campaigns in Ireland and the Netherlands, replaced purveyance and entrepreneurial victualling by a contracting system underwritten by the state. For the next three hundred years the attitude of successive governments to the supply of rations for the Army appears to have been dominated by the following criteria: that the least possible cost should accrue to the Nation; that the daily ration should be the minimum that the soldier would tolerate without mutiny; and that as much responsibility as possible for raising the soldier above a subsistence diet should be transferred to the individual regiments and their officers. The maladministration and suffering which flowed from these principles have been chronicled for the period of the Civil Wars by Sir Charles Firth and Charles Carlton, for the Restoration by John Childs, and for the War of the Spanish Succession by Major R E Scouller.[3] Various historians have briefly considered the soldier's diet during the Napoleonic Wars, but with the exception of the Crimea, questions of cuisine during the 'long peace' have been largely neglected.

That it was a question of importance was readily admitted by contemporary officers and politicians; what they found difficult was securing agreement on a judicious and practical solution to the problems of the soldier's diet in the face of Government apathy. For throughout the nineteenth century, even during periods of peace when supply was normal, the official ration was found wanting in quantity, variety, and nutritional value. The arrangements made for its inspection, preparation, and consumption were inefficient and wasteful. Only sporadic and usually ineffective attempts were made by the authorities to ensure that the soldier could prepare his ration in a manner that would render it appetising, and little was done to provide him with an appropriate environment in which to eat it. The onus for improving the soldier's cuisine was thus thrown on to regimental funds and initiative. As a result there was a standard ration for the Army at home, but there was no such thing as a standard diet. What the soldier ate in peacetime varied from regiment to regiment, depending upon the philanthropy of the officers and the conscientiousness of the non-commissioned officers. That a matter of such fundamental importance to the well-being of the Army - food did after all largely determine the health, morale and discipline of the soldier - should be delegated to individual regiments was, to say the least, short-sighted. It was therefore fortunate that two events during the century concentrated attention upon the

Cookhouse of the 8th Hussars, Crimea, 1855

Photograph taken by Roger Fenton

NAM. neg no 4591

Army's diet. The first was the experience of the Crimean War and the subsequent public outcry and the second the introduction of short service as part of the Cardwell reforms.

The soldier's official ration during service in the United Kingdom was fixed in 1813 at three-quarters of a pound of meat and one pound of bread per day. It was still at that level at the end of the Boer War. When serving overseas most troops received an extra allowance of a quarter of a pound of meat on the grounds that foreign meat was inferior to that produced in England, and the same addition was granted to troops at camp. The disparity between the meat ration at home and overseas stations was made greater for married men by the fact that their ration issue in the United Kingdom had to suffice for both the soldier and his family, while in India in 1876 for example, the ration for a married soldier was two pounds of both meat and bread.[4]

The daily ration was divided between two meals, breakfast at 0730hrs or 0800hrs and dinner at 1230hrs or 1300hrs-the former usually consisting of bread and a basin of tea and the latter of beef and potatoes. All food in excess of the official ration had to be purchased regimentally using money deducted from soldiers' pay, or by the soldiers individually from local tradesmen. The only cooking utensils were two coppers, one for potatoes and the other for meat, which meant that the principal fare of the day was invariably boiled beef, there being no equipment available for baking or roasting. On occasion, soldiers would send their ration to be baked out of barracks, but this inevitably diminished the money available to them for the purchase of vegetables or condiments. This lack of variety, which must have added significantly to the boredom and monotony of barrack life, would have been a major drawback to Army food even if the ration had been prepared adequately, but more often than not its preparation removed all the flavour and tenderness from the meat. That this could happen with predictable regularity was due to the complete absence of trained cooks within the regiments.

The British soldier had a marked aversion to any contact with his food before it appeared on the barrack-room table, and his profound lack of knowledge of even the most basic of culinary arts amazed Hanoverian soldiers in the Peninsula and French soldiers in the Crimea. August Schaumann, a Deputy-Assistant-Commissary-General with Wellington in Portugal, was astounded by the Army's fatalism concerning this most important of subjects; 'It is strange but true, that Englishmen would rather starve than trouble themselves about cooking; that is why it is so hard to be an English war commissary; for the men, together with their officers, are like young ravens - they only know how to open their mouths to be fed'.[5] In the absence of a 'Tradesman Cook' each company of a regiment appointed a cook for the week and an assistant cook daily. In most units the men selected were chosen because they were the least efficient soldiers not because they possessed any knowledge of cooking. Some regiments did at least attempt to make their reluctant chefs look the part;

> 'Each company is to be furnished with cooking dresses made of strong brown linen, consisting of four frocks and four caps ... The purchase and washing of these dresses are to be at the general expense of the unmarried men of the company, and the cooks will parade every Thursday and Sunday at - o'clock with clean dresses ...[6]

For the soldier, however, the proof of the cooks was in the eating and many men preferred to forego their ration altogether; 'each soldier took the portion that suited his fancy; but at least half a dozen men, after a look at the dish, lit their pipes and went off to the canteen'.[7] Even for those few companies who could call upon a man with a passing acquaintanceship with the basic techniques of cooking it was but a temporary reprieve; once out-post or detached duty broke a regiment into sections the majority of the men were again cast on to their own totally inadequate culinary resources. In most respects the conscript armies of Europe were more fortunate than Britain's volunteers, for the *'levée en masse'* inevitably drew some professional cooks into the ranks. Once there they were treated with infinite consideration, particularly by the French who, although most of their troops were perfectly capable of cooking an appetising meal, recognised the importance of the true professional; 'These conscript cooks did not fight; they were left in the rear; we would not expose their precious lives. A captain falls; his lieutenant takes his place: but tell me, if you please, how you would replace a cook'.[8] The need for British troops to do their own cooking when not on active service was a relatively new burden, for until a general programme of barrack building was initiated in 1792 the majority of men stationed in Britain were quartered in inns with the landlord providing their food ready prepared.

Whether the official ration arrived in an edible state or not it only provided two meals per day. During the nineteen-hour gap between dinner at 1230hrs and breakfast at 0730hrs the soldier either went hungry, filled his stomach with beer, or bought extra food. An evening of drink on an empty stomach was bad for both health and discipline and some commanding

Troops Bevouack'd near the Village of Villa Velha, on the Evening of 19th May 1811 *(detail)*
Coloured aquatint engraved by C Turner after Major T St Clair, 1812

NAM. 7102-33-507-8

officers introduced, on their own initiative, a third daily meal paid for by a stoppage of pay agreed to by the men. The regimental canteens, known officially by the somewhat forbidding title of 'Regimental Institutes', had originally been opened for the sale of alcohol, but gradually they began to provide groceries to supplement the official ration. The tenant of each canteen was appointed by the Master-General and Board of Ordnance and he had a monopoly of supply within the barracks although the troops were allowed to patronise local shops for provisions. In 1840 a third meal, consisting of 'tea or coffee, with a portion of bread', was sanctioned by Horse Guards and it was usually served at 1600hrs or 1630hrs.

The responsibility for the supply of food to the bulk of the Army rested with the Ordnance Department who issued the necessary contracts. This system, however, was not uniformly

M. Soyer's Camp and Bivouac Kitchen in The Crimea. General Pélissier tastes the fare at the opening of the Kitchen, 27 August 1855

Wood engraving after E A Goodall from The Illustrated London News, *22 September 1855*

applied even throughout the United Kingdom; the arrangements for Ireland operated on one principle, those for England and Scotland on another, while the Guards and the Artillery supplied themselves on a regimental basis.[9] In 1853 the Treasury set out to change this system and suggested that in the interest of economy all contracts in the United Kingdom should be placed by the Commissariat. The transition was not immediate but by the time the Army of the East set sail for the Crimea the move towards uniformity was well under way.

The privations suffered by the British soldier in the Crimea were given contemporary prominence by the pens of William Howard Russell, *The Times* special correspondent, and other less skilled writers. Since then, the difficulties which beset the supply of food to the Expeditionary Force as a result of the shortcomings of the Commissariat have been chronicled by many historians; but what is often overlooked is that an absolute shortage of rations was rare, and that a comparable if not greater problem for the men on the Heights of Sebastopol was again the inability to deal with the ration once it had arrived. Failures of supply which did occur were often spectacular - the six weeks' delay in issuing the 20,000lbs of lime juice which were in store at a time when the army was ravaged by scurvy, or the loss of 336,000lbs of vegetables aboard the ship *Harbinger* at Balaclava because no one would unload the cargo were only two examples - but a protracted failure in the issue of rations was not the general experience of the Army. Much depended on the location of particular regiments and Mr E G Parker, the Chaplain to the 1st Division between 28 November 1854 and 23 January 1855, stated before the Select Committee on the Army before Sebastopol that at no time were the men of the Division without rations.[10] The greatest cumulative problems were the complete absence of a means of cooking which did not involve the daily consumption of tons of firewood, and the pervasive lack of knowledge of how to gain the greatest benefit from the food available. The remedy for both was to be provided by a civilian, the former chef to the Reform Club, Alexis Soyer, who travelled to the Crimea at his own expense in March 1855. Before leaving, Soyer was interviewed at the War Office by Lord Panmure, Secretary of State for War 1855-58, who asked him to do all that he could to reform the Army's methods of cooking and specifically to design a new stove to replace those that Russell had described as 'wretched affairs ... of thin sheet iron ... mere poison manufactories'.[11] Within days Soyer had dispatched a model of a new portable cooking stove to the War Office where it received an enthusiastic welcome from both Lord Panmure and the Duke of Cambridge.

After re-organizing the hospital kitchens at Scutari and Loulali and vastly improving the quality of the patients' diet, Soyer turned his attention in May to the culinary problems of the troops before Sebastopol. Their cooking was dependent upon twelve-pint kettles, one of which was issued to every eight men. Many of the kettles had been left behind at Varna by soldiers too ill to carry them and these unfortunates were reduced to using mess-cans as their only means of preparing food. These difficulties were compounded by the Commissariat which supplied green coffee, which the troops had somehow to roast and mill before it could be used, and by the initial failure to supply bread instead of the biscuit on which the soldiers' scorbutic gums could make no impression. The contrast with the French camp, where the troops were supplied with fresh, wholesome bread and hot dinners each day only made matters worse.

Soyer's intervention was mercurial and flamboyant, but effective, and he concentrated first on the need to show the Army how to prepare its ration of salt meat. Using his newly invented stoves, which had been manufactured by Messrs Smith & Philips of Snow Hill, London, Soyer began courses of instruction for the men selected as cooks by each battalion. With straightforward recipes[12] devised by Soyer and printed by Headquarters the cooks quickly mastered the stoves, which being portable and not showing fire even when cooking was taking place, could be used equally well in the trenches as in camp. On their first day of instruction the cooks of the 1st Battalion, Coldstream Guards

Meal-time for the Natal contingent to the Diamond Jubilee celebrations in a barrack room in Chelsea Barracks, 1897

NAM. neg no 27457

produced 428lbs of perfectly cooked meat using only 47lbs of wood instead of the normal 1,760lbs of fuel. Soyer calculated that the use of his stoves would save an army of 40,000 men 90 tons of fuel per day while on campaign. He personally supervised the soldier-cooks' first encounter with his stoves as regiment by regiment came for instruction, issuing his recipes to all. The regimental officers were universally impressed by the improvement which took place in the preparation of the men's rations and Soyer collected a library of testimonials;

'Camp, Kamara, 1st June 1856

> I have much pleasure in bearing my testimony to the great advantage of Monsieur Soyer's field-stove over the usual method of cooking practised by an army, from the economy in fuel, the little attention it requires when the fire is once lighted, and its construction enabling the soldier to cook in the open air in all weathers. The slow process of boiling, also, which is easily regulated by the men after a day's instruction, produces a more nutritious soup, and renders the meat more tender than when cooked in the ordinary way. Altogether, I consider the improvement one of great utility.

To Monsieur Alexis Soyer   John Douglas, Lieut-Col
                                Commanding 79th Highlanders[13]

Soyer's stove carried all before it; 400 were ordered for the Crimea and it was adopted for the use of the entire Army at home and overseas. Modified versions of the stove were still in operation with the Territorial Army in the 1950s.

Soyer's work in the Crimea had shown how easily and economically an improvement in the soldier's cuisine could be effected, and as the troops returned to Britain there were many people within the Army and Parliament who were determined to capitalise upon the progress that had been made. The Crimean Commission of Sir John McNeill and Colonel A M Tulloch had submitted a highly critical report on the Army's supplies in the Crimea in January 1856 and during the next five years there were to be repeated exposures of the inadequacy of the soldier's diet. It quickly became apparent that whatever the problems surrounding the method of supply of the official ration, nutritionally it was the wrong type of food. The Crimean Commissioners had called upon the expert advice of Dr Robert Christison[14] of Edinburgh University who compared the nutritive principle of the British soldier's ration in the Crimea (i.e. one pound salt meat, one pound biscuit, two ounces sugar) with three similar diets;

ounce of Nutritive Principle

Hessian soldier	32.96
British sailor	28.5
Perth Prison	25.16
British soldier	23.52

The diet of a man in a Scottish prison was thus found to be more nutritious than that of the British soldier fighting and digging before a besieged city. In 1857 the Army Sanitary Commission placed the responsibility for the inadequacy of the soldier's rations firmly with the Government whose duty it was;

> 'to see that the soldier is supplied with and consumes a diet so composed as to keep him, as far as possible, at all times and in all climates in health and efficiency ... a mere bread and meat ration, even if increased in quantity, could never ensure health, even with the addition of vegetable food.[15]

The Commissioners also underlined the futility of improving the soldier's ration without first ensuring an equal improvement in his ability to prepare and cook it.

Practical improvements did follow, notably through the work of Sidney Herbert,[16] but they were largely restricted to the arrangements made for preparing rations at the camps at Aldershot, the Curragh, and Shorncliffe. At Aldershot and the Curragh a commissariat staff corps comprising butchers, bakers and 'issuers' was formed and given instruction in their tasks. The bakers produced 20,000 rations daily (40,000 on Saturdays) from standing ovens at Aldershot and from small portable ovens at the Flying Camp at Woolmers.[17] The regiments in the camps furnished the men for the corps and they were then permanently embodied in the Commissariat by Royal Warrant. A body of men trained in baking, slaughtering and ration distribution for a force of 20,000 troops had thus been formed, but there was no facility for returning these men to their regiments after they had received instruction, nor was it any part of the corps' duties to become involved with the cooking of the soldiers' rations which would remain a regimental responsibility.[18] Mr J W Smith, the Commissary-General-in-Chief, agreed with the suggestion of the Select Committee that it would be beneficial to the troops if the ration facilities at Aldershot and the Curragh were extended to other fixed stations, but he thought that this development would be unlikely to occur due to considerations of economy.[19] Only in areas where comparatively large numbers of troops were concentrated therefore would the benefits of centralised bread and meat preparation be available to the soldier.

In most regiments therefore, little had changed and the major responsibility for ensuring that the soldier's diet was conducive to contentment and health remained with them. In 1864 the British daily ration was still inferior to that issued in the French Army, the latter consisting of nearly as much meat, half as much again of bread, nearly twice as much coffee plus vegetables and wine or brandy.[20] The British soldier did receive one penny per day as beer money, and, when on active service, a gill of rum or arrack in addition to his basic ration of one-and-a-half pounds of bread or one pound of biscuit, one pound of meat, a third of an ounce of coffee, one sixth of an ounce of tea, two ounces of sugar, half an ounce of salt, and one 36th of an ounce of pepper.[21]

During the nineteenth century the variations in the soldier's ration at home, at sea and abroad, were reflected in the stoppages deducted from his pay and these were a source of endless confusion to the authorities and baffled grievance for the soldier. A stoppage of

Orderly-men receiving meat rations, *1898*

Process engraving after R Caton Woodville from Social Life in
the British Army by a British Officer, *London (1900)*

NAM. neg no 54714

sixpence for the daily ration was instituted in 1794 and this continued until 1854 when it was reduced to fourpence-halfpenny. The soldier's pay had remained throughout at one shilling per day with the addition in 1800 of a supplement of one penny as beer money.[22] Thus in 1860 a soldier in the United Kingdom paid fourpence-halfpenny for his ration of three-quarters of a pound of meat and one pound of bread. If he were serving overseas, however, threepence-halfpenny was stopped from his pay for a ration of one pound of meat and one pound of bread, and while he was on board ship sixpence per day was deducted for an Admiralty ration. Should he request a spirit ration while at sea he paid an additional stoppage and if he was admitted to hospital tenpence was stopped from his pay.

On top of the official deductions came a further stoppage of threepence or threepence-halfpenny for extra food supplied by his regiment. It was thus difficult for anyone to give the soldier a clear and accurate account of his pay and in 1873 it was decided that the gordian knot should be cut, and the daily ration was henceforth issued free of any stoppage. In the seven years between 1882 and 1889 the average cost to the Government of each free ration was 5.59 pence per day.[23]

In 1863 new regulations were promulgated which removed canteens from the hands of the private tenants and transferred ownership to the regiments. The commanding officer now appointed a canteen committee and was able to purchase provisions competitively from tradesmen. Any profit made by the canteen was to be spent for the benefit of the men of the regiment. Two drawbacks to this system quickly became apparent and they were characteristic of the problems which arose from the policy of leaving the provision of a major portion of the soldier's food in the hands of the regiments. Individual units obtaining food on their own behalf surrendered the benefits of large scale purchase, and as so few regimental officers possessed the experience to deal adequately with often unscrupulous contractors, much of the responsibility for operating the canteens passed to non-commissioned officers or canteen stewards. This is not to say that all regiments maintained inadequate canteens but the system was open to abuse and it was the soldier who ultimately suffered.

In the last quarter of the nineteenth century the introduction, through the Army Enlistment Act of 1870, of short service led to a general reduction in the age of soldiers stationed

CHAPTER
82
EIGHT

in Britain, and the men's diet again became a matter of some concern to the War Office. General Sir A J Herbert stated the essential problem at a meeting of the Royal United Service Institution in January 1891; 'at the present time we are inundated by a great mass of young, immature lads, who require more feeding than they do drill; and the greatest attention should be paid to the messing'.[24] Many regiments had indeed been paying considerable attention to the men's diet and some, notably the 1st Battalion, Royal Irish Rifles and the 2nd Battalion Northumberland Fusiliers, adopted an evangelical role. The standing orders of the Fusiliers in 1882 devoted no less than 55 pages to the subjects of cooking and messing, including descriptions of how to operate seven types of stoves and ovens, recipes ranging from 'Turkish Pillaff', 'Indian Collops' and 'China Chilo' to 'Crimean Kebbobs', 'Bomb Shells' and 'Cannon Balls', and detailed instructions for inspecting cuts of meat. The soldier's food was now clearly divided into rations and groceries, the latter being provided entirely through the regiment. A grocery book was kept by each company and the daily stoppage of threepence or threepence-halfpenny plus a proportion of the profits from the sale of dripping, kitchen refuse and the canteen, were credited to this account. On the standard of management of the grocery books depended the quality and variety of the regiment's diet. In the Royal Irish Rifles, who devoted a great deal of attention to the provision of extras, the men's official breakfast ration of bread and coffee was supplemented during an average week by bacon and eggs (two ounces bacon and one egg per man), porridge, liver, mutton chops and butter. Dinner was always accompanied by a basin of soup and instead of a tea-meal the men received a supper which might consist of Irish stew, fresh fish, rice and milk, porridge or a dish of haricot beans with extra bread. Today it hardly sounds a mouth-watering bill of fare, but in the 1880s it represented a considerable regimental achievement and the system of messing used by the Royal Irish Rifles was earnestly recommended to other units.

In those regiments which did not achieve the standard of variety and nutrition attained in the diet of the Royal Irish Rifles, the men were necessarily more dependent upon the quality of the official ration. This appears to have varied considerably from station to station, with contemporary comments on the condition of the meat supplied ranging from approbation for that generally available in Britain, to outright condemnation of the ration in Ireland. The quality of the meat and bread consumed by the soldier depended upon the integrity of the contractor and the vigilance of the regimental officers who were responsible for inspecting the ration supply. Lieutenant P J Thorpe, the Quartermaster of the 1st Battalion, Royal Irish Rifles, had few illusions concerning the scruples of most army contractors;

> 'Reject a diseased carcass to-day, and he will bring up an old cow tomorrow; send
> that back, and next day witnesses the advent of a tough old bull; condemn that, and
> prepare yourself to inspect a malodorous old ram on the following day.[25]

Not all officers could call upon the level of knowledge which Lieutenant Thorpe obviously possessed and in the opinion of Colonel D Makgill-Chrichton-Maitland most officers did 'not know old bull from old cow'.[26] Occasionally officers of the Army Service Corps made surprise inspections of the rations but the responsibility for ensuring, in the words of the

Sergt. The Bread Sir is slightly imprefsive, and the meat good but bony Sub on Duty. U-a-a-all right.

Regimental Duties, *c1850*

Watercolour, artist unknown, from a series entitled Life in an
Infantry Regiment, *c1850*

Commissariat contract, that the soldier's meat was 'well-fed, good, sound, sweet, and wholesome' invariably rested on the orderly officer of the day. The quartermaster who was responsible for ensuring that the quantity of the meat was correct was not permitted to comment upon its quality. An attempt was made to overcome the officers' natural antipathy to discussing mutton and beef by holding instructional classes at Aldershot in 'the method of judging the quality of provisions'.[27] Each regiment of cavalry, division of Royal Artillery, and battalion of infantry stationed at Aldershot was to send one officer to the classes which were held four times a year. Frozen meat which could be inspected well in advance by Commissariat officers and Garrison Boards had been instinctively rejected by the troops, one battalion registering a protest by dumping its frozen meat dinner in the middle of the barrack square.

The meat now fared better at the hands of the cooks than it had before the Crimean War, for in 1883 an instructional kitchen was formed at Salamanca Barracks, Aldershot. From there one sergeant-cook was appointed to every regiment and battalion to supervise all cooking carried out in regimental cook-houses. Assistant cooks were appointed for longer periods and a second cook could be sent from the regiment to Aldershot for training. Cooking was still by no means a popular duty in the Army for it necessitated working indoors from dawn till dusk, but the standard of preparation of the men's food had noticeably improved by the end of the century.

While meat now arrived on the barrack-room table in a more appetising form, it was still widely felt that the ration itself was too small. Although twelve ounces of meat was issued per man it was reduced during cooking to at best eight ounces and at worst four ounces, and most soldiers found that they required an extra half pound of bread each day. The third meal of the day which often, even in the 1890s, consisted of only tea and bread was considered inadequate to carry a man through from 1600hrs until breakfast at 0800hrs next morning. The government usually responded to these complaints by arguing that the soldier's diet was far superior to anything he would enjoy in civilian life and that it could always be supplemented by regimental groceries. On the question of increasing the content of the third meal and the possibility of serving it at a later hour they pointed to the soldier's habit of walking-out in the evenings, which would be disrupted by a meal at 2000hrs. It was undoubtedly true that the troops stationed in towns and cities did value their time away from barracks and many remained out until midnight, but contemporary opinions were divided as to the superiority of the soldier's ration over the diet he could expect as a civilian. It seems certain that the soldier received more meat than the civilian although the latter's diet would have greater variety. Recruits obviously carried the prejudices gained in civilian life concerning food into the Army, and Colonel A G Raper of the 2nd Battalion, North Staffordshire Regiment believed that 'during the first two or three years of their service, young recruits, especially when working at their drill, can put away as much as you can give them and with advantage ...'[28] The recruit was often taken aback by the conditions of messing in the barrack room which Lieutenant Thorpe condemned in no uncertain terms;

> 'Go into any barrack room you like to pick out at the tea hour, and this is what you will find: a bare table, not too clean in appearance, on which stand a number of basins filled with a greasy-looking fluid, which is dignified by the name of tea. Loaves and pieces of loaves are strewn about the table, without any show of arrangement. Look up at the shelves, and you will find there several basins of tea, which the men have put up there to drink later in the evening ... The atmosphere is laden with the particles of dirt which the men are knocking off their clothes and boots.[29]

Although day rooms where the men could eat their meals were provided in India it was the exception rather than the rule to find dining rooms in barracks in Britain. One or two regiments were able to provide a separate area where the men could eat but the Quartermaster-General's Department was already stretching the accommodation in barracks in an attempt to satisfy demands for libraries, school and games rooms, and adequate sleeping space.

The size of the daily ration and the conditions in which it was consumed do seem to have created the impression amongst the working classes, at least, that the soldiers of many regiments were half-starved and this had a detrimental effect upon recruiting. Once the recruit had joined he often felt that he had been misled by the declaration on the recruiting posters that he would receive a 'free ration'. This of course applied only to the official ration and no mention was made of the stoppage of threepence for groceries. Many officers believed that this was a legitimate and widespread cause of grievance and those called to give evidence before the Committee on the Terms and Conditions of Service in 1891 argued strongly for corrective action.

At the end of the nineteenth century, as at its beginning, the soldier's diet was essentially a matter of local custom rather than central policy. Although there had been improvements in the quality of rations the majority of officers and men still considered them to be inadequate in quantity and variety. Even with the groceries supplied by regiments, soldiers were spending fourpence per day on extra food and some as much as one shilling at weekends. Government still granted its attention to the problem reluctantly and spasmodically, there were still too few cooks, the fuel supplied for cooking was still too little to ensure adequate preparation, and there was a marked lack of modern culinary equipment in most barracks. As 'Tommy Atkins' received the plaudits of his countrymen on his return from South Africa he might, with justification, have echoed Molière's words: '*Je vis de bonne soupe et non de beau langage*'.

TEMPERANCE AND ITS REWARDS IN THE BRITISH ARMY

STEPHEN WOOD

Drink was traditionally associated with the British Army. The ranks were largely filled by men drawn from classes brutalised by poverty and alcohol abuse. The officers came mainly from a social milieu where Temperance was equated with Religious Dissent, not altogether unjustly, and shunned accordingly. The men's beer canteen and the officers' mess were inseparable parts of regimental life and although the spirit ration had been abolished in 1830, it persisted for soldiers on active service. Drinking was not actively discouraged but drunkenness was savagely punished and officers could be cashiered for habitual intoxication. Inspiration and the setting of example formed less of a part of the leadership process than did ingrained habits of paternalism enforced as necessary by the use of the lash.

Among the civilian population the growth of temperance organizations owed much to the rise of the evangelical movement in the late eighteenth century. The twin causes of slavery and drunkenness were those with which early evangelicals like Thomas Clarkson and William Wilberforce especially associated themselves.

With Temperance however, as with so much else innovatory about the nineteenth-century British Army, several factors combined to produce a positive climate from one so apparently inhospitable. These factors were: the new type of officer, middle-class, serious, and with little private money; India, that cradle of reputations, and the Baptist faith.

Foremost among the evangelical officers was Lieutenant Henry Havelock[1] whose community of like-minded officers, christened 'Havelock's Saints' by Havelock himself, was established in Rangoon in 1823. The place of establishment of such a group is significant in the history of temperance movements in the Army since it was in India more than in any other part of the Empire that the temptations offered to the common soldier were greatest. Havelock had exchanged from the Rifle Brigade to the 13th (or the 1st Somersetshire) Regiment in 1822 to experience service in India. His active proselytising of the Christian ethic in the mid-1820s, and eventual conversion to the Baptist faith in 1829, succeeded in creating a social gulf between him and his brother officers. The Baptist evangelical crusade against the perils of alcohol was aimed at servicemen through the medium of such periodicals as *The Soldier's Magazine and Military Chronicle*, which began circulation in 1828.

While Havelock's adoption of the tenets of the Baptist faith may have made him unpopular in his regiment, it undoubtedly furthered both his career and the cause of Temperance in the

Army. His career was given a boost by his appointment to the adjutancy of the 13th in 1834, an appointment directly influenced by the Governor-General,[2] and this position of regimental authority enabled him to put certain of his ideas to work. He founded a Regimental Temperance Society in the 13th in 1836, the first of its kind, and it soon reached the point where its membership numbered 274. So encouraged was Havelock by the success of his brain-child that he wrote to the adjutants of other British regiments in India on the subject. Within two years, 30 other units possessed Regimental Temperance Societies and figures available indicate[3] that their average membership, of about a quarter of regimental strength, was similar to that of the 13th. Such societies depended, of course, to an enormous extent upon the personal supervision of committed officers such as Havelock. His detachment from the 13th for staff duty in Afghanistan in 1838 may well have weakened the influence of the Temperance Society over his regiment's morals and certainly Staff-Sergeant Percival made no mention of it when recalling his service in the 13th in 1846.[4]

Life for British soldiers in India was not always nasty, brutish and short but it often contrived to be at least one of the three. Boredom was the chief enemy. Since the multitude of native servants and the generally oppressive climate combined to promote idleness and to ensure that the majority of garrison soldiers spent most of their time off duty and in barracks it is not surprising that drunkenness grew to be such a problem. Spirits were cheap, plentiful and often of the poorest, rawest quality and, before the days of India Pale Ale, British beer was almost unobtainable. Forms of recreation were restricted to the most unenergetic kind and little attempt was made to induce the soldiers to use their off-duty periods constructively. Apart from that exerted by the few officers like Havelock little influence was brought to bear on British soldiers in India prior to the Mutiny to try and reduce the problem.

It seems that Regimental Temperance Societies were confined to India, on the occasions when they existed at all. Typically, a regiment would establish one on arrival in India but disband it on leaving, either for active service or for peacetime posting out of India. No satisfactory explanation has been found for this since, while the provision in India of cheap, poor-quality alcohol for intoxication and apparently unlimited servants for the relief of tedious duties is well-known, these factors were equally present in other hot-weather stations where there is no evidence that Regimental Temperance Societies existed either with the same profusion or at all. Corfu, Gibraltar, St Helena, the Cape of Good Hope, the West Indies and even Ireland all presented the commanding officers of regiments posted there with problems linked to the abuse of alcohol and, with the exception of Ireland, wines and spirits were cheap and readily available in all those stations. The Regimental Temperance Societies in India remained the only institutionalised form of military temperance for more than twenty years, until the establishment of Regimental and Garrison Institutes reached the sub-Continent at the end of the 1850s.

The soldiers fortunate enough to be based in Britain in the first half of the nineteenth century, and thus less excluded from the prevailing moral climate, came increasingly to be influenced by the growing number of temperance societies. These had begun as a purely American phenomenon, the first being founded at Saratoga in 1808. Going from strength to strength via the Massachusetts Society for the Suppression of Intemperance (1813) to the

A hussar, an infantryman and a dragoon scrambling for the entrance to the canteen, c1890.

Watercolour by 'DGL', after Harry Payne, c1890

NAM. 7402-110

American Society for the Promotion of Temperance (1826) the movement became firmly established across the Atlantic in 1829 with the formation of the Ulster Temperance Society. By 1830 the movement was established in Yorkshire and Lancashire and its mouthpiece, the *Temperance Societies Record*, estimated that there were 60,000 associated abstainers in that year.

The Regimental and Garrison Institutes had begun just before the Crimean War in a number of garrison towns in southern England which had recognised the need to channel the energies of their soldier population along less disruptive routes than those traditionally followed. The Institutes began with one founded at Sandgate, near Shorncliffe Camp outside Hythe in Kent, by Miss Lucy Papillon, a spinster whose evident desire to aid the welfare of soldiers stationed there contrasted curiously with the implications presented by her surname. Her example was followed by the Reverend Carus-Wilson who established a Soldiers' Home in Portsmouth. Both institutions seemed to have suffered not only from an apparent lack of managerial efficiency but also in their main purpose, since they were apparently so uninviting and dull that they presented little competition to the more traditional and well-established places of soldierly recreation. By odd coincidence and contrast the two largest Institutes, and the most successful ones, were founded almost simultaneously in Britain's oldest and youngest military centres: Chatham and Aldershot.

These two Institutes had much in common and were deliberately unlike the ones previously founded by well-meaning civilians. The aim of their founders was to keep the soldiers out of the towns, with their associated temptations, and inside the barracks by providing centres of entertainment and recreation that were not inextricably linked with the perilous pleasures presented by gin-palaces and prostitutes. The Institutes which failed had done so because they only attracted soldiers already committed to temperate behaviour and even those had to leave barracks in order to attend them.

In the case of Chatham, a group of conscientious citizens gained the support of the Barrack-Master[5] who lobbied the War Office on their behalf, representing the disquiet felt by those citizens at the numbers of drunken soldiers in their streets and the sort of people attracted to Chatham by the soldiers' needs and ability to pay for them. In a letter to the Brigade-Major at Chatham, the Barrack-Master expressed eloquently what was wrong with the existing arrangement;

'At present the soldier on leaving his barrack room has, with the exception of the canteen, but one place to which he can retire - viz. the Library, where, it is true, he can sit and read, but where you look for him in vain, as it has not sufficient attractions; he cannot play a game of chess, draughts, backgammon, dominoes or bagatelle, smoke his pipe, drink his cup of coffee, or make himself comfortable, and really feel at ease and at home. Failing these inducements to detain him within the barracks, he goes to the low public houses or the haunts of vice, where too frequently he lays the foundation of future misery....[6]

His verbosity did the trick and, privately financed, the Chatham Garrison Institute began functioning in 1857. It had only guarded support from the Horse Guards, which insisted on the nature of the financial arrangements and that its title should be 'Institute' and not 'Club'.

Three years later, however, the authorities were taking the idea of Institutes sufficiently seriously to commission a Report[7] on facilities for soldiers in the new garrison town of Aldershot. The Report's author, Captain Pilkington Jackson,[8] Royal Artillery, had already verbally demolished the Carus-Wilson Soldiers' Home in Portsmouth and so, one suspects, fired with enthusiasm, he set to work on Aldershot. Although dismayed by what he found provided in the town by way of diversion for the soldiers, he recorded it all in meticulous and censorious detail. There were eighteen canteens, 25 Public Houses where 'the attendance of Prostitutes ... is encouraged' and 47 Beer Houses,[9] 'Public Brothels of the worst description'. On one day he visited 25 Public and Beer Houses and 'found 80 Prostitutes in them drinking and ... playing Cards with Soldiers'; one has to admire both his stamina and the strength of his stomach. Aldershot was, Jackson observed '... inhabited principally by Publicans, Brothel Keepers, Prostitutes, Thieves and Receivers of Stolen property' and, because it had been allowed to grow up adjacent to the various barracks, '... the Men quartered there have the minimum taxation of time and trouble upon frequenting the Village and the maximum of temptation to vice'.

Jackson's suggested remedy indicates both an illuminating contemporary view of what was felt to be good for the soldier and an insensitivity for his own peer group that may well have contributed to his rather abrupt quitting of the Army in 1868. He suggested that the Officers' Club be converted to an Institute housing a library, rooms for reading, writing and refreshments, other rooms for playing billiards, bagatelle, draughts and chess, two workshops, the usual offices and, significantly, a Museum. 'Manly games' could be catered for outside. There would be no gambling or sale of alcohol; religion, party politics and military matters would be prohibited from discussion. Concerts, lectures, lantern-slide shows and arms practice would all be encouraged.

Both the General Officer Commanding in Aldershot[10] and the Duke of Cambridge were horrified by the suggestion that an officers' building should be relinquished for the use of other ranks; a wooden hut with a conveniently adjacent skittle alley was produced as an alternative. The Secretary of State for War overruled them and the Aldershot Institute began life.

In the civilian world, the Temperance Movement was sufficiently strong in 1860 to enable George Cruickshank to raise a corps of Temperance Rifle Volunteers in Southwark. This corps, designated the 24th Surrey Rifle Volunteer Corps in 1861, had been given the sub-title 'Havelock's Own' by its founder who also became its captain-commandant. Like so many of its contemporary corps the 24th Surrey did not last, being disbanded in 1862. Cruickshank was not to be deterred. Crossing the Thames he raised the 48th Middlesex Rifle Volunteer Corps (Havelock's Rifles) in March 1862 and became its lieutenant-colonel. Cruickshank's enthusiasm for temperance had been proclaimed since 1847 when he published a series of savage caricatures entitled *The Bottle*, followed in 1848 by *The Drunkard's Children*. It may be that his enthusiasm was overdone in the Rifle Volunteer Movement because he resigned the lieutenant-colonelcy of the 48th Middlesex in 1868 and the corps dropped their titular association with Havelock in 1870.

Total abstainers were not to be outdone by their rivals in the temperance movement. It would be as wrong to describe total abstinence as a particularly Presbyterian trait as it would be to describe the Rifle Volunteer Movement as entirely middle-class. Thus it may be no more

Major-General Sir Henry Havelock KCB in staff uniform,
c1856.

Line engraving by Charles Holl, published by James S Virtue, c1856

NAM. 6008-118

than coincidental that the only Rifle Volunteer Corps formed from total abstainers were raised in the lowlands of Scotland. Total abstainers composed No 16 Company of the Queen's Rifle Volunteer Brigade, Edinburgh, raised in 1860, and the 3rd Edinburgh Rifle Volunteer Corps, raised in 1867. The 54th and 82nd Rifle Volunteer Corps of Lanarkshire comprised total abstainers and, raised in 1860, subsequently became part of the 3rd Lanarkshire Rifle Volunteer Corps.[11]

Halfway across the globe, similar developments were taking place; we must now return to India. The cantonment at Dum Dum near Calcutta had an empty building, once the officers' mess of the Bengal Artillery, and in February 1860 the cantonment chaplain wrote to Sir James Outram[12] to suggest that it be used to provide much-needed facilities for officers and other ranks. Mr Norman drew (surely unnecessarily) Sir James's attention to 'the habit of drinking which [is] the natural result of unemployed hours hanging heavily on the hands of uneducated men' and proposed that the disused mess building be used to provide reading rooms for officers and men, together with a lecture room for the men and, yes, a Museum. The chaplain's suggestion was welcomed by the Council, implemented by a committee and the first Outram Institute was born. At some point during the process of its establishment, the idea of incorporating officers into it was quietly dropped.

The Outram Institutes were not a great success. In 1864 the Commander-in-Chief in India[13] ordered that their progress be studied and a report produced. As a result of the survey the factors which were slowing their development became clear: they were not alcohol-free, they were non-regimental in arrangement and they offered too few amenities. Despite the identification of these deficiencies, the Outram Institutes had to wait until 1887 before being offered a serious chance of improvement; this chance involved formal association with a body that was everything which the Institutes were not, the Soldiers' Total Abstinence Association.

The Association was founded in 1862 by a Baptist missionary, working in Agra since 1858. It had been in Agra that Havelock had done much of his remedial work among soldiers and there that he had built a Baptist chapel. The missionary, the Reverend John Gelson Gregson, was assuming Havelock's mantle.

The two men had met briefly, in Cawnpore in 1857 after Havelock had re-occupied it following the Massacre, and their acquaintanceship is described in the biography[14] of

An Aldershot Canteen, 1886. *Soldiers from a number of units are present, including men of the 10th Hussars, the 1st and 2nd Dragoons, the Royal Horse Artillery and the Royal Field Artillery.*
Watercolour by T P Chapman, 1886

NAM. 7003-7-3

Havelock by his son-in-law John Marshman. In the copy of the biography in the library of the Scottish United Services Museum in Edinburgh Castle, Gregson's own copy, these details are underlined in reverent red pencil. Other details, such as the fact that the beleaguered garrison at Jellalabad in 1842 had fought on despite being without alcohol, are heavily marked in fanatical blue.

Gregson realised rapidly in 1858 that the old Regimental Temperance Societies had been a successful idea and would be strengthened if a degree of federation could be brought to bear upon them. This he did, beginning in 1862 with the 35th (Sussex) Regiment, from the ranks

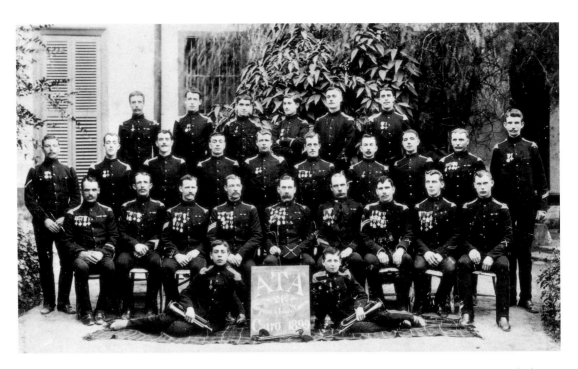

An officer and men of the 21st (Empress of India's) Lancers branch of the Army Temperance Association, photographed in Cairo in 1899. The majority of the men, even the boy trumpeters, have managed to achieve at least six months' temperance. The officer in the centre has achieved eight years' temperance.

NAM. neg no 41760

of which he recruited 37 members. Within a year he had formed thirteen more regimental societies, added 323 members and formed the Association.[15] By 1866, the Association had 1,125 members in 29 societies. Gregson went home for six years between 1866 and 1872 and the Association declined. On his return he redoubled his efforts and in 1876 succeeded in gaining a measure of recognition from Government, which gave him a monthly grant of 150 rupees to cover the purchase of tracts and medals, and travelling expenses. In 1872 there were 53 societies with 4,324 members; by 1877 there were 110 societies with 10,886 members. In 1879 the Government grant was doubled and Gregson concentrated solely on the cause of military temperance.

In 1879 Gregson went on active service to Afghanistan, attached for the purpose as Presbyterian chaplain to 72nd (Duke of Albany's) Highlanders. If the comments contained in his published reminiscences[16] of the campaign can be relied upon, and it is unlikely that he was economical with the truth, he did not enjoy the experience. He saw that the British soldier on active service was a very different animal from the same soldier in peacetime, and that temperance broke down under such conditions. He also witnessed a Highland regiment, the 92nd (Gordon) Highlanders, celebrating Hogmanay; a spectacle guaranteed to make most sensitive Englishmen suddenly find an excuse to be elsewhere. He witnessed flogging in the field as a punishment for stealing the rum ration and he collected the *topi* and *poshteen* in which he was photographed for the frontispiece of his book.

Despite, or perhaps because of, his experiences in Afghanistan, Gregson and the Association blossomed during the 1880s. In 1885 there were 144 societies with 12,321 members and Gregson's Government grant, now more of a salary, was 400 rupees a month. He attracted

A selection of the medals awarded by Army temperance societies:

Top row, *the Soldier's Total Abstinence Association, India*

1. Medal for one year with clasp for a second year of temperance

2. The Beatty Star, awarded for three years' temperance

3. The Cruickshank Medal for six months' temperance.

NAM. 5211-67-2, -3, -1

Middle row, *the Army Temperance Association (India)*

4. The White Star for five years' temperance

5. The Havelock Cross for seven years' temperance

6. Medal for eight years' temperance.

NAM. 5211-67-6, -5; 6611-9-5

Bottom row, *the Army Temperance Association (Home Organisation)*

7. Medal for six years' temperance

8. Medal for 15 years' temperance

9. Medal (Royal Army Temperance Association) for 20 years' temperance

NAM. 5211-67-11, -8, -9

the attention of Lord Wolseley,[17] commanding the Gordon Relief Expedition in 1885, who asked him to help eradicate drunkenness among the troops in Cairo. He was noticed by Sir Frederick Roberts[18] while the latter was Commander-in-Chief in Madras between 1881 and 1885 and, when Roberts became Commander-in-Chief in India in 1885, the two men were able to be of considerable use to each other and to the cause which they held dear.

In 1884, when sending his annual subscription to the Secretary of the Association, the Reverend J G Gregson, Roberts wrote;

> 'I am making enquiries as to the possibility of meeting your wish to have a recognized room set apart in each set of barracks for the branch society of the association. I quite understand how desirable it is that your temperance work should be placed on a permanent basis, and it would be a pleasure to me to help you in this, or indeed in any other way …
>
> It is difficult to give statistics in support of the assertion, but I have little doubt it could be proved that serious crime in the army is almost entirely due to the effects of drink. I am not an abstainer myself, and if I thought that soldiers could trust themselves to drink in moderation, I would not advocate their taking the pledge … I am always glad when I hear that a soldier, especially a young soldier, has joined your society.[19]

Later in the same year Roberts had the opportunity of publicly airing his views on the subject of drink and crime when addressing a Temperance meeting at Secunderabad;

> 'Drink and crime, as you all know, go together; if there were no drunkards in the army there would be little or no crime. A few years ago Lord Napier of Magdala, when commander-in-chief in India, caused a return to be prepared, showing the class of men by whom offences had been committed during a certain number of months. The return proved that total abstainers were wholly guiltless of crime, that partial abstainers were practically equally guiltless, and that the drunkards were responsible for the whole of the crime in the army.[20]

Although both men wanted to improve the lot of the British soldier it is clear that they had differing views on how such an improvement might be achieved. The final return home of Gregson in 1886 allowed Roberts to put his ideas into practice without hurting the missionary's feelings too directly. Roberts felt that a policy of temperance would succeed where one of total abstinence was too obdurate to do so and he took the opportunity of the celebrations connected with the Queen's Golden Jubilee in 1887 to combine the old Outram Institutes with the Soldiers' Total Abstinence Association and create the Army Temperance Association in the following year.

Once amalgamation had been achieved, a programme of Institute building was undertaken, constantly prodded by Roberts. Institutes were provided in ten sizes and each included a

Temperance room. By the time Roberts left India in 1893, the Army Temperance Association had 23,000 members.

Roberts was able to describe a typical institute in Rangoon to an audience at Meerut in 1888;

> 'On entering the building, I found myself in the Temperance room - a spacious, airy apartment, in which 300 to 400 men were assembled. Some were playing games, others were talking and amusing themselves ... Waiters were bustling about with tea, coffee and light refreshments. Neither beer nor other intoxicating drinks were, of course, allowed in this room ... Further on I found myself in the Refreshment, which was much about the same size as the Temperance room. At one end of it was a Coffee shop, where all kinds of oilman stores and regimental necessaries could be purchased at a cheap rate and where very inviting looking suppers were being prepared ... Here several men were enjoying their evening meal, with which those who wished for it could have beer brought to them from the neighbouring canteen ...
>
> There was, as I said before, an air of real comfort about the whole place; and I thought to myself, "Is a soldier likely to prefer wandering about the dirty bazaars and backslums of Rangoon to joining the fun and partaking of the comfort of the Institute?"[21]

Gradually the Army Temperance Association became accepted as the one organization for the Army and the objections of the earlier dogmatic and denominational societies were overcome. In 1890 Roberts had been able to provide the Viceroy, the Marquess of Lansdowne, with figures that indicated the worth of the Army Temperance Association in reducing the numbers of soldiers punished for crimes. Between 1888 and 1889, he said, the number of cases of insubordination with violence in Bengal had decreased by 50, the number of cases of drunkenness tried by court-martial had decreased by 51 and the number of men sentenced to imprisonment with hard labour had decreased by 176. The number of convictions by court-martial had decreased in Bengal by fourteen per cent, in Madras by one per cent and in Bombay by seventeen per cent.[22]

Predictably, Roberts' arrival home led rapidly to the extension of the ATA to Britain and the Army Temperance Association (Home Organisation), as it was called, rose from having 3,732 members in 1894 to 13,119 in 1896; in the same year the ATA in India mustered 22,810 members. Organized under the authority of the Chaplain-General the movement spread throughout the Army, each regiment having its own branch. Becoming the Royal Army Temperance Association in 1902 the movement continued until after the Second World War when, with the higher standard of recruit, it died a natural death in 1958.

The reasons that soldiers joined total abstinence and temperance societies would be as hard to define as the reasons why others did not, and continued drinking. It is doubtful whether many soldiers became officially temperate in their habits in order to qualify for one or more of the large variety of medals awarded by the societies to commemorate periods of abstinence or temperance. If qualification for medals was the only reason then those whose motives were so amoral must have been well satisfied. Large numbers of medals were awarded by all the major societies, civilian and military, and several regimental branches also presented their own medals, notably the Royal Berkshire Regiment, the Royal Fusiliers and the Royal Dublin Fusiliers. Six months' temperance was rewarded by the Cruickshank Medal and thereafter a medal or clasp was awarded for each successive year of ignored temptation. The medals, which were not to be worn in uniform except on relevant occasions, were to be worn on the right breast and impressive groups could be amassed by soldiers of strong will and principles. The one-year medal awarded by the Soldiers' Total Abstinence Association, India, and probably the most often encountered, was continued by the Army Temperance Association after 1897. Many of the medals bore titles associating them with persons active in the cause, for example: the Beatty Star after the Reverend Edward Beatty, first Secretary of the Army Temperance Association; the White Star after Sir George White,[23] the Havelock Cross and the Roberts Badge.

The gradual success of the temperance movements in the British Army is a barometer of the social change that affected that institution through the passage of the nineteenth century. Life at home was very different from that in India and the Army Temperance movement never really caught on in Britain as it had done in the sub-Continent. The degree to which its success was attendant upon the zeal first of Havelock, then Gregson and finally Roberts, is difficult to calculate but the figures indicate that their organisations fulfilled a desperate need. As the study of military history progresses away from the viewpoint of the tactician or the constructor of memoirs and towards the study of the men of all classes who made up the Armies of Britain, more will doubtless be revealed, if the sources allow, about their lives, aspirations, conditions and deaths.

SMALL ARMS AND THE BENGAL CAVALRY, 1840-1841

DAVID HARDING

For the Bengal Army the Afghan campaigns of 1839-42 ended a period of comparative peace which had lasted since the Burma Expedition of 1824-26 and the Bhurtpore siege of 1825-26. It does not take many years of quiet garrison duty for an army to begin to lose touch with the practicalities of war, and in 1840 and 1841, in the light of the opening campaign in Afghanistan, the Bengal authorities perceived a need to re-examine the whole subject of cavalry training and equipments. This article examines the opinions expressed on the topic of what firearms, if any, the Bengal Light Cavalry regiments ought to have been carrying. The various reports bring into sharp and fascinating focus both the current armament of the Bengal cavalry and, above all, the views of experienced officers regarding basic fighting techniques and soldier psychology.

To fill in the background; since 1810 the scale of issue of small arms in the Bengal Light Cavalry had stood at a pair of pistols per man and fifteen carbines per troop.[1] These arms were provided by the East India Company from London, and all still used flintlock ignition.[2] The pistols were carried on most occasions in capped holsters on either side of the horse's neck and the carbine in a leather bucket normally near the trooper's right leg.[3] As yet, there had been no move to imitate recent changes in the British Army in England, where the pistol had fallen into disfavour and had been withdrawn to a great extent in 1838: in the British service pistols were now issued only to lancers (one per man) and to sergeant-

The Sepoy of the Cavalry

Watercolour by an Indian artist, c1830

Note the holster in front of the thigh. Sepoy actually refers to a private soldier in the infantry; in the cavalry he was known as a sowar.

NAM. 5602-179

97

majors and trumpeters of non-lancer cavalry regiments.[4] To turn to the Bengal Irregular Cavalry, at the period in question the Bengal Government issued pistols (the same English-made flintlocks as used by the regulars) for the native officers and *duffadars* (sergeants in cavalry regiments) only;[5] beyond that, each regiment provided itself with Indian-made matchlock longarms for the men.

SIR JOSEPH THACKWELL'S REPORT, 1840

The discussions were opened in July 1840 when the Commander-in-Chief in India, General Sir Jasper Nicolls KCB,[6] asked for the opinions of Major-General Sir Joseph Thackwell KCB and KH,[7] 'late in Command of the Cavalry of the Army of the Indus' (i.e. during the first phase of the Afghan war).[8] As Thackwell came from the Royal Service and was currently Colonel of HM 3rd Light Dragoons, it is not surprising to find that he advocated a change in the direction of the current armament of Her Majesty's Light Dragoons in India;

> '... with respect to the mode in which the Light Cavalry are armed it occurs to me that instead of 15 carbines per Troop only and a pair of Pistols for each Man it would be more advantageous if the Regiments were equipped in this particular the Same as the Light Dragoons in Her Majesty's Service in this country, every Sepoy (the Sergeants Band Trumpeters and Farriers excepted) being provided with a good Carbine and one Pistol the Non Commissioned Officers etc to retain the two Pistols now in their possession.

Thackwell offered several arguments in favour of an increase in the proportion of carbines. Firstly he found they were needed in 'jingles [*sic*], Mountain defiles, Ravines, Broken ground and in situations where the sword cannot be used'. Secondly fifteen carbines per troop were 'insufficient to keep in check the Matchlocks of the enemy' even if they could be concentrated, and in fact they were invariably dispersed for the protection of the baggage, he said. Thirdly, with only fifteen carbines per troop there was little prospect of the men in general becoming good shots. Though it lies a little outside the sphere of small arms, it is worth noting that Thackwell added a remark that the 'present sword' (evidently the East India Company's copy of the Royal Service's Light Cavalry pattern of 1821) was too heavy for the native troopers: they could not cut with it, and preferred the old pattern (evidently the Light Cavalry pattern of 1796, with its curved blade more suited to slashing, as was the native *tulwar*). These feelings about swords were to have their effect on the question of small arms.

Thackwell's remarks met with little encouragement; 'The Right Honble. Governor General of India in Council[9] considers it to be quite unnecessary to make any alteration in the Fire Arm equipment of the Light Cavalry', was the official response. Only in the matter of swords was His Lordship amenable to change, asking how many remained in store, to see if a reversion to the old pattern were possible.[10]

THE INCIDENT AT PURWAN DURRAH, 1840

Later in 1840, Bengal's concern about cavalry armaments was given greater stimulus by an unfortunate incident which led to the disbandment in disgrace of the 2nd Bengal Light Cavalry. During an action on 2 November 1840 at Purwan Durrah in Afghanistan, two squadrons of the 2nd had refused to follow their officers in a charge upon a body of the enemy believed to be led by Dost Mahomed, the Afghan *Amir*, or lord, at Kabul. The adjutant, doctor and an Engineer officer were killed, several officers were severely wounded, and numbers of the men were cut up while fleeing. A Court of Enquiry decided the débacle was caused by 'sheer cowardice', but there were suggestions that the men had been unwilling to charge with the sword - and that a similar lack of confidence in their arms was general in the Bengal Light Cavalry. In advocating the raising of an irregular cavalry regiment to replace the 2nd, Major-General Sir William Casement KCB[11] confirmed that this reluctance to rely on the sword was general in the Light Cavalry; 'Native Troopers ... place great reliance on their Pistols, and almost invariably on going into action make use of them instead of their swords ....'[12] He maintained that the *sowars* did not understand the use of the point, and proposed issuing the more curved native *tulwars*, with which the men were much more at home. He also suggested equipping one entire troop with carbines, and leaving each man with just one pistol.

CAVALRY OFFICERS' REPORTS, 1841

Stimulated by the incident at Purwan Durrah and the remarks made about it, the Bengal Government re-opened discussion of the current state of the Bengal Light Cavalry, this time on a wider basis. They now consulted 26 senior cavalry officers on a series of specific points, embracing equitation, uniform, saddlery, bladed weapons and small arms.[13]

The views expressed on small arms are easily summarised. On the distribution of carbines, nine officers preferred the current scale of fifteen per troop; four officers preferred restricting the carbines to distinct troops within the regiment; and thirteen advocated issuing a carbine to each man. As for pistols, three officers wanted two per man as at the time of reporting; seventeen officers wanted only one per man; and six officers were 'against the weapon altogether'. But these statistics say little, except that opinions were divided. It is the opinions themselves which are so fascinating, however contradictory they may be.

Most officers were aware of a conflict between European theory and Indian reality. The prevailing theory, which most of them subscribed to, was that the sword was the proper weapon for cavalry, and to thrust or charge with the point was the most lethal way of using it. But at the same time most officers were all too aware (as Thackwell had noted) that their *sowars* did not share this view: the men placed great reliance on firearms, and this undesirable dependence was increased by the men's yearning for curved slashing swords like their traditional *tulwar*.

Captain James MacKenzie[14] commanding the 6th Bengal Irregular Cavalry gave the best expression to these notions of Indian reliance on firearms;

'It is well known that all asiatic natives have great Confidence in fire Arms and in this feeling our Cavalry, Regular and Irregular, fully participate ... The Natives of India are of opinion that ... Superior fire Arms have been the Chief Auxiliary in our Conquests in Hindoostan. It is the Confidence he places in his Musquet which makes the gallant Infantry Sepahee Advance against the Enemy secure of Victory.[15]

No-one disagreed with this fundamental observation, but many officers clearly regretted its incompatibility with their own native European doctrine of the *arme blanche* and the use of the point. The Commander-in-Chief and his Adjutant-General of the Army (Major-General J R Lumley[16]) clashed, Nicolls expressing 'regret' that Lumley should have supported his advocacy of the carbine by asserting 'that no native cavalry ever met an enemy with the sword alone, except in pursuit'. But much as he disliked the assertion, Nicolls could not say it was untrue.

PISTOLS AND CARBINES

Whatever their cherished theories, one by one, the officers who had been consulted admitted there were several legitimate uses for small arms, including pistols. Above all there were occasions (as pointed out the year before by Thackwell) when the enemy simply could not be reached with a sword.

Many officers who professed to despise the pistol themselves emphasised that their men liked the weapon and the enemy feared it. One of the reporting officers, J. Sutherland, Agent Governor-General, Rajpootana Agency,[17] gave typically grudging acknowledgement to the need for pistols; '... an enemy may have some respect for this weapon', he wrote, 'those carrying it should not - a few rounds of ammunition would be sufficient'.[18] Some officers were unwilling to make allowance for the men's preferences and opposed having any pistols at all,

East India Company flintlock cavalry pistol, 1819-39.

East India Company flintlock cavalry carbine, 1811

but they were in a minority.

The life-saving aspect of the pistol's usefulness led several officers to discuss how it was best to be carried. Lieutenant-Colonel R E Chambers[19] of the 5th Light Cavalry asserted that 'No man should go into action without a Pistol', which should be carried in a 'leather pipe … attached to the left of the sword belt to receive the Pistol when the trooper is on foot duty so that he may always carry his arms about him'.[20] Such 'pipes' were already used in his regiment at inspection parades, Chambers added. They were '5½ inches long open at both ends - with a nich [*sic*] at the upper end to receive the Guard', and were provided at the expense of troop officers. Brigadier James Blair[21] Commanding the Nizam's Cavalry Division agreed; '… carried at the waist it is more easily drawn and returned than when in a holster'.[22] (It is interesting that the term 'holster' was only used for a pistol container attached to the saddle, and not one attached to the waist belt).

Blair also advocated attaching a lanyard or cord to the pistol, to be looped round the trooper's neck (as he said was done already in the 3rd Irregular Cavalry) which '… secures it from being dropt, and when the Trooper gets unfortunately unhorsed, and His horse runs over to the enemy (which our Horses always do on account of the Mares) he is not parted from his Pistol and Ammunition'. The explanation may be partly that many pistols of earlier patterns without the ring remained in use, but even with the new pistols the lanyard could not have been attached to the trooper's person as long as the regulations stipulated that the Light Cavalry must carry their pistols in the holsters on the saddle - such an arrangement would have meant the trooper would have to disconnect the two lanyards every time he dismounted, and he risked being strangled by them if unhorsed accidentally. An Adjutant-General's Circular of 1829 had directed that regiments be '… completed with the full proportion of swivels, to enable the men to sling their pistols'.[23] This suggests that the ring on the butt had sometimes been used to attach the pistols to the crossbelt, much as the carbine was attached in action (see below), but the lack of references to this practice in the officers' reports makes one suspect it had never caught on.

It was left to Major-General Thackwell to distil the final conclusion on the pistol; 'It is true that no fire Arms ought to be used in a melee, but a Pistol may on occasion be the means of saving a man's life and it would not be prudent to let the men have a prejudice that they were sent into action improperly armed'.[24]

It was generally agreed that the carbine was a dangerous weapon to fire from horseback, but that it had its uses on foot; thus Brigadier James Blair;

'In my opinion the Mounted Carbineer is of little or no use, from the fiery and restive nature of our Indian Horses, but dismount him, and in the absence of Infantry, he comes into play to clear broken and Jungly ground, to attack Villages and Heights and in short, he is invaluable for all dismounted work.[25]

The dangers of firing a short carbine, as used by the regular light cavalry, from horseback, were bluntly emphasised by Captain James MacKenzie; '… if his horse swerves during the act of firing the Trooper is as likely to shoot his neighbour or his own horse as his Enemy'.[26] This danger was one reason why the irregular cavalry preferred their long-barrelled matchlocks, but MacKenzie also believed the long matchlock gave improved accuracy, 'If I had a choice I should prefer the Matchlock to our present Carbine although the former misses fire twice out of five discharges and is nearly useless in wet weather still when it does go off it sends a Ball a long distance with considerable precision'. He concluded that the best carbine would be '… a light percussion gun with a barrel 30 inches in length, to be slung to the back like a rifle or in the manner the match locks of the Irregular Horse are carried'.

Blair's recommendation about how to carry the carbine was a departure from current practice. The carbine was normally carried in the leather bucket attached to the saddle. Before going into action it could be attached to a hook and swivel on the man's crossbelt, so that he could simply let go of it after firing, without fear of it dropping to the ground and being lost. Freedom of handling was preserved by the swivel being a loose fit, so as to slide freely up and down the crossbelt, and by attaching the hook to a ring which itself slid easily along a bar on the side of the carbine.

The apparent accuracy of matchlocks, as claimed by Blair, may have been due to their having rifled barrels, but only one officer (Major C Newbery[27] of the 9th Light Cavalry) advocated adopting 'Rifle barrelled Carbines' of European manufacture in the regular cavalry - this was an idea which was still somewhat before its time.[28]

There were numerous adverse remarks on the quality of the small arms currently in use (which seem to have been a mixture of old and new patterns), but the feeling was that the impending introduction of new weapons fitted with percussion ignition would remove the problem. One can add that the Bengal Army was habitually critical of its arms, while the Madras and Bombay Armies and British Army units in India were well satisfied with the same arms, made in the UK to the specification of the East India Company and subject to a strict inspection.[29]

CONCLUSIONS

The final recommendation of the Commander-in-Chief, Sir Jasper Nicolls, was strictly in line with the numerical analysis of officers' opinions as summarised above: he was in favour of issuing a carbine and one pistol to each man, 'with the ammunition carried as at present', in a pouch on the back of the crossbelt which was slung across the left shoulder. On 28 August 1841 the Governor-General, Lord Auckland, endorsed Nicolls' conclusion 'That carbines and a single pistol should be given to all the men of the Cavalry'. No-one seems to have been conscious that this was in fact a reversion to the pre-1810 scale of issue.

Yet despite this clear conclusion, the only change in armament which resulted from the enquiries of 1840-41 concerned swords. The Bengal Light Cavalry was now given some choice, on a regimental basis, as to whether they retained the current pattern sabre or reverted to the generally preferred earlier pattern of 1796, of which there were still 5,872 available in store in Bengal magazines. It was acknowledged that the men's misgivings about their swords were adding to their undesirable dependence on pistols.

The reason for inaction on small arms seems to have been caused initially by Bengal waiting for the arrival of percussion carbines from London, rather than issuing obsolescent flintlocks from store. By the time the new carbines arrived in Bengal in late 1844, it appears the new scale of issue decided upon in 1841 had either been quietly dropped on a change of key personnel (Lord Auckland left India in 1842, and Sir Jasper Nicolls was replaced as Commander-in-Chief by Sir Hugh Gough in August 1843) or else the bureaucracy simply suffered a failure of institutional memory. In 1847 pistols were withdrawn from those men carrying carbines.[30] A further enquiry in 1852[31] decided in favour of withdrawing all pistols and giving every man a carbine, but this measure was also stillborn, despite being ratified by the Court of Directors in 1854.[32] In 1857 it was realised that no change had yet been implemented,[33] but a still further delay was incurred when the Bengal Government decided they must await the arrival of new carbines on the Minié rifled principle, as seen in the Enfield or Pattern 1853 rifled musket. Thus when the Bengal Light Cavalry regiments disappeared in the holocaust of the Mutiny they still carried their pair of pistols and their fifteen carbines per troop, all of them smoothbore weapons with percussion ignition.

'A NEW NAVAL AND MILITARY DECORATION'

THE VICTORIAN SOLDIER AND THE VICTORIA CROSS

LESLEY SMURTHWAITE

On a bright, summer morning in June, 1857, large crowds gathered in Hyde Park, London, to witness a ceremony at which Queen Victoria personally invested 62 veterans of the Crimean War with a newly instituted award for outstanding gallantry in the field, appropriately named the Victoria Cross. Indeed, the Queen herself had taken a particular interest in the design and creation of the Cross, which was to be the first and only medal for gallantry in the face of the enemy for which officers and men of all ranks serving in Her Majesty's Forces were eligible.[1] The first 85 awards, announced in the *London Gazette* of 24 February 1857, were made retrospective to the beginning of the Crimean War in autumn 1854.[2]

After a long period of peace, Britain's military and naval involvement in the war with Russia, and an increasing public awareness of the heroism and sufferings endured by her soldiers and sailors overseas, had prompted the Government to consider new ways of rewarding individual acts of gallantry. To some extent this need was met in 1854 by the institution of the Distinguished Conduct Medal, for the Army, and in 1855 by the Conspicuous Gallantry Medal, for the Royal Navy. These awards, however, were available only to other ranks, and while junior officers of the French forces were decorated for bravery in the Crimea with lower grades of the *Légion d'honneur*, no equivalent award existed in Britain, since eligibility for the Order of the Bath was generally restricted to officers of field rank and above. The first announcement of a decision to remedy this deficiency was made by the Secretary of State for War in Parliament in January 1855, and a year later, on 29 January 1856 the Royal Warrant for the institution of the Victoria Cross was signed by the Queen.[3] It was to be 'a

Prototype Victoria Cross, 1856

NAM. 6310-59

Lieutenant Frederick Sleigh Roberts VC, Bengal
Horse Artillery, 1859

NAM. neg no 1101

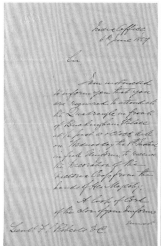

Letter to Lieutenant F S Roberts, *from the Military Secretary,
India Office, instructing him to attend at Buckingham Palace to
be invested with the Victoria Cross, 6 June 1859.*

NAM. 5504-64-14

Awards of Field Marshal Lord Roberts VC. *From left to right: Victoria Cross 1858; Volunteer Officers'
Decoration 1907; Queen Victoria's Diamond Jubilee Medal 1897; Edward VII Coronation Medal 1902; George
V Coronation Medal 1911; Indian Mutiny Medal 1857-58, with clasps: Lucknow, Relief of Lucknow, Delhi;
Indian General Service Medal 1854-95, with clasps: Looshai, Umbeyla, Burma 1885-7; Abyssinia Medal
1867-68; 2nd Afghan War Medal 1878-80, with clasps: Peiwar Kotal, Charasia, Kabul, Kandahar; Kabul to
Kandahar Star 1880; Queen's South Africa Medal 1899-1902, with clasps: Cape Colony, Paardeberg,
Driefontein, Johannesburg, Diamond Hill, Belfast*

NAM. 6310-73

New Naval and Military Decoration, which We are desirous should be highly prized and
eagerly sought after by the officers and men of Our Naval and Military Services' and under the
terms of the Warrant it would 'only be awarded to those ... who have served Us in the presence
of the enemy, and ... have performed some signal act of valour, or devotion to their country'.

The original prototype of the Victoria Cross, submitted to and approved by Queen Victoria in 1856, is in the Collections of the National Army Museum (National Army Museum 6310-59). Produced by the London jewellers, Messrs Hancocks and Co, who are still responsible for the manufacture of the Victoria Cross, the design is of a bronze cross *pattée*,[4] bearing on its obverse, the Royal Crest, a crowned lion *statant gardant* upon a crown, beneath which a scroll bears the words 'For Valour'. Queen Victoria is said to have suggested these words in preference to the proposed motto: 'For the brave'.[5] The reverse of the Cross is engraved with the date of the act of gallantry, and the reverse of the suspender bar bears the recipient's name, rank and unit. The earliest Crosses were cast from the bronze of Russian guns captured in the Crimea, later to be superseded by that of Chinese guns. The ribbon worn with the Cross was originally dark blue for Crosses awarded to Royal Navy recipients, and crimson (described in the Warrants as 'red') for the Army. This continued to be the case until 1918, when with the formation of the Royal Air Force, a crimson ribbon was adopted for recipients of all the services.

Succeeding Royal Warrants, of which there have been no less than fourteen, seven of them between 1857 and 1914, made a number of changes and amendments to the original terms and conditions set out for the award of the Victoria Cross in 1856. Recognising the heroism of civilian volunteers during the Indian Mutiny, a Warrant published in 1858 extended eligibility for the Cross to 'Non-Military Persons'. In a Warrant of the same year[6] provision was made for the VC to be awarded in cases of 'Conspicuous Courage and Bravery Displayed under Circumstances of Danger but not before the Enemy'. However, the provision for awarding the Cross under non-combat circumstances was short-lived, and since 1881 awards have only been made for acts of gallantry performed in the presence of the enemy. In 1867[7], in recognition of services performed by local auxiliary units during the Maori uprisings in New Zealand, eligibility was extended to local forces serving with Imperial troops. However, after the withdrawal of British troops from New Zealand in 1867, those forces could no longer be eligible for the VC, a situation which led to the institution of the New Zealand Cross (as described elsewhere in this publication). A Royal Warrant of 1881, however, extended eligibility to officers and men serving in naval and military auxiliary and reserve forces.[8] No allowance was made in the instituting Warrant for posthumous awards, although it became the practice to grant these during the Boer War. The first posthumous recipient was Lieutenant the Hon F H S Roberts (only son of Lord Roberts), who was killed at Colenso in 1899 although such awards were not published in the *London Gazette* until 1907, and it was not until 1920 that specific provision for posthumous awards was made in a Royal Warrant[9]. A further important amendment to the original conditions of award came in 1911, with the extension of eligibility to native officers and men of the Indian Army.[10] The 1920 Warrant also made provision for awards to officers and men of the Forces of the Empire and the Mercantile Marine, women of the nursing and hospital services and civilians of both sexes serving with Forces of the Empire. As yet no women have qualified for the award, although in India in 1859 a gold representation of the Cross was presented by the officers of the Regiment to the wife of the Officer Commanding the 104th Bengal Fusiliers, Mrs Webber Harris, for her 'indomitable pluck' in nursing their men during a severe outbreak of cholera that claimed 27 victims in one night.

Between the institution of the Victoria Cross in 1856 and the outbreak of the First World

War in 1914, a total of 522 Crosses were awarded. Of this number 348 went to the British Army, 95 to the East India Company's forces and Indian Army, 30 to members of Dominion and Colonial forces and four to civilians.[11] The greatest number of VCs won for any single campaign during the reign of Queen Victoria was undoubtedly during the Indian Mutiny, which broke out in 1857, shortly after the first investitures took place. In this conflict 182 Victoria Crosses were won, and nine are now in the Collections of the National Army Museum. Perhaps the most renowned military figure among the recipients of these early awards was Lieutenant Frederick Sleigh Roberts, who went on to win many further honours and eventual promotion to the rank of Field Marshal and Commander-in-Chief of the Army before his death in 1914. Born at Cawnpore in 1832, Roberts was commissioned lieutenant in the Bengal Horse Artillery in 1857, and at the outbreak of the Mutiny was attached to the Delhi Field Force. His was the first act of gallantry to win a Victoria Cross in 1858, when as one of a squadron commanded by Major George Younghusband, he took part in a cavalry charge at Khodagunge, between Cawnpore and Delhi. The citation, published in *The London Gazette*, 24 December 1858, describes how;

Field Marshal Sir Henry Evelyn Wood VC, in the uniform of Colonel, Royal Horse Guards, c1907

NAM. neg no 78046

'Lieutenant Roberts's gallantry had on every occasion been most marked. On following up the retreating enemy on the 2nd January 1858, at Khodagunge, he saw in the distance two sepoys going away with a standard... They immediately turned round and presented their muskets at him, and one of the men pulled the trigger, but fortunately the caps snapped and the standard-bearer was cut down by this gallant young officer... He also on the same day, cut down another sepoy who was standing at bay with musket and bayonet keeping off a sowar. Lieutenant Roberts rode to the assistance of the horseman, and rushing at the sepoy with one blow of his sword cut him across the face killing him on the spot.

In this attack Major Younghusband fell mortally wounded, Roberts however saved the standard, and the life of a sowar, and for these two acts of gallantry, he was awarded the VC (NAM. 6310-73).

Later in 1858, another young lieutenant who went on to achieve the rank of Field Marshal after a career scarcely less distinguished than that of Roberts, won the VC for his gallantry in India. Born in Essex in 1838, Henry Evelyn Wood (later Sir Evelyn Wood), had served as a midshipman in the Royal Navy during the Crimean War, when his conduct had received high praise from his senior officers and an unsuccessful recommendation for the Victoria Cross. Leaving the Navy in 1855 he obtained a commission in the 13th Light Dragoons, transferring to the 17th Lancers in order to go to India when the Mutiny broke out in 1857. He was awarded the VC for his gallantry at Sindwaho and Sindhora on 19 October 1858, while attached to the 3rd Bombay Light Cavalry. Evelyn Wood's Victoria Cross was announced in *The London Gazette* 4 September 1860;

'Henry Evelyn Wood, Lieut., 17 Lancers. For having, on the 19th Oct. 1858, during an action at Sindwaho, when in command of a troop of the 3rd Light Cavalry, attacked with much gallantry,

'How Lieutenant Wood won the VC at Sindwaho, 19 October 1858'

Seeing rebel troops of the 36th Bengal Native Infantry forming a square, Lieutenant Wood spurred at and killed the corner man, but was then pursued by another sepoy with a bayonet. The latter made the fatal error of clubbing his musket at the last moment, and Wood promptly ran him through.

NAM. neg no 77936

Awards of Field Marshal Sir Evelyn Wood VC. *From left to right: Victoria Cross 1858; Queen Victoria's Diamond Jubilee Medal 1897; Edward VII Coronation Medal 1902; George V Coronation Medal 1911; Crimean War Medal 1854-56, with clasps: Inkermann, Sebastopol; Indian Mutiny Medal 1857-58; Ashantee War Medal 1873-74, with clasp: Coomassie; South Africa Medal for Zulu and Basuto Wars 1877-79, with clasp: 1877-8-9; Egyptian Medal 1882-89, with clasp: The Nile 1884-85; Légion d'honneur, France, 5th Class; Order of the Medjidie, Turkey, 5th Class; Turkish Crimean War Medal 1855, Sardinian type; Khedive's Egyptian Star 1882-91*

NAM. 9303-39

almost single-handed, a body of rebels who had made a stand, whom he routed; also for having subsequently, near Sindhora, gallantly advanced with a Duffadar and Sowar of Beatson's Horse, and rescued from a band of robbers, a Potail, Chemmum Singh, whom they had captured and carried off to the jungles, where they intended to hang him.

Lieutenant Wood was twice mentioned in Despatches (*London Gazette*, 24 March and 5 May, 1859). He was later to distinguish himself in Africa, during the Ashanti War 1873-74, where he raised and commanded 'Wood's Regiment', and for which he was again mentioned in Despatches and created a Companion of the Order of the Bath (CB).

Captain Hugh Shaw VC,
18th (Royal Irish)
Regiment, c1865
NAM. neg no 30732

For his services in the South African War 1877-79, where he won an action against the Zulus at Kambula, and commanded a column at the Battle of Ulundi, Evelyn Wood received further commendations and numerous mentions in Despatches. As a major-general, he concluded peace negotiations with the Boers in the Transvaal in 1881, was further highly commended for his services commanding a brigade in Egypt in 1882, and in the Sudan 1884-85 where he organised the lines of communication on the Nile, receiving the Government's thanks for his efforts in conducting this monumental task. Sir Evelyn Wood had been knighted in 1879, and in 1881 was created a Knight Grand Cross of the Order of St Michael and St George (GCMG). In 1903 he was honoured by Edward VII with the rank of Field Marshal. One of only four Field Marshals to have won the Victoria Cross, (Lord Roberts,

Awards of Major-General R W Sartorius VC, late 6th Bengal Cavalry. From left to right: Order of St Michael and St George, Companion Badge, 1874; Victoria Cross 1874; Indian Mutiny Medal 1857-58; Indian General Service Medal 1854-95, with clasp: Bhootan; Ashantee War Medal 1873-74, with clasp: Coomassie; 2nd Afghan War Medal 1878-80

NAM. 6710-66

Captain Reginald William Sartorius VC, and his dog 'Bell', who accompanied him throughout the Ashanti War, 1874.

Sir George White and Viscount Gort were the other three), his baton and magnificent array of Orders and medals, British and foreign are testimony to an outstanding and highly colourful military career (NAM. 9303-39).

Fifteen VCs were won during the 2nd Maori War, in New Zealand, between 1860 and 1866. The last of these to be awarded was to Captain (later Major-General) Hugh Shaw, 2nd Battalion, 18th (Royal Irish) Regiment. Born in India in 1839, Hugh Shaw had served with the 18th Regiment in the Crimea and the Indian Mutiny, before going to New Zealand in 1864, where he was mentioned in Despatches, and for his bravery during a skirmish at Nukumari, on 24 January 1865, was awarded the Victoria Cross. According to the citation in *The London Gazette*, 28 November 1865, Captain Shaw advanced 'under heavy fire with four privates of the regiment, who volunteered to accompany him, to within thirty yards of the bush occupied by the rebels, in order to carry off a comrade who was badly wounded.'

His later career included service in the Sudan in 1884-85 where he commanded the 1st Battalion, Royal Irish Regiment, which had been sent from India to assist in the abortive Gordon Relief Expedition. Shaw, now a colonel, was again mentioned in Despatches and awarded a CB in 1885. His medals also include the New Zealand Campaigns Medal 1845-66, 2nd Afghan War Medal 1878-80, Egypt Medal 1882-89 and Khedive's Egyptian Star (NAM. 6105-1). Retiring with the rank of major-general in 1887, he died in England in 1904.

Four Victoria Crosses were awarded as a result of the Ashanti Expedition to West Africa, 1873-74, under General Sir Garnet Wolseley. One of these was to Major Reginald William Sartorius, of the 6th Bengal Cavalry. He and his brother, Euston Henry, both attained the rank of major-general and the added distinction of winning the Victoria Cross, which had only been conferred upon one other pair of brothers (General Sir Charles and General Sir Hugh Gough, during the Indian Mutiny). Reginald, the eldest of the three sons of Sir George Rose Sartorius, GCB, Admiral of the Fleet, was born in 1841 and obtained a commission in the Indian Army in 1858, very soon winning medals for his service in the Indian Mutiny and later in the Bhootan Expedition, 1864-66. Sartorius distinguished himself during the Ashanti War, during which he was twice mentioned in Despatches, promoted to major and received the Victoria Cross. *The London Gazette* for 26 October 1874, states that the award was made for his 'having during the attack on Abogoo, on the 17th Jan. last, removed under a heavy fire Sergt.-Major Braimah, Doctor [*sic*], a Houssa non-commissioned officer, who was mortally wounded, and placed him under cover'.

Sartorius later took part in the campaign in Afghanistan, 1878-80, in which his younger brother was to win the VC. He retired from the army as a major-general in 1897. Sartorius had been appointed a Companion of the Order of St Michael and St George (CMG) in 1874. In addition to his Orders and medals (NAM. 6710-66) the Museum also has in its Collections the gilt dog-collar which was presented by the 'Ladies of Lancashire' to Sartorius in 1874 for his faithful dog 'Bell' who had accompanied him on the Ashanti campaign (NAM. 6710-75).

During the Second Afghan War, 1878-80, sixteen Victoria Crosses were won, all at the expense of great courage and personal risk on the part of their recipients. Outstanding among them was the award to Captain O'Moore Creagh, of the Bombay Staff Corp, decorated for gallantry on 21 April 1879 at Kam Daka, on the Kabul River. Born in County Clare, Ireland, in 1848, the seventh son of a Royal Navy captain, O'Moore Creagh was educated at Sandhurst and at eighteen was commissioned ensign in the 95th Regiment. Embarking for India in 1869, he entered the Bombay Staff Corps in 1870 and was made Adjutant to the Marwara Battalion in 1871. At the outbreak of the Afghan War, the Battalion volunteered for service, and Captain Creagh took part in subsequent operations, as second-in-command. For his services, he was promoted to major, and received the Victoria Cross. The citation, published in *The London Gazette*, 18 November 1879, describes how;

General Sir O'Moore Creagh VC, *c1909*

NAM. neg no 77934

> 'Captain Creagh was detached from Daka with two companies of his battalion, to protect the village of Kam Daka, ... against a threatened incursion of the Mohmands, and reached that place the same night. On the following morning, the detachment (150 men) was attacked by the Mohmands in overwhelming numbers (about 1,500 men); and the inhabitants of the Kam Daka having themselves taken part with the enemy, Capt Creagh found himself under the necessity of retiring from the village. He took up a position in a cemetery not far off, which he made as defensible as circumstances would admit of, and this position he held against all the efforts of the enemy, repeatedly repulsing them with the bayonet until three o'clock in the afternoon, when he was relieved by a detachment sent for the purpose from Daka. The enemy were then finally repulsed, and being charged by a troop of the 10th Bengal Lancers, under the command of Capt D M Strong, were routed and broken, and great numbers of them driven into the river. The Commander-

in-Chief in India has expressed his opinion that, but for the coolness, determination, and gallantry of the highest order, and the admirable conduct which Capt Creagh displayed on this occasion, the detachment under his command would, in all probability have been cut off and destroyed.

Above: The Afghan Campaign - the Fifty-Ninth Regiment storming a Hill near the Sebundi Pass
From The Graphic, *27 December 1879*

NAM. neg no 77935

Above right: Lieutenant Euston Henry Sartorius VC, *59th Regiment, younger brother of Reginald, c1880*

NAM. neg no 77933

Awards of Major-General E H Sartorius VC, *late 59th (2nd Nottinghamshire) Regiment. From left to right: Victoria Cross 1879; Order of the Bath, Companion Badge 1897; Queen Victoria's Diamond Jubilee Medal 1897; Edward VII Coronation Medal 1902; George V Coronation Medal 1911; 2nd Afghan War Medal 1878-80; Egyptian Medal 1882-89; Order of the Osmanieh, Turkey, 3rd Class; Khedive's Egyptian Star 1882-91*

NAM. 6710-67

Victoria Cross 1879 awarded to Corporal C F Schiess, Natal Native Contingent

NAM. 5811-96-1

In his subsequent career, O'Moore Creagh continued to serve with distinction in India, on the North-West Frontier and in China in 1900. Rising to the rank of general, he became Commander-in-Chief, India, in 1909. His Orders and medals (NAM. 7606-3) include the Knight Grand Cross of the Order of the Bath (GCB) and the Japanese Order of the Rising Sun, 2nd Class.

A no less impressive Victoria Cross was earned in Afghanistan by Captain Euston Henry Sartorius, 59th (2nd Nottinghamshire) Regiment, younger brother of Reginald William who had so recently gained the same distinction for his gallantry in the Ashanti War. Captain Sartorius, born in Portugal in 1844, and educated at Sandhurst, had already displayed his considerable courage when, as a young lieutenant in June 1869, he received the Royal Humane Society's Bronze Medal for saving the lives of three girls from drowning in the sea at Broadstairs in Kent. He passed the Staff College examinations in 1870 and served as Instructor in Military Surveying at Sandhurst for four years. During the Afghan War, Sartorius commanded a company of the 59th Regiment and served as Assistant Field Engineer at the occupation of Kalat-i-Ghilzai in 1879. He was twice mentioned in Despatches, and was awarded the Victoria Cross for gallantry at Shahjui on 24 October 1879. His citation, in *The London Gazette*, 17 May 1881, describes how he was;

> 'leading a party of five or six men of the 59th Regiment against a body of the enemy, of unknown strength, occupying an almost inaccessible position on the top of a precipitous hill. The nature of the ground made any sort of regular formation

impossible, and Capt Sartorius had to bear the first brunt of the attack from the whole body of the enemy, who fell upon him and his men as they gained the top of the precipitous pathway; but the gallant and determined bearing of this officer, emulated as it was by his men, led to the most perfect success, and the surviving occupants of the hill-top, seven in number, were all killed. In this encounter Capt Sartorius was wounded by sword-cuts in both hands, and one of his men was killed.

Sartorius was promoted to major, and was specially commended and thanked by the Indian Government for his work in connection with the Survey Department. As Deputy-Assistant-Adjutant-General in the Egyptian Campaign, 1882 Sartorius was again mentioned in Despatches and received the 3rd Class of the Turkish Order of the Osmanieh. He was made a CB 1896, and appointed to the rank of major-general in 1899. Retiring from active service in 1903 he died in Chelsea in 1925. In addition to campaign awards for Afghanistan and Egypt, the decorations of General Sartorius include Queen Victoria's Diamond Jubilee Medal 1897, and the Coronation Medals of Edward VII (1902) and George V (1911), (NAM. 6710-67).

In the course of the relatively brief but bloody campaign against the Zulus, in South Africa, in 1879, no less than 23 Victoria Crosses were won, eleven of these on 22 and 23 January, in the defence of Rorke's Drift. This disused mission station had become a Commissariat post manned by a garrison of eight officers and 131 men, mostly of the 24th (2nd Warwickshire) Regiment. Among their number, however, was a soldier of Swiss birth, Corporal Christian Ferdinand (also recorded as Ferdinand Christian) Schiess, who was serving in the 2nd Battalion, 3rd Natal Native Contingent. Schiess gained the twin distinctions of being the only Swiss national and the first man serving with South African forces to be decorated with the supreme British award for gallantry. Little is known of his background. He was born at Burgdorf, Switzerland in 1856, raised in an orphanage, and at an early age travelled to South Africa, where he settled in Natal. The citation for his Victoria Cross, published in *The London Gazette*, 29 November 1879, which records him simply as 'Schiess, Corpl', relates how;

> 'in the defence of Rorke's Drift Post on the night of 22nd January, 1879, ... in spite of his having been wounded in the foot a few days previously, he greatly distinguished himself when the Garrison were repulsing with the bayonet, a series of desperate assaults made by the Zulus, and displayed great activity and devoted gallantry throughout the defence. On one occasion when the Garrison had retired to the inner line of defence, and the Zulus occupied the wall of mealie bags which had been abandoned, he crept along the wall, without any order, to dislodge a Zulu who was shooting better than usual and succeeded in killing him, and two others, before he, the Corporal returned to the inner defence.

Schiess received his Victoria Cross from the hands of General Sir Garnet Wolseley on 3 February 1880. Just six years later he was found starving on the streets of Cape Town, and a subscription was raised to pay his fare to England on board the *Serapis*. The effects of poverty on his health were sadly such that he did not survive the voyage. His Victoria Cross, unclaimed

Lance-Corporal James Murray VC, 94th Regiment, 1881

Sergeant John Danagher VC, *2nd Battalion Connaught Rangers, c1890. Danagher was serving with Nourse's Horse, a locally-raised South African Unit, when he won his VC.*

by any relative, was found many years later at the War Office, and is now in the National Army Museum (NAM. 5811-96-1).

During the First Boer War, 1880-81, in which Britain suffered heavy losses in the Transvaal, six Victoria Crosses were won, two of them by Irishmen, on the same day and in the same action. At Elandsfontein, near Pretoria, Private James Murray, 94th Regiment, later 2nd Battalion, Connaught Rangers, and Trooper John Danagher (also recorded as Danaher) of Nourse's Horse, a locally raised South African unit, together risked their lives to rescue two privates of the 21st Regiment who had been shot and badly wounded by the Boers. Their awards were published in *The London Gazette*, 14 March 1882 and the citation for John Danagher states;

'For gallant conduct (with L.-Corpl. James Murray, 2nd Battn. The Connaught Rangers) during an engagement with the Boers at Elandsfontein on the 16th Jan. 1881, in advancing for 500 yards, under a very heavy fire from a party of about sixty Boers, to bring out of action a private of the 21st Foot who had been severely wounded; in attempting which L.-Corpl. Murray was himself severely wounded.

Of the two privates they attempted to rescue, one, Private Byrne, was mortally wounded during the operation. The second, Private Davis, was taken prisoner with Murray, who had ordered Danagher to make his escape. They were freed shortly afterwards by the Boers, however, and allowed to return to their units, Davis sadly dying a few days later from his wounds. Both Murray and Danagher survived and were promoted to lance-corporal and sergeant respectively. Danagher subsequently joined the Connaught Rangers and added to his Victoria Cross the Army Long Service and Good Conduct Medal (NAM. 6007-4), while Murray, whose medals include the South Africa Medal for Zulu and Basuto Wars 1877-79 with the clasp '1879', and the George VI Coronation Medal 1937 (NAM. 5109-33), died in 1942, at the age of 85.

A number of Victoria Crosses were won during campaigns on the North-West Frontier of India in 1897 and 1898. The first of these was awarded to another young man of Irish descent, Lieutenant Edmond William Costello. He was born in 1873 at Sheikh Budin, North-West Frontier Province, the son of a colonel in the Indian Medical Service. Educated in England,

Lieutenant Edmond William Costello VC, c1890

NAM. neg no 25587

he was commissioned in the West Yorkshire Regiment, but soon transferred to the Indian Army, and joined the 22nd Punjab Infantry. In 1897 he was appointed to the Indian Staff Corps, and was serving with the Malakand Field Force, under General Sir William Lockhart, when he gained the Victoria Cross for gallantry on 26 July 1897, at Malakand. His citation, published in *The London Gazette*, 9 November 1897, describes how, that night 'Lieutenant Costello went out from the hospital enclosure, and with the assistance of two sepoys, brought in a wounded lance-havildar who was lying sixty yards away in the open on the football ground. This ground was at the time overrun with swordsmen and swept by a heavy fire both from the enemy and our own men who were holding the sapper lines.' Costello was twice wounded within the next few days, was mentioned in Despatches, (*London Gazette*, 5 November 1897: 'Lieutenant E W Costello, 22nd Punjab Infantry, has behaved excellently well, and is the subject of a separate recommendation') and received the India Medal 1895-1902 with two clasps. He took part in operations in the Mohmand country in 1908, for which he received the India General Service Medal 1908-35 and promotion to major in 1910. Graduating from the Staff College, Quetta, in 1914, Costello rejoined his regiment as second-in-command and further distinguished himself during the First World War, serving in Mesopotamia with the 17th Brigade of the 6th Indian Division and commanding the 12th Indian Brigade in 1918. He was mentioned in Despatches five times and received the Distinguished Service Order in 1917 (*London Gazette*, 25 August 1917). Costello retired from the regular Army in 1923, with the honorary rank of brigadier-general, continuing to serve with the Territorial Army Reserve of Officers until 1930. He died in 1949 at the age of 75. His group of Orders and medals includes the French *Croix de Guerre* with palms, as well as the CMG, and Companionship of the Royal Victorian Order (CVO), which he received in 1918 and 1920 respectively (NAM. 6009-65).

The South African War, 1899-1902, when British troops encountered a well-armed and determined opponent, saw some of their most outstanding feats of individual heroism and self-sacrifice. Seventy-eight Victoria Crosses were won during the campaign, seven of them at the disastrous Battle of Colenso on 15 December 1899, where two batteries of the Royal Artillery were virtually wiped out , and in efforts to rescue the guns from an almost impossible position of exposure to enemy fire, many more brave officers and men were killed or wounded. The young Lieutenant the Hon Frederick Hugh Sherston Roberts of the King's Royal Rifle Corps, an aide-de-camp to General Buller, and the only son of Field Marshal Lord Roberts, was one of three officers and seven men who bravely responded to Buller's call for volunteers. Lieutenant Roberts was mortally wounded in the heroic but ill-fated attempt to save the guns and became the first VC winner to 'receive' his award posthumously (*London Gazette*, 2 January 1900). His decorations (NAM. 6310-76) include the Indian General Service Medal 1854, and India

Lieutenant the Hon Frederick Hugh Sherston Roberts, *King's*
Royal Rifle Corps, killed at Colenso, 15 December 1899

Oil on canvas, by Julian Story (1857-1919), painted posthumously, 1901

NAM. 6005-320

Awards of Lieutenant the Hon F H S Roberts VC, *King's Royal Rifle Corps. From left to right: Victoria Cross 1899; Queen Victoria's Diamond Jubilee Medal 1897; Indian General Service Medal 1854-95, with clasp: Waziristan 1894-95; India Medal 1895-1902, with clasp: Relief of Chitral 1895; Queen's Sudan Medal 1896-97; Queen's South Africa Medal 1899-1902, with clasps: Relief of Ladysmith, Natal; Order of the Medjidie, Turkey, 4th Class; Khedive's Sudan Medal 1896-1908, with clasp: Khartoum*

NAM. 6310-76

Medal 1895-1902, in recognition of his services on the North-West Frontier of India, for which he was also mentioned in Despatches. In his short but distinguished career he had also served in the Sudan, receiving the Queen's Sudan Medal 1896, the Khedive's Sudan Medal and 4th Class of the Turkish Order of the Medjidie, in addition to his Queen's South Africa Medal 1899-1902.

Another disastrous incident in the War occurred on 31 March 1900 when, after the occupation of Bloemfontein on 18 March, a column on its way there, including two batteries of the Royal Horse Artillery, was ambushed by Boer marksmen at Korn Spruit. Most of the baggage train and several guns were captured. 'Q' Battery, under the command of Major Edmund Phipps-Hornby, managed to gallop away and bring their guns into action. One of the gunners was Isaac Lodge, who had worked as a farm boy and gamekeeper in his native Essex before joining the Army and serving in India, Ireland and South Africa with 'Q' Battery. Under deadly enemy fire, Lodge's comrades were shot down and he became the only man in his section able to serve the guns. Phipps-Hornby was eventually forced to give the order to retire, and Lodge, together with the surviving gunners and drivers, succeeded in bringing all but one of their guns to safety. After the action, the award of Victoria Crosses was proposed. Such was the gallantry of every man in 'Q' Battery that Rule 13 of the Victoria Cross Warrant was applied, under which one officer was to be nominated by his fellow officers, one non-commissioned officer by the NCOs and two gunners or drivers by the drivers and gunners. The gunners' choice fell on Lodge, and together with Phipps-Hornby, Sergeant Charles Parker and Driver Horace Glasock, he was decorated by Lord Roberts in Pretoria that October. Lodge was promoted to corporal in 1903, and six years later, on being discharged from the Army, he became a Keeper in the Royal Parks. His medals include the Army Long Service and Good Conduct Medal which he received in 1907, as well as the Queen's South Africa Medal 1899-1902 with five clasps, and the rare George V Coronation Medal awarded to Royal Park Keepers in 1911 (NAM. 8309-68).

Between the end of the Boer War in 1902 and the outbreak of the First World War in 1914 only ten Victoria Crosses were awarded. Of these, three were won in an action that took place on 22 April 1903, during the campaign in Somaliland. Captain William George Walker, 4th Ghurka Rifles, was one of the three officers who distinguished themselves by their bravery on that occasion. Born 40 years earlier, in Naini Tal, India, Walker was the eldest son of Deputy Surgeon-General W Walker, Indian Medical Service, who became Honorary Physician to Queen Victoria. William entered the Army as a University Candidate, and was commissioned into the Suffolk Regiment in 1885, transferring

Gunner Isaac Lodge VC

Cigarette card No 53 from the series 'VC Heroes - Boer War', issued by Taddy & Co.

NAM. 8310-13-8

Awards of Corporal Isaac Lodge VC, Royal Horse Artillery. From left to right: Victoria Cross 1900; Queen's South Africa Medal 1899-1902, with clasps: Relief of Kimberley, Paardeberg, Driefontein, Transvaal, South Africa 1901; George V Coronation Medal, Royal Parks 1911; Army Long Service and Good Conduct Medal 1907

NAM. 8309-68

Above: Awards of Major-General W G Walker VC, late 4th Gurkha Rifles. From left to right: Victoria Cross 1903; Indian General Service Medal 1854-95, with clasps: Samana 1891, Waziristan 1894-95; Africa General Service Medal 1902-56, with clasps: Somaliland 1902-04, Jidballi; 1914-15 Star; British War Medal 1914-20; Allied Victory Medal 1914-19, with oakleaf for Mention in Despatches; Delhi Durbar Medal 1911

NAM. 8905-184

Right: Captain William George Walker VC, Bikanir Camel Corps, Somaliland, 1903

NAM. neg no 62335

to the Indian Army in 1887. Posted to the 1st Battalion, 4th Ghurka Rifles, he first saw active service in the second Miranzai Expedition (1891), receiving the Indian General Service Medal 1854-95 and clasp, to which he added a second clasp in the Waziristan Expedition, 1894-95. From 1902 to 1904 Captain Walker took part in British operations in Somaliland, and while serving with the Bikanir Camel Corps, was present in the actions at Daratoleh and Jidbali. He was three times mentioned in Despatches, awarded the Africa General Service Medal, with two clasps, and received the Victoria Cross. The citation for his award, published in the *London Gazette*, 7 August 1903, recounts the dramatic incident in which Captain Walker, together with a fellow officer and four men, all displayed exceptional courage;

> 'During the return of Major Gough's column to Donop on 22nd April last, after the action at Daratoleh, the rearguard got considerably in rear of the column, owing to the thick bush, and to having to hold their ground while wounded men were being placed on camels. At this time Captain Bruce was shot through the body from a distance of about twenty yards, and fell on the path unable to move. Captains Walker and Rolland, two men of the 2nd Bn King's African Rifles, one Sikh, and one Somali of the Camel Corps were with him when he fell. In the meantime the column, being unaware of what had happened, were getting further away. Captain Rolland then ran back some 500 yards, and returned with assistance to bring off Capt Bruce, while Capt Walker and the men remained with that officer, endeavouring to keep off the enemy, who were all round in the thick bush. This they succeeded in doing, though not before Capt Bruce was hit a second time, and the Sikh wounded. But for the gallant conduct displayed by these officers and men, Capt Bruce must have fallen into the hands of the enemy.

Captain Bruce unfortunately succumbed to his wounds. All those involved in the rescue attempt received gallantry awards or commendations; Walker, Captain Rolland and Major John Edmund Gough, who commanded the column, and whose father and uncle had both won VCs during the Indian Mutiny, were decorated with the Victoria Cross, while Sergeant Nderamani and Corporal Surmoni of the King's African Rifles together with Sowar Umar Ismail, Somali Camel Corps, all received the Distinguished Conduct Medal. Walker was in addition promoted to major and brevet lieutenant-colonel for his services. During the First World War he commanded the 1st Battalion, 4th Gurkha Rifles in Egypt and France, taking command of the 2nd Division in 1915 and receiving promotion to the rank of major-general in 1916. He was mentioned in Despatches three times. Retiring from the Army in 1919, after a most distinguished career, General Walker died in Sussex in 1936, at the age of 73. In addition to the Victoria Cross, his decorations include the CB, awarded in 1914 (NAM. 8905-184).

The Victoria Crosses now in the National Army Museum's Collections represent a small proportion of the heroic deeds performed by individuals throughout Britain's military history since 1854. For every soldier successfully recommended for the VC a number have been equally deserving. A product of the Victorian age, however, it was then as it is still, the highest award for gallantry to which men could aspire, not to be approached in status until 1940 with the institution of the George Cross for non-operational acts of gallantry. There is no doubt that it served its purpose in encouraging and inspiring, by the example of all those who won it, officers and men alike throughout the many greater and lesser campaigns in which the British Army was involved during the years since the first investiture. Yet, ironically perhaps, its greatest need would be felt in the global conflicts of the twentieth century. After 1904 no further awards would be made until the outbreak of the First World War in 1914. Thereafter, in a period of less than five years, a staggering figure of 633 Victoria Crosses were to be won, a prospect that Queen Victoria herself, in instituting the award could never have foreseen.

VICTORIA CROSSES AWARDED 1856-1914 IN THE COLLECTIONS OF THE NATIONAL ARMY MUSEUM

- Corporal J McGovern, 1st Bengal European Fusiliers, Delhi, India, 23 June 1857   6609-138-1
- Colonel R H M Aitken, 13th Bengal Native Infantry, Lucknow, India, 30 June-22 November 1857   5612-2
- Sergeant J McGuire, 1st Bengal European Fusiliers, Delhi, India, 14 September 1857   5602-276
- Private T Duffy, 1st Madras European Fusiliers, Lucknow, India, 26 September-1 October 1857   5809-1-1
- Private J Ryan, 1st Madras European Fusiliers, Lucknow, India, 26 September 1857   6210-68-1
- Lieutenant (later Field Marshal) F S Roberts, Bengal Horse Artillery, Khodagunge, India,
  2 January 1858   6310-73-1
- Lieutenant (later General) W M Cafe, 56th Bengal Native Infantry, Fort Ruhya, India, 15 April 1858 6310-89-1
- Lieutenant H E Wood (later Field Marshal Sir Evelyn Wood),17th Lancers (Duke of Cambridge's Own),
  Sindwaho, India, 19 October 1858   9303-39-1
- Captain H M Clogstoun, 19th Madras Native Infantry, Chichumba, India, 15 January 1859   6105-7-1
- Captain (later Major-General) H Shaw, 18th (Royal Irish) Regiment, Nukumari, New Zealand,
  24 January 1865   6105-1-1
- Major (later Major-General) R W Sartorius, 6th Bengal Cavalry, Abogoo, Ashanti,
  17 January 1874   6710-66-1
- Corporal F C Schiess, Natal Native Contingent, Rorke's Drift, Zululand, 22 January 1879   5811-96-1
- Captain (later General) O'Moore Creagh, Bombay Staff Corps, Kam Daka, Afghanistan, 21 April 1879
     7606-3-1
- Major (later Major-General) E H Sartorius, 59th (2nd Nottinghamshire) Regiment, Shahjui, Afghanistan,
  24 October 1879   6710-67-1
- Private F Fitzpatrick, 94th Regiment, Sekukuni's Town, South Africa, 28 November 1879   5102-17-1
- Lance-Corporal J Murray, Connaught Rangers, Elandsfontein, South Africa, 16 January 1881   5109-33-1
- Sergeant J Danagher, Nourse's Horse, Elandsfontein, South Africa, 16 January 1881   6007-4-1
- Lieutenant (later Brigadier-General) E W Costello, 22nd Punjab Infantry, Malakand, Indian Frontier,
  26 July 1897   6009-65-1
- Lieutenant the Hon F H S Roberts, King's Royal Rifle Corps, Colenso, South Africa, 15 December 1899
     6310-76-1
- Gunner (later Corporal) I Lodge, Royal Horse Artillery, Korn Spruit, South Africa, 31 March 1900
     8309-68-1
- Captain (later Major-General) W G Walker, 4th Gurkha Rifles, Daratoleh, Somaliland, 22 April 1903
     8905-184-1

NOTE

For reasons of space, the awards illustrated in this article *do not*, in every case, include the recipient's *complete* entitlement of Orders, decorations and medals. The groups of decorations illustrated are, to the best knowledge of the National Army Museum, in the order in which they were worn by the recipients.

SEBASTOPOL AFTER THE SIEGE, 1855-1856

MARION HARDING

'We visited a house which had evidently been a Russian restaurant ... Upon the long open corridor or balcony on the first story ... we found a photographer, who, by his potent chemistry, was commanding the ruins of Sebastopol to reflect themselves for the amusement of the stay-at-homes of London and Paris.[1]

The Crimean War was the product of the long-cherished desire of Russia to secure her shortest sea route to the outside world by gaining control of the Bosphorus and the Dardanelles and the equal determination of the European powers to prevent her from achieving that aim. To this end Britain, France, Turkey and later Italy, represented by Sardinia, united to forestall any future threat to their own trade routes by seizing Sebastopol, the fortified naval base in the Black Sea, and destroying the Russian fleet which had taken refuge there.

THE SIEGE

In September 1854 a combined force of 63,000 men was landed 30 miles north of Sebastopol. Declining a costly assault on the northern defences the Allies moved round to take up position before the south front on the plateau known as the Chersonese Upland. The delay involved in this manœuvre and in bringing forward the siege artillery was put to good use by the town's garrison who so strengthened their defences that the results achieved when the bombardment finally commenced were insufficient to justify an assault.

The terrible conditions which prevailed throughout the winter months, for which the British Army at least was totally unprepared, prevented the Allies from seriously prosecuting the siege, but during 1855 they pushed their front line of entrenchments forwards across the plateau towards the anchorage and military installations. A cordon of trenches and rifle pits, batteries and strongpoints were the chief physical obstacles to the advance.

The two most important Russian strongpoints were the Malakoff and the Redan. The Malakoff occupied the most commanding position and formed the key to the southern fortifications. It consisted of a semi-circular masonry tower, mounting five heavy guns around which was a circular entrenchment with a short flank at each end armed with a further ten guns. It overlooked the rear of all the defensive works on the eastern side of Sebastopol, including the Redan, and from its position on an independent high knoll it afforded a good site from which to repel assaults.

The fortifications of the Redan were also formidable. Built on what had once been a vineyard 306 feet above sea level it had two faces, each 70 yards long, meeting at an angle of 65 degrees. The base from which it jutted out was a fortified line of earthworks spanning the ridge. In front of it was a ditch roughly twenty feet wide and fourteen feet deep and above this the Redan rose to a height of fifteen feet making its escarpment nearly 30 feet from top to bottom. Between it and the nearest parallel constructed by the British was approximately 450 yards of ground, much of it uphill and all of it exposed to Russian batteries on the right and left. Guns mounted in embrasures in the faces of the Redan itself also commanded a wide field of fire and the Russian gunners were protected by mantlets, tough rope mats slung across the embrasure with a collar through which the muzzle of the gun protruded. There were secure bomb-proof shelters for the officers and men constructed of old ships' timbers, some of them over two feet in diameter. Nearly every magazine was wired so as to be capable of being exploded electrically if required.

An assault on 18 June 1855, though costly and unsuccessful, left the Russians under no illusion that this set-back to the Allies afforded little more than a respite. The final assault took place on 8 September after an artillery bombardment lasting three days and though no permanent success was achieved along the greater part of the line, including the British sector before the Redan, the capture of the key position of the Malakoff by the French made the defences untenable and the remnants of the Russian garrison withdrew across the harbour during the night, blowing up the magazines and firing buildings in the city's southern sector as it went.

ATTITUDES TOWARDS PHOTOGRAPHY

The Crimean War was the first to be subjected to full press coverage in anything approaching the modern sense. Newspaper correspondents, war artists and photographers were all present. The first, in the person of William Howard Russell of *The Times* presented a stark word-picture of the realities of war; the second, represented by artists such as William Simpson certainly depicted killed and wounded and the burial of the dead but the interposition of an intermediary between the subject and the viewer blurs the reality and softens the impact. Though the technical limitations of his equipment did not allow him to record scenes of violent action, Roger Fenton, the photographer most closely identified with the campaign, had ample opportunity to photograph the aftermath of battles. Instead he concentrated on scenes such as *The Cookhouse of the 8th Hussars*, a convivial party of French and English officers entitled *L'Entente Cordiale* and views of camps. It is unclear whether the reason for this 'censorship' was political or commercial. Fenton's expedition was made under royal patronage and with the assistance of the Secretary of State for War and it may have been understood that the photographs should reassure the public by reflecting the improvement in conditions which were largely the result of Russell's revelations. On the other hand, the trip was financed by the Manchester publishers Thomas Agnew and Sons and it may have been thought that it was not commercially prudent to produce pictures which might have been considered upsetting or offensive.

The Interior of the Redan. *Photograph by James Robertson. 'The interior of the Redan was a wide level space, filled with debris of all kinds - fragments of gabions, broken guns and carriages, beams hurled from exploded magazines, and chasms made by bursting shells'.*

Lieutenant-Colonel E Bruce Hamley, The Story of the Campaign of Sebastopol, *Edinburgh (1855) p136*

NAM. neg no 4450

THE PHOTOGRAPHERS

'I should advise you not to bring a camera ... a camera with all its appurtenances would immensely increase your baggage ... I suppose it would require a cart (Mr Fenton had a large van) ... the town of Sebastopol, which affords the best views for the camera, has already been photographed from every possible point of view, and I imagine that by this time many of the impressions are in London.[2]

Photographs taken by two photographers, both amateurs, who followed Fenton to the Crimea, though once again avoiding portrayals of the human wreckage of war do provide at least a glimpse of the attendant chaos and destruction.

James Robertson was Superintendent and Chief Engraver at the Imperial Mint in Constantinople. Some of his best photographs were taken as British troops passed through on the way to the front and several were reproduced as woodcuts in *The Illustrated London News*. Lieutenant-Colonel Frederick Campbell of the 46th Regiment wrote of Robertson in a letter home;

'Since Mr Fenton was here a man of the name of Robertson, who has an establishment in Constantinople, has taken a great many views, superior, I think to Fenton's. He went to Constantinople, about a month ago to have them printed off, and promised to let me have £5 worth, but I have heard no more of them. He had the great advantage of being able to take the interior of the Malakoff, Redan and other places almost immediately after their capture.[3]

Altogether Robertson produced some 60 photographs[4] but sales were very slow and his unsold stocks were auctioned with those of Fenton between 15 and 19 December 1856. Interest in the photographs had waned as the War drew to a close and ceased almost completely once the peace treaty had been signed.

In April 1986 the National Army Museum purchased a set of twelve photographs taken by G Shaw-Lefevre entitled 'Photographic Views of Sebastopol taken immediately after the Retreat of the Russians, September 8, 1855'.[5] They were published by J Hogarth in 1856 and cover much the same ground as those of Robertson: the Redan, the Malakoff and the ruinous suburbs of the town. If indeed they were taken immediately after the retreat then his vantage points must have been very carefully chosen, for not a single dead or wounded man is to be seen, and the task of removing the wounded and burying the dead would have occupied several days.

George John Shaw-Lefevre was born in London on 12 June 1831, the only son of Sir John George Shaw-Lefevre. He derived from his father a keen interest in politics and a taste for foreign travel. He was educated at Eton and at Trinity College Cambridge and the year after taking his degree in 1853 was called to the bar by the Inner Temple. In 1863 Shaw-Lefevre was elected MP for Reading in the Liberal interest and filled successive positions as Secretary to the Board of Trade, Under Secretary at the Home Office, Secretary to the Admiralty, and,

Searching for wires connected with the powder magazine in the Carronade Battery flanking the ditch in the Redan. Photograph by G Shaw-Lefevre.

NAM. neg no 69869

The Interior of the Malakoff. *Photograph by James Robertson 'Before us rose that celebrated hill, still crested with the low ruins of the tower destroyed by our siege artillery ... and on that top was a flagstaff and a telegraph'.*
Anonymous, Inside Sebastopol and Experiences in Camp, *p215*

NAM. neg no 25646

with a seat in the cabinet, First Commissioner of Works and President of the Local Government Board in the Liberal administrations which held power between 1868 and 1895. After suffering defeat at the polls in the latter year he decided not to stand for re-election. He represented the Haggerston Division of the London County Council in 1897 and in 1906 was raised to the Peerage as Baron Eversley of Old Ford but seldom attended the House of Lords. In 1912 increasing deafness induced him to retire to his country home, Abbotsworthy House near Kingsworthy, Winchester where he resided until his death in 1928.

In 1874 Shaw-Lefevre married Lady Constance Emily, only daughter of the third Earl of Ducie. They had no children and the barony became extinct on his death. In marked contrast to his political career virtually nothing is known of Shaw-Lefevre as a photographer. His entry in the *Dictionary of National Biography* states only that 'In September 1855 he sailed in Sir Edward Colebrooke's yacht to the Crimea, taking with him an early form of photographic camera'.[6] Sir Edward Colebrooke himself is equally uninformative: in his *Journal of Two Visits to the Crimea*[7] published in 1856 he mentions Shaw-Lefevre only twice; 'joined by G Lefevre, who gladly availed himself of my offer of a berth' and 'Saturday 1st September. Took Lefevre to the front'.

THE PHOTOGRAPHS

The method of photography employed by both Robertson and Shaw-Lefevre was the wet plate or wet collodion process. A quantity of collodion (a form of gun-cotton dissolved in ether) containing potassium iodide was poured onto a perfectly clean glass plate which was then manipulated until the whole surface was evenly covered. When the ether had almost evaporated, leaving a tacky coating, the plate was immersed in a bath of silver nitrate to sensitize it. The plate was loaded into a plate holder, exposed in the camera, and immediately developed, washed and fixed. The collodion negative could record fine detail and subtle tones with exposures of only a few seconds, but suffered from the major disadvantage of requiring the mobile or itinerant photographer to transport considerable quantities of equipment and material wherever he went.

A comparison between similar views taken by Robertson and Shaw-Lefevre at Sebastopol may perhaps reflect the degree of enthusiasm for photography and thus the level of skill acquired. Robertson seems to have a better eye for composition - his photographs of the Redan, the Malakoff and the Karabelnaia suburb, for example, capture the scenes of destruction the more vividly of the two and the introduction by Shaw-Lefevre of soldiers into some of his views, while adding human interest, also gives them a somewhat posed, artificial feel. Nevertheless, his photographs do show various aspects of the siege, such as the search for the wires laid by the Russians to explode the magazines, or the Russian general's bunker in the Redan which might otherwise have gone unrecorded visually.

Shaw-Lefevre's pictures and more particularly those by Robertson are reminiscent of some of the scenes on the Western Front made familiar to us by the official photographers of the First World War and serve as a reminder that although the technology may change the cost of war in both human and material terms does not.

Ruined House behind the Malakoff. *Photograph by G Shaw-Lefevre. 'We now arrived at that much knocked-about group of houses called the Karabelnaia suburb. Lying underneath the Malakoff, all the missiles which overtopped that fort fell into this suburb ... and the whole place was an utter wreck'.*
Anonymous, Inside Sebastopol and Experiences in Camp, *pp215-16*

NAM. neg no 69876

'DEVOTION AND LOYALTY'

THE 3RD MIDDLESEX RIFLE VOLUNTEERS, 1859-1898

IAN ROBERTSON

12th Middx (Barnet) RV, 1859

The hat is adorned with a plume of black cock's feathers.

From E T Evans, Records of the Third Middlesex Rifle Volunteers ... from 1794-1884, *London (1885)*

NAM. neg no 77976

'The origin of the custom of volunteering for military service in this country is of very ancient date, and indeed, ever since we have possessed a standing army, recruiting for that army has been carried out on voluntary principles.' So wrote Lieutenant Edward T Evans, an officer in the 3rd Middlesex Rifle Volunteers, at the beginning of his book *Records of the Third Middlesex Rifle Volunteers ...*, which was published in 1885.[1] An understanding of this volunteer spirit is fundamental to an appreciation of what the Volunteers represented and why expressions of surprise were uttered even at the peak of the Volunteer Movement.[2] 'Indeed it is a matter for astonishment to the "regulars" that men can be found', wrote Evans (p30), 'to place themselves voluntarily under the Army Discipline Act and cheerfully rough it on the Hampshire Hills for such very small reward as the Government grants them, but there is nothing that gives the enthusiastic volunteer more enjoyment than this annual week of soldiering in Aldershot garrison'.

Whatever the military value, if any, of the Volunteers - formed as they were initially into numerous corps and detachments of about 100 men each - under-pinning the whole concept was a sense of devotion and loyalty to the Crown which was explicitly recognized in the general orders issued on 25 June 1860 (Evans pp19 & 20) in which it is stated that;

'Much as her Majesty's admiration was excited by the soldier-like bearing of the various corps passed in review, a still deeper impression has been made in her mind by the proof which the Volunteer movement throughout the country affords of their devotion and loyalty, and their anxiety to second her endeavours to insure the security and, thereby, the prosperity of the kingdom. The General commanding-in-chief is further directed by her Majesty to mark especially her sense of the zeal displayed by the officers commanding brigades of corps, and to notice particularly those battalions and companies which, regardless of personal inconvenience and expense, came from distant counties to join the display of loyalty and patriotism which will render the 23rd of June, 1860, memorable in the annals of our times.

14th Middx (Highgate) RV, 1859

The officers are shown in full and undress uniform.

From E T Evans, Records of the Third Middlesex Rifle Volunteers ... from 1794-1884, *London (1885)*

NAM. neg no 77977

In addition, in the early days of the Movement in 1859-60, when invasion by France was thought a distinct possibility, there was very much a fashionable modernity about the Volunteers. For example, the 12th Middlesex (Barnet) Rifle Volunteers wore, 'a so called "Garibaldi" hat (black, broad-brimmed, with a plume of black-cock feathers), from which the corps obtained the sobriquet of "the Garibaldians"'. At the Hyde Park Volunteer Review on 23 June 'the "Garibaldians" were present with a strength of 50 rank and file, "were recognized by Her Majesty and greeted with a ringing cheer by the spectators" *(Times)*, anything Garibaldian being at this period intensely popular with the British public' (Evans, pp71 & 73).

As well as being a Volunteer and in accord with public opinion, a sense of locality was a prerequisite for success in the early days of the Movement. Not only does Lieutenant Evans seek to establish links between the revived Volunteer Movement of 1859-60 and the earlier

Volunteers who came forward during the wars with Revolutionary and Napoleonic France, but he is at pains to record the success or failure of the attempt to recruit in particular villages in that part of central north Middlesex with which he is concerned. Middlesex was an extensive county and it should not be forgotten that other Volunteer corps therein were in time to become affiliated to the Royal Fusiliers, the King's Royal Rifle Corps, and the London Regiment, as well as to the Middlesex Regiment.

One of the most interesting units, in respect of local associations, is the 41st Middlesex Rifle Volunteers, raised at Enfield Lock from the employees of the Royal Small Arms Factory. It was a large unit, which in 1868 reached its greatest strength, with an all ranks total of 733 (Evans, p173). Thereafter, the establishment was reduced and it is noted that in 1873 'a considerable number of men also resigned; this was caused by the discharge of a large proportion of the factory hands consequent on the introduction of machinery to replace hand labour, and also to a diminished out-turn' (Evans, p174). Evans further recorded that 'the introduction of machinery and great fluctuations in work at the Royal Small Arms Factory have had a very detrimental effect on its numbers, very few young men having been engaged during the last few years, and it will probably never reach the great total of 1869, when the corps was at its apogee as regards numbers' (p177). These quotations suggest that recruitment for the 41st Middlesex (Enfield Lock) Rifle Volunteers was intensely localized and if men were not available from the immediate area then the size of the unit declined, rather than recruits being taken in from elsewhere.

Because of the voluntary, local and almost private nature of the Volunteer Movement, with the members paying so many of the bills to augment a Government Capitation Allowance, it follows that historians are challenged for some corps by a paucity of records. Nationally, the responsibility for the Volunteers lay first with the Home Office and then with the War Office; the records of these Departments of State are in the Public Record Office; however, as Peter Boyden points out elsewhere in this publication, the records of individual corps may, if they exist at all, be in local record offices or in private collections. For example, in the Archives of the National Army Museum are a collection of printed orders of the Civil Service Rifles 1873-1907 and the 25th Middlesex (Bank of England) Volunteers 1896-1907 (National Army Museum 7302-27). There are also the regimental books of the 11th Wimbledon (Rifle) Volunteers, later 2nd Volunteer Battalion, the East Surrey Regiment 1860-1913, including committee minutes, orders, nominal rolls, correspondence, clothing agreements books, notices and results of shooting competitions (NAM. 8411-95 to -103, -106, -107, -121 to -123, 8901-134). In the area of personal memorabilia there are the scrapbook and loose papers collected by Colonel E H H Combe, 2nd Volunteer Battalion, the Norfolk Regiment 1883-96 (NAM. 8805-50).

In 1992, the National Army Museum received as a donation the highly important Collections of the Middlesex Regiment Museum Trustees and these include a manuscript continuation of Evans' book, which, he notes, 'was one of the first works of its kind' and in the same preface (pviii) mentions this manuscript continuation. In addition, there are the Minutes of the Finance Committee and Clothing Sub-Committee as well as the Building Accounts for 1894-6 (NAM. 9309-88). Evans' book and its manuscript continuation form the basis of this review of the activities of those corps which were to make up the 3rd Middlesex

Rifle Volunteers. Also included in the former Middlesex Regiment Archives are two watercolours executed by Evans in 1884 which appear as illustrations in this article.

The military purpose of the Volunteers, both riflemen and gunners to man coast artillery batteries, was set out in the War Office Circular of 25 May 1859 and so far as the infantry are concerned one paragraph neatly summarizes the principles involved;

> 'The nature of our country, with its numerous inclosures and other impediments to the operations of troops in line, gives peculiar importance to the service of volunteer riflemen, in which bodies each man, deriving confidence from his own skill in the use of his arm and from his reliance on the support of his comrades - men whom he has known, and with whom he has lived from his youth up, intimately acquainted, besides, with the country in which he would be called upon to act - would hang with the most telling effect upon the flanks and communications of a hostile army (Evans, p296).

The Circular insists on the effective use of the rifle and it is clear that this instruction was carried out assiduously in the Middlesex Rifle Volunteers about whom Evans wrote, with the acquisition of sites and construction of rifle ranges being chronicled as well as the results of shooting matches. Taking just one example; in his manuscript continuation Evans gives details of the shooting match held on 12 September 1885 between the NCOs of the 3rd Middlesex Rifle Volunteers and the NCOs of the Depot of the 57th Regiment; 'Shot at Childs Hill. Ranges 200, 500 and 600 yards. Seven shots at each. Wimbledon conditions. Wind from left, very boisterous. Cloudy'. The regular Army NCOs of the Depot won all three categories and overall by twelve points, thus reversing the win by the Rifle Volunteer NCOs at Hounslow in the previous year. Great stress was placed on Volunteer marksmanship and, in addition to formal drills, efforts were made to set up rifle clubs to continue to foster this most desirable of skills.

So far as harassing the flanks and communications of a hostile army was concerned, this particular training took the form of outpost drill and Evans reports of the 2nd Administrative Battalion, Middlesex Rifle Volunteers that;

> 'On October 25th, [1879] the battalion was practised in night out-post duty, forming a line of picquets facing north, eight in number, extending from the High Road at Upper Edmonton to Brent Bridge, Hendon. This is the first instance, it is believed, that this practice was ever engaged in by volunteers on any practical scale, and owes its institution to Lieutenant-Colonel Warner. A signalling party from the Hampstead Corps was present under Lieutenant H E Millar (p224).

As for the 3rd Middlesex Rifle Volunteers, in 1881 he notes that;

> 'On October 29th [1881] an outpost drill took place under Major Church. The regiment was divided into opposing forces, the western force (Hampstead,

Highgate and Barnet), forming picquets at East Barnet, Cock Fosters and Beech Hill Park; the eastern force having picquets on the Ridgeway, at Chase Cottage and Grovelands Park; the Enfield Lock Detachment forming a support at Enfield Station, Great Northern Railway. Every officer engaged sent in a report (p244).

41st Middx (Enfield Lock) RV, 1860

Officers in full and undress uniform with a private in full dress.

From E T Evans, Records of the Third Middlesex Rifle Volunteers ... from 1794-1884, *London (1885)*

NAM. neg no 79778

That this outpost drill was officially approved is clear from the approbation of the Major-General Commanding Home District which was communicated after the 1879 exercise and by the fact that in 1881 Lieutenant-Colonel J H Warner offered two prizes to be competed for 'by officers for the best essay on the following subjects: Part I - Infantry Outposts - The best mode of combining the duties of observation and resistance by day, and by night, in an open and an inclosed country. Part II - The practical application of the principles laid down to a line of country to be selected by the writer, within the district of the regiment' (Evans, pp245-46).

Outpost drills continued to be held and there is a particularly detailed manuscript report for 24 October 1885. Headed 'Outpost Drill' the entry reads as follows;

'For the first time since these drills were instituted in 1879 by Lieut.-Col. Warner, the battalion had a tangible opponent, the 5th (West) Middlesex R.V. The 9th (Harrow and Stanmore) Corps was to have been present, on the opposing side, but did not parade. The weather was very inclement, the night being very dark with rain and wind.

The 3rd Middlesex were supposed to cover a force encamped near East Barnet and formed a line of picquets from the junction of the Totteridge and Mill Hill Roads at Highwood Hill on the right, to Finchley Station, G.N.R. on the left, the opposing picquet line being (roughly) from Hendon, on the right to the Hale near Edgware on the left, covering a force at Harrow. The picquets and supports were to be in position at 6pm before which time no movements to the front or flanks were to take place.

The ground occupied was quite new to the battalion and entailed considerable work on the field officers and adjutant in preparing the plan of the operations. Major Walker was in command of the left of the picquet line and Major Clay of the right.

Also among these manuscript records is a copy of a memorandum dated 20 January 1886 from Horse Guards headed;

'Outpost Duty - Memorandum from the General Commanding the Home District: The Major-General has much pleasure in noticing the great care and general intelligence shown in the Outpost Duty Reports of the officers of the 3rd Middlesex Rifle Volunteers. The instructions issued by the field officers were good and clear, and the results were very satisfactory. On future occasions the importance of the use of the 'Countersign' may be brought forward with advantage, more especially on dark nights, such as the one in question. Reports and sketches herewith returned. By order J H Hall Col. AAG.

Josiah Wilkinson, Major Commanding the 2nd Administrative Battalion (3rd Hampstead, 13th Hornsey, 14th Highgate)VRC, *c1861*

Coloured lithograph by and after Henry Fleuss, published c1861.

NAM. 7301-46

While good shooting and effective harassing of the enemy remained essential components of the training regime for Rifle Volunteers from the time of the 25 May 1859 Circular throughout the existence of the corps, in another important respect there was a significant deviation from the original instructions. In the 1859 Circular it was clearly stated that;

'It should not be attempted, therefore, as regards Rifle Volunteers, to drill or organize them as soldiers expected to take their place in line, which would require time for instruction that could ill be spared; but it should be rather sought to give each individual Volunteer a thorough knowledge of the use of his weapon, and so to qualify the force to act efficiently as an auxiliary to the regular army and militia, the only character to which it should aspire. It is evident that this object will be best attained by the enrolment of Volunteers in small bodies, in companies, consisting of an establishment of one captain, one lieutenant, one ensign, and 100 men of all ranks, as a maximum, or in subdivisions, and even sections of companies, with the due proportion of officers, and composed of individuals having a knowledge of and thorough dependence upon each other personally; and it should rarely, if ever, be sought to form them into larger corps, entailing the necessity of a lengthened and complicated system of drill instruction (Evans, pp295-96).

This Circular revived a concept of volunteering which would have been familiar to those who had served in the very earliest years of the nineteenth century, but in practice, an organization based upon numerous, independent, localized corps was soon abandoned. On 28 November 1860 the 2nd Administrative Battalion Middlesex Rifle Volunteers was formed, comprising the 3rd (Hampstead), 13th (Hornsey), and 14th (Highgate) Middlesex Rifle Volunteers, while in 1880 the 3rd Middlesex Rifle Volunteer Corps was formed as a consolidated unit to include the amalgamated 2nd and 6th Administrative Battalions, with detachments in due time at Hampstead, Barnet (12th), Hornsey, Highgate, Tottenham (33rd), Enfield Lock (41st), Enfield Town, and a Drill Station at Hendon.[3] The effect of these administrative reorganizations was not only to produce greater obvious standardization as in the uniform worn, but also ultimately to lead to greater centralization in the handling and disbursement of the Government Capitation Allowance. These developments also led to far larger bodies of men being paraded than was envisaged in the 1859 Circular; for example, in the manuscript records it is reported that at the Annual Inspection by Colonel C Tucker on 4 July 1885 there were 754 all ranks on parade.

A manuscript account exists of this particular parade and it is worth quoting as a detailed example of how the Volunteers performed on such a day;

'1885 July 4th

The Annual Inspection took place again this year at Col Church's "Red Barn" Field, Southgate, the parade being formed at about 6.30pm, the men being in 'marching order', without great-coats. Col Tucker CB arrived on the ground soon after the above hour, accompanied by his brigade-major, Captn Graham (77th). A general salute having been given, Colonel Tucker minutely inspected the men's arms and accoutrements; after which the battalion wheeled into column and marched past in column, quarter-column and at the double. The battalion was then put through the manual and firing exercises by Major Walker, on the conclusion of which the two right companies (Hampstead and Barnet) were detached for company-drill, through which ordeal nearly every subaltern had to pass, Captn Graham superintending.

In the meantime, the remaining six companies were drilled in battalion by Major Clay and the captains in succession. The whole battalion being again formed up, the attack formation was very creditably carried out under the command of Captain Grove White, the Adjutant. It was now nearly dark and, quarter-column having been reformed, Col Tucker briefly addressed the battalion, expressing satisfaction with what he had seen, but calling attention to the condition of certain of the rifles which he had examined. Col Church subsequently addressed the officers, thanking them for the assistance they had rendered him, and specially mentioning the Adjutant, through whose indefatigable exertions, he considered the present efficient state of the battalion to be to a large extent due. There were 754 of all ranks on parade, being the largest recorded muster of the battalion.

The signallers and buglers were separately inspected, also the transport party.

Not only do we read of increasing numbers of battalion drills but also of brigade drills, as well as the famous Volunteer Reviews, involving substantial numbers from a variety of corps travelling and parading. For example, at the Easter Monday Review in Brighton in 1885 the manuscript records that 16,787 men of all ranks were on parade as well as 312 horses and 30 guns. These larger numbers made possible the famous 'sham fights' and marching columns which gave officers the opportunity to manoeuvre substantial numbers of troops in the field. Numbers were maintained by the creation of Provisional Battalions for exercises and officers were clearly relieved at having transported hefty contingents of men to and from field days and camps without loss and without incident.

At regimental level, the consolidation of small units facilitated the establishment of specialist detachments, for example in the 3rd Middlesex Rifle Volunteers a regimental transport detachment was formed and a wagon purchased. An ambulance detachment and a signalling detachment were added to the strength in about July 1884, of which it is reported that at the Easter Monday 1885 Review at Brighton;

'a detachment of signallers consisting of 2 sergeants and 3 men accompanied the detachment of the battalion on the Marching Column. Two sergeants and six men were present at the field-day on Easter Monday and were attached to the 4th (West) London R.V. when they were of signal service in bringing up reinforcements when the extended line was attacked by the Middlesex Yeomanry.

In accordance with prevailing trends a further specialist detachment was raised, that of mounted infantry.

A particular influence by the regular Army on the Rifle Volunteers was through the medium of training. In addition to Volunteers attending, since 1859, at the School of Musketry at Hythe, attachment to regular regiments at Aldershot had been introduced for the purpose of instruction in drill. In 1870 a School of Instruction for Volunteer Officers was established at Wellington Barracks and certificates of proficiency issued. Indeed, in a

Rifle Contest, Wimbledon, 1864

Chromolithograph by Leighton Bros. after A Hunt, published by The Illustrated London News, *1864*

NAM. 7212-7

manuscript entry dated 30 September 1885 it appears that a certain Lieutenant Evans had been awarded the best marks at Aldershot and received the Commander-in-Chief's special commendation! Besides training for officers, from the earliest days of the Volunteer Movement, Militia instructors had been permitted to assist Volunteer Rifle Corps and, in due course, sergeant-instructors and adjutants from the regular Army were appointed. These staff and commanding officers with regular Army experience must have had a significant influence on the way in which the Rifle Volunteer Corps developed.

Particular mention may be made of Colonel Reginald Hennell DSO, who assumed command of the 3rd Middlesex Rifle Volunteers in the autumn of 1891 and who, it is clear from the manuscript minutes of the Finance Committee, sought to promote the concept of a regiment rather than a mere amalgam of detachments. He promoted the idea of an officers' mess and, in 1896, he was instrumental in purchasing 'The Elms', 'an important freehold mansion' at Hornsey, as the headquarters for the 3rd Middlesex Rifle Volunteers, as part of its Centenary Building Fund. Unable to meet the total conversion cost of £2,900 Colonel Hennell reported in March 1897 that he had obtained a Government loan of £2,200 under the terms of the Military Works Loan Act of 1892, 'repayable by yearly instalments with interest at $3^{1}/_{2}$ per cent., extending over 35 years. The whole Estate becomes, on full payment, the property of the Corps'.

While little can be deduced at present concerning the social composition of the 3rd Middlesex Rifle Volunteers, nevertheless enough may be gleaned from the records deposited at the National Army Museum to determine whether or not the wish was fulfilled as stated in the May 1859 Circular, 'to induce those classes to come forward for service as Volunteers who do not under our present system enter either into the regular army or the militia' (Evans, p295). The original Rifle Volunteer Corps were essentially democratic, middle-class organizations and it was quite usual for the officers to be elected from amongst the rank-and-file who, in a restricted locality, might well have been neighbours of the same social class. For example, in a circular letter to members of the 14th Middlesex (Highgate) Volunteer Rifle Corps of 5 November 1859 Captain Wilkinson stated on behalf of his fellow officers and himself that he wished, 'to express our sense of the compliment you have paid us in inviting us to undertake the duty of commanding you, and to assure you that our best exertions shall be applied to qualify ourselves for the posts which it is your pleasure we should occupy' (Evans, p116). In 1885 Evans commented on this statement as follows; 'Extraordinary as such expressions would now appear in a circular addressed by a commanding officer to the men under his command, they were at that time usual and such as were expected, discipline being by no means understood as it is now; the relation of officers to their men being rather that of officials of a friendly club than of officers of a military body' (p117).

The situation of officers being selected from the rank-and-file to command men of the same social class as themselves on the one hand caused difficulty to the mid-nineteenth century military establishment, but on the other, appealed precisely to those who would not have contemplated willingly serving in either the regular Army or the Militia. Although the Rifle Volunteers achieved a substantially improved military bearing as time progressed, this probably coincided with a decrease in the number of middle-class volunteers in the ranks. For example, on 22 May 1884, at the Annual Officers' Dinner, a presentation was made to Lieutenant-Colonel Joseph Henry Warner on the occasion of his retirement from command of the 3rd Middlesex Rifle Volunteers. In his speech of thanks Colonel Warner, so it is reported, 'referring to the present state of the force, laid great stress upon the advantage of having a leaven of the middle classes in the ranks and expressed his opinion that the best volunteer officers were those who had thus served' (Evans, p273). Moreover, in the manuscript Minutes of the Special Finance Meeting held on 7 November 1894, when the funding difficulties of the Corps meant that the mounted infantry detachment would have to become dismounted, it was urged that 'every endeavour must be made to obtain a wealthier class of Recruit for Mt. Infantry'.

So far as Volunteer officers were concerned, it was desirable that they should at least aspire to be gentlemen, but essential that they should have sufficient income to be able to defray the expenses of their corps after the receipt of the Government Capitation Allowance. The existence of the latter, paid on the basis of the number of effective men in a unit, and more exacting standards of military efficiency, encouraged officers both to recruit and train their men.

Finance was a vital element in the business of a Volunteer corps and although unit property was vested in the commanding officer in the case of the 3rd Middlesex he was assisted under the Corps Rules of 1880 by a Finance Committee, which could and did have a number of sub-committees, of which those dealing with the band and clothing were the most significant. The manuscript Finance Committee Minutes covering the period 1886-98 reveal the pressures under which the Corps performed. There were the costs, for example, of the field days and camps (not least the purchase of railway tickets), repayments for bread, straw and candles, forage for horses and so on. Then there were the prizes awarded for the rifle shooting contests, the cost of the band, or of signalling equipment, or the hire of horses for the mounted infantry detachment. Not surprisingly, it is minuted of the deliberations held on 29 June 1893 that 'This meeting lasted 5 hours'! The financial pressures were such that the Finance Committee Minutes record examples of the Corps seeking advance payments of the Capitation Allowance, loans from the Bank (including, for example, one in November 1894 with Colonel Hennell giving his own personal guarantee), while in December 1895 an enquiry was held into the parlous financial state of the Highgate Detachment. These financial difficulties affected the military activities of the Corps, not simply in arresting the development of the mounted infantry detachment, but also because, at its February 1895 meeting, the Finance Committee 'decided that it was impossible for financial reasons for the Regiment to take part in the Brigade Field Day ordered for the 18th May next, or in any other (save the Aldershot week) during the present year'.

The overall impression is that the 3rd Middlesex Rifle Volunteers was not a wealthy organization and that finances were carefully controlled as well as being increasingly centralized. It would be quite wrong to see the 3rd Middlesex Rifle Volunteers as a high-spending, social organization; throughout their manuscript records it is clear that a premium was placed on military efficiency and, although officers relished the permission to retain their rank and wear their uniform after retirement, social functions seemed to be restricted essentially to concerts to raise money to help defray the costs of running the Corps.

Because of the twin needs for uniformity and control of expenditure, the subject of clothing crops up regularly in the Finance Committee Minutes, when recommendations from the Clothing Committee were considered. While space precludes a review of the detailed changes, it is worth drawing attention to the matter of the introduction of the Slade Wallace equipment. In the manuscript Minutes of a Special Meeting of the Finance Committee on 30 October 1889 Colonel Church reported that, through the good offices of the Lord Mayor of London, a grant had been made from the Patriotic Volunteer Fund towards equipment to the sum of £501-13s-4d (with £5-16s-2d towards debt). This money was allocated for the purchase of 'the equipment known as the Slade Wallace Equipment'. A representative of the supplier was on hand and the prices are noted, including a waistbelt in brown leather at 2s 4d; pairs of braces at 3s 4d apiece; and a mess tin costing ninepence-halfpenny. The Finance Committee decided to buy the Slade Wallace equipment without the valise and haversack, a decision re-examined subsequently. Apparently, the acceptance of the new equipment was not without difficulty, for at the meeting on 12 November 1891 it was minuted, 'The fitting of the Slade Wallis Equipment is then discussed. It is apparent that only one Officer has taken the trouble to get the equipment properly fitted. This is the reason for the general complaint. We have the equipment and must therefore make the best of it. Instructions accordingly'.

Of particular interest are the Clothing Committee Minutes of the Easter meeting held on 16 April 1892 at the Chatham Brigade Camp, when it is noted that;

'1. Major Bentley reported that an active service jacket pattern as for 60th Rifles
   Wd..cost 26s/- Badges 3s/-
   Norfolk jacket pattern 33s/- (60th pattern)
   Decided.-
   That the fatigue jacket for the Regt: shall be that worn by 60th Rifles (active service pattern) Buttons to be small silver Buttons with crown & bugle -
   The jacket to be perfectly plain without piping or facing of any sort.-
   It was further decided.-
   That the Fatigue Cap for the Regt: shd be active service pattern as for 60th Rifles, no ornament or red piping but fastened in front with Mess jacket studs made of silver.-

2. The Committee proposed to make the following further alterations in the dress of Officers of the Regiment.
   Gloves.- The regulation gloves for the Regt to be Brown regulation gloves as laid down for the Regular Army.-
   Mess jackets.- Mess jackets not to have any red piping on - and collars are to be similarly braided -
   It was further decided to inform Messrs Silver & Co that they must in future issue to officers, uniform of one pattern only as approved -
   Boots.- Shooting Boots to be worn on parade when gaiters are worn. plain fronted Boots at other times.

Considerable difficulty was experienced with Messrs Silver & Co, the contractors of the day, on account of their inability to achieve consistency in the quality of the grey cloth supplied. The result of these deliberations was that at a meeting of the Clothing Committee on 24 January 1893 it was;

'unanimously decided that in future one contractor be employed throughout the Regiment. To be supplied with or supplying a pattern of cloth and sealed patterns of all articles of clothing and equipment which shall be examined and

2ⁿᵈ ADMINISTRATIVE BATTALION MIDDLESEX
RIFLE VOLUNTEERS.
1876.

2nd Administrative Battalion Middlesex Rifle Volunteers, 1876

Watercolour by Lieutenant E T Evans

Private in Review Order, presenting arms.

NAM. 9309-89-1

passed at the beginning of every Volunteer Year by the Clothing Committee. This resolution to have effect from the commencement of the next Volunteer Year viz 1st November 1893.

At the Clothing Committee meeting on 2 March 1893 it was 'unanimously decided by ballot that a selected number of firms be asked to tender'. At the same meeting the matter of the officers' dress was discussed and it was decided that 'Mess dress not to have any red piping as is to be found on old Mess Jackets. All red piping to be taken off by 2nd Mess Dinner. Jackets to be made according to Colonel H's [Hennell's] pattern which all the officers who have joined in the last two years are provided with'. The Mess waistcoat was to be 'similar' while on the trousers 'grey braid to be substituted for red piping - similar to that worn on Patrol Jacket'. The CO's pattern was to be followed for the patrol jacket, Norfolk jacket, forage cap and fatigue cap. At a subsequent meeting on 29 June 1893 various tenders were received and that of Messrs Samuel Brothers was accepted with the following prices for the main articles of clothing: Coat 15s 9d; Trousers 9s 6d; Helmet 5 shillings, making a total of £1 10s 3d. This decision was based on Colonel Hennell being satisfied that the materials and workmanship matched the sealed pattern.

Amongst the most interesting papers in the 3rd Middlesex's manuscript archive are those of the Regimental Finance Committee, from the meeting held on 10 November 1897 onwards. The purpose of that meeting was to discuss the question of whether the accounts of the Corps should be taken over by the Regimental Finance Committee with the Capitation Grant being administered from HQ, which was linked to the need to appoint a salaried quartermaster-sergeant. However, this was over-shadowed by a much more serious problem which arose from a War Office Memorandum, 'in which it is proposed by the Secretary of State for War to reduce the establishment of the Corps from 908 to 800. This is also proposed as regards a large number of other Battalions in the Home District'. In the discussion which followed the point was made that this reduction 'would mean the destruction of one whole Detachment or the Reduction of a two company Detachment to one'. An alternative solution apparently lay in the Rifle Volunteers 'going into red and assuming the title of 1st Vol Bat DCO Middlesex Regiment. Para 51 Vol. Reg. of 96 says that an application would be favourably considered'. Colonel Hennell continued, 'I propose we should apply for permission to make this change'. In addition, he also wished to submit a request that rather than a reduction to 800 there should be an increase to 1,000, 'viz 10 companies of 100 each. I have reason to believe that in a few months this establishment would be reached with the new uniform'. This statement was made despite it having been just reported that, 'For years past we have never touched 900 and have been gradually decreasing'.

These Minutes of 1897 will be read with surprise by anyone who thought that the linking of regular Army, Militia and Volunteer battalions was achieved in practice as opposed to being secured in theory by the reforms of 1881! Evans appears to ignore the changes in his book, which was published in 1885, although it is clear from these manuscript Minutes that the independence of the 3rd Middlesex Rifle Volunteers did not go unnoticed at the War Office. There is a tantalizingly brief minute of the Finance Committee of 3 May 1887 which runs: 'The CO also stated that in reply to a communication from the War

3rᵈ MIDDLESEX RIFLE VOLUNTEERS.
1882.

3rd Middlesex Rifle Volunteers, 1882
Watercolour by Lieutenant E T Evans
Private in Marching Order, arms at the slope.

NAM. 9309-89-2

Office he had fully stated reasons why the Mess should not become a Vol. Batt. of the Middlesex Regt'. Although no changes appear to have taken place in the next decade, continued independence was not to be. By the time of the Finance and General Committee meeting of 23 February 1898, the matter was well on the way to being settled in that;

'Colonel Hennell opened the Proceedings by reading the letter from the Secretary of State for War announcing the approval of HM to the 3rd Mid. R. Vol adopting the title of 1st V/B Duke of Cambridge's Own Middlesex

Regiment and the scarlet and white facing of the Middlesex Regiment. The brown leather equipment would be retained. No full dress to be considered until 1905. The minutes of the last meeting are read and the question on whether adoption of a Tunic or a Kersey is fully discussed and the votes being taken it is finally decided to adopt the Kersey.

Amongst related decisions is one to adopt the Middlesex Regiment badge, whereas originally it had been hoped that in adopting the uniform the badge of the 3rd Middlesex Rifle Volunteers could be retained; however, the latter was to be 'retained for non official writing paper'. The Committee then went on to consider the prices of the various articles of uniform submitted by Messrs Samuel Brothers which were as follows: Sergeant's Kersey 14 shillings; Private's Kersey 11s 3d; Trousers 10 shillings; Helmet with Badge 5s 9d; Field Service Cap with Middlesex Regiment Badge 2s 8d; Leggings (black leather) 3s 3d.

The last entry in the Finance Ledger is a statement of numbers present when 'the Corps was mobilized for Practice with the West London Brigade on 5 March 1898', in accordance with the Mobilization Scheme. On 31 March we find Colonel Hennell signing himself as Colonel Commanding 1st VB Middlesex Regiment.

In retrospect, it is clear from these archives that the achievement of the 3rd Middlesex Rifle Volunteers and its constituent corps between 1859 and 1898 was to develop a strong tradition of apparently effective military training, notwithstanding all the financial pressures which could have deflected the interest of the officers and other members. Although the demise of the Volunteer Rifle Corps was over-shadowed nationally by the debate concerning the possible introduction of conscription as a means of being able to match the reserves upon which putative continental adversaries could draw, nevertheless, with the benefit of hindsight, Lieutenant Evans was right when he maintained that volunteering was at the basis of Army service in the United Kingdom, for conscription has never proved politically acceptable for any length of time during periods of peace.

The lesson of the Volunteer Movement is that an interest in matters military can be diffused amongst the population at large and if the threat to the United Kingdom is perceived as being sufficiently great substantial numbers of people, who would not otherwise contemplate the rigours of military life, will volunteer for service. It is true that in the nineteenth century the regular Army never came to terms with, and therefore made best use of, this volunteering spirit, not least because members of Volunteer Corps could resign upon giving fourteen days notice. Equally, it can be argued that the Army, which in the earlier nineteenth century had seen part of its role as the training and reformation of the lowest orders of society, while at the same time maintaining an officer class firmly rooted in the landed interest, was not disposed to cope with, nor seek positively to attract, a 'better class' of recruit.

If the Army failed to utilize the full potential of the Volunteers, then part of the blame must rest with successive Governments, whose traditional policy was to rely on the Royal Navy for home defence, while at the same time never sufficiently differentiating, and therefore making appropriate financial provision for the three very different functions of an Army Reserve, namely, supporting garrisons and operations throughout the Empire, for home defence, and for fighting a European war.

Had invasion been attempted in the latter part of the nineteenth century, then the Volunteers would have had to mobilize and fight; on the evidence of the records under consideration, there is no doubt that considerable efforts had been made to ensure that they were prepared for that task. The Rifle Volunteers were never conceived as, nor intended to be, a reserve for an Imperial Army, but to have the much more limited role of being effective sharpshooters and harrying an enemy once invasion had begun; on that basis there is no reason to think that the 3rd Middlesex Rifle Volunteers would not have acquitted themselves adequately and fought to the very best of their ability. Whether the Volunteers as a whole could have provided the only effective reserve, as they might have had to do during the Anglo-Boer War, when the number of Regular Army Battalions in the United Kingdom was so seriously depleted, is quite another matter.

THE NEW ZEALAND CROSS, 1869

LESLEY SMURTHWAITE

New Zealand Cross 1869, awarded to Constable Henare Kepa Te Ahururu, No 1 Armed Constabulary, New Zealand

The New Zealand Cross awarded to Constable Henare Kepa Te Ahururu, No 1 Division Armed Constabulary, for his bravery in the engagement at Moturoa on 7 November 1868 (NAM. 8711-104), represents one of the rarest of all gallantry decorations and one which is perhaps unique in the circumstances under which it came to be conferred.

The Cross, peculiar to New Zealand, where it ranks as highly as the Victoria Cross, and to the period of the 2nd Maori War of 1862-72, came into being as a result of the limited terms of eligibility for the VC in force at the time.

By 1867 the British Government had withdrawn all Imperial troops from New Zealand, leaving it in the hands of the Governor and his locally raised forces, consisting of Militia, Volunteers and an Armed Constabulary, to restore and maintain peace between the European settlers and Maori inhabitants who were conducting a renewed and vigorous guerrilla campaign to win back their confiscated lands. Under the terms of a Royal Warrant of January 1867, the Victoria Cross could not be conferred upon members of local colonial forces unless they were serving with Imperial troops, or under the command of an Imperial officer. Colonel G S Whitmore, recently appointed commander of the Government forces, by report a man of considerable energy and initiative, urged the Governor, Sir George Bowen, to institute a local decoration equivalent to the VC. This would provide tangible recognition for bravery, urgently needed to encourage loyalty among the troops, and raise morale in the face of a skilled and tenacious enemy, who combined cannibalism and mutilation of their fallen opponents with highly developed tactics of ambush and military engineering, which incorporated trench and bunker fortifications of a sophistication scarcely matched in Europe until 1915.[1]

The Governor responded by instituting an award, initially referred to simply as the 'Decorative Distinction', by an Order in Council of 10 March 1869, and immediately conferred five medals, of which Constable Kepa Te Ahururu's was the first. It was an unprecedented act on the part of a colonial Governor, who in carrying it out had neither sought nor awaited the approval of the Sovereign. It was to earn him a severe rebuke from the Secretary of State for the Colonies, Earl Granville, who on receiving a copy of the Order in Council, together with the Governor's letter of explanation, replied in no uncertain terms that Sir George had over-reached his authority. While it was appreciated that his hasty action had been prompted by the 'critical circumstances of New Zealand', it was emphasised that 'no precedent may be established for taking a similar step hereafter, either in New Zealand or any other British Colony without the cognizance of Her Majesty's Government, and the personal sanction of the Queen'.[2]

Faced with a *fait accompli* however, five awards having already been made, Queen Victoria had little choice but to ratify the Order, and in 1871 approval was given for the design of the Cross, in form loosely based on that of the Victoria Cross, to be made in gold and silver by the goldsmiths Phillips Bros of Cockspur Lane. A total of 25 crosses was struck, for issue to members of the Militia, Volunteers and Armed Constabulary. In the event, however, only 23 were awarded.

Constable Henare Kepa Te Ahururu, not only the first recipient but one of only three Maoris to be so honoured, received his Cross for gallant conduct during the disastrous assault on an enemy *pa* (stockade) at Moturoa, during which the Government forces were routed and suffered severe casualties. According to an account given in the Roll of the New Zealand Cross, 'the Storming Party, failing to find an entrance, passed round to the enemy rear of the *pa*. Constable Kepa heroically climbed to the top of the palisading surrounding the *pa* to reconnoitre the position and on doing so was shot through the lungs, yet he nevertheless walked out of the action'.[3] Despite the seriousness of his injury Constable Kepa survived and although it was reported that he had later deserted, there is fairly reliable evidence to the effect that he was taken prisoner by the enemy and, having escaped, returned to serve honourably with the Armed Constabulary for several more years.[4]

Taking a Maori Redoubt, 1860

Coloured lithograph by McFarlane and Erskine, c1860

Though relating to the period before the New Zealand Cross was instituted the scene is typical of the type of action for which it was awarded.

NAM. 6702-15

'CADS ON CASTORS'

A HISTORY OF BRITISH MILITARY BICYCLING TO 1914

MARION HARDING

T he bicycle made its first appearance on the military scene in Italy when, at the
manœuvres in Somina in 1875, cyclists were successfully employed to maintain contact
between the Quartermaster-General and the battalion commanders. In 1884, by order of the
Austrian Minister of War, a party of cyclists from the Military Academy undertook a five-day
ride in full field order. The result of the experiment was presumably satisfactory since cyclists
were employed on a large scale as messengers in the manœuvres of 1885. In Switzerland,
France and Germany cyclists were used to carry messages during manœuvres and to maintain
contact between frontier fortresses and outpost forces.

THE EARLY DAYS

The first employment of cyclists on military duties in Britain is credited to Colonel W C
Tamplin, 1st Volunteer Battalion, Royal Sussex Regiment, who successfully used them as
scouts during the Easter manœuvres of 1885, though according to a memorial in the now
disused church of St Margaret in Brighton it is to the Adjutant of that same battalion, Major
J A Bloomfield, that this honour should be given. The memorial records that Bloomfield,
observing that his opponents in the manœuvres could muster mounted men to oppose his
infantry, armed the latter with revolvers borrowed from the Coastguard and furnished them
with 'penny-farthings' or 'ordinaries' as they were then known, thus achieving extra mobility
and the element of surprise.[1]

It was not until 1887 that cyclists achieved public prominence in England. In that year
Colonel H H D Stracey, Scots Guards, Commander of the Dover Marching Column, finding
himself short of cavalry used cyclists as scouts on the flanks of his line of march. The
newspaper report of the incident stimulated the interest of Lieutenant-Colonel A R Savile,
Professor of Tactics at the Staff College, Camberley, and an enthusiastic cyclist, in the tactical
aspect of the experiment. He contacted Stracey and offered to command his cyclist section.
Savile subsequently described the first parade of military cyclists at Canterbury;

> 'We were certainly a mixed lot and motley crowd to look at. Some were officers
> serving in the Army and others were retired; there were volunteers of all ranks,
> also members of Cycling Clubs ... everyone who possessed a uniform wore it,

altering it for cycling purposes according to his own fancy; the remainder were in plain clothes of every pattern, age, and description. Some were armed to the teeth with swords, rifles, bayonets, revolvers and field glasses; others seemed prepared to encounter an enemy with the aid of no better weapon than a heavy spanner.

The common purpose which united them was a determination to prove that they were not 'cads on castors' as they had been dubbed in some press reports.

On the first day of the manœuvres the Cyclist Corps carried out a reconnaissance towards Faversham. The main body, composed chiefly of tricyclists, moved along the centre road whilst the bicyclist flankers scoured the country from eight to ten miles on each side. They had to negotiate the Whitstable Marshes, by-lanes, and footpaths, hop plantations, ploughed fields and locked gates. Each patrol had been told the places it was to visit and the final rendezvous. Colonel Savile left it to the discretion of the patrol commanders to take what they considered to be the best route across country, sometimes riding and sometimes wheeling the machines and lifting them over obstacles, but always keeping in touch with the parties on the left and right. On the following day, the cyclists acted as scouts for the marching column along a front of about 30 miles from Ashford to Ramsgate. On Easter Mon-

Lieutenant-Colonel A R Savile, *the pioneer of military cycling. Between 1888 and 1892 he commanded the 26th Middlesex (Cyclist) Volunteer Rifle Corps, at that time the only body mounted exclusively on bicycles.*
Photolithograph after Percy Keyton, 1897

day, after one hour's drill on the review ground, the corps marched past the Commander-in-Chief, Field Marshal HRH The Duke of Cambridge, in creditable style. The verdict of the War Office on the performance of the cyclists was 'very satisfactory'.[2]

On 2 December 1887 Savile was officially appointed president of a Committee which was to inquire into various aspects of Volunteer cycling.[3] It was to draw up precise specifications of types of cycles suitable for military requirements, and to consider the clothing, arms, equipment and training of a volunteer cyclist. The Committee's report was published in three parts, the first on 12 March 1888 and the remainder on 29 May of that year.

The Committee's first step was to notify the manufacturers of bicycles and their accessories that it would be prepared to examine any inventions relevant to military cycling which might be brought to its notice. The response was enthusiastic and the merits of each invention were carefully considered. The next step was thoroughly to inspect those machines and equipments which appeared to be most useful. The examinations were carried out at St Stephen's Hall, Westminster on 8 and 9 February 1888: 51 manufacturers were represented. The Committee concluded that;

> 'If it were intended that volunteer cyclists should be employed solely as messengers ... the ordinary bicycle would fulfil most of the requirements of a military machine, but as we are aware that the wish of the War Office authorities is that volunteer cyclists shall be efficient Infantry soldiers, capable of rapidly moving considerable distances in compact bodies, and carrying their arms, a large amount of ammunition, and their kits, on all kinds of passable roads, and of conveying their machines when dismounted over any kind of country, we at once abandoned all thoughts of the ordinary bicycle, and decided in favour of the rear-driving safety bicycle, which, by reason of its diminished height and longer wheelbase, is to be preferred to the ordinary bicycle; while in that it occupies less space ... is lighter, more speedy and easier to handle, the rear-driving safety bicycle is better adopted to the use of the rank and file than even a tricycle.

They were unable, however, to recommend any of the machines which they had viewed as being suitable in all respects and drew up their own special specification of a safety bicycle.

The Committee stated that the training of a cyclist should include both foot and mounted drills. It was recognised that foot drills, where they were devoted chiefly to extended order movements, the duties of advanced and rear guards, outpost work, patrolling and reconnoitring, would be of direct service to the bicyclist. It was therefore desirable that officers commanding cyclist sections should time their mounted drills so as not to coincide with foot drills of this nature. The primary object of the training was to be efficiency in 'cycle-marching'. Each section was to be taught to move in close formation at a rate of between five and eight miles per hour over distances of up to 50 miles in a single march. The Committee also recommended that a uniform system of cycle drill should be adopted by all units.

On 24 February 1888, fifteen days before the publication of the first part of the report, official notification of the formation of the 26th Middlesex (Cyclist) Volunteer Rifle Corps was published in *The London Gazette*.[4] It had an authorised establishment of 120 all ranks. A detachment under the command of Captain F P F Vane took part in the Easter manœuvres of that year and distinguished itself by its smartness, riding ability and general efficiency. In the same year, a scheme for training regular soldiers as cyclists was instituted at Aldershot under the supervision of Major G M Fox, Assistant Inspector of Gymnasia, and Volunteer battalions were granted permission to raise cyclist sections within their establishments, the strength to be one officer, two non-commissioned officers, from twelve to twenty privates and one bugler.

In August 1887 a series of instructions dealing with the formation of cyclist sections and offering guidance to officers commanding them were issued by the War Office. The

Cyclist Section, 1st Volunteer Battalion, Dorsetshire Regiment, c1896.

instructions covered the selection of the men, their dress, training and duties. They also indicated the intention of the authorities to use cyclists not merely as messengers, but as a fighting force carrying out the duties of mounted infantry. It was in this latter respect that Britain's plans for its bodies of military cyclists differed from that of the Continental armies, where they continued to be used only in duties of minor importance.

When the cyclist sections of Volunteer battalions were assembled under Savile's command for the manœuvres of Easter 1888 the aim was to discover whether they could be used as an effective fighting force.[5] On the Saturday, the cyclists were told off in two bodies to act against each other offensively and defensively along the road between Salisbury and Winchester. One body, representing a rear-guard, took up defensive positions on favourable ground and awaited attack - the first operation of its kind. It quickly became apparent that a distinct advantage lay with the defenders as long as they were opposed by cyclists only. Good defensive positions were chosen usually at the top of a long incline with a downward slope close behind. The attackers would then reconnoitre these positions with their advanced scouts and when the main body came under fire it would dismount, assume attack formation and advance. The aim of the defenders was never to allow the attacking party to come to grips, retiring swiftly on their cycles as soon as the position became untenable, only to repeat these tactics at the next favourable spot. The attackers were never able to move as quickly for they had to retrace their steps in order to recover their cycles.

Experience gained in these manœuvres enabled both the advantages and the disadvantages of bicycles to be assessed objectively. There were many points in their favour. Great stress was laid on the speed which could be attained by the cyclist compared with infantry: even under the worst possible conditions it was estimated that the cyclists' 'marching' power would be approximately three times greater both in pace and distance. Over good roads the gain would be even greater and a day's march of 100 miles was not thought unreasonable for a body of cyclists in proper training, whereas small parties of cavalry undertaking experimental 'distance rides' had achieved only 40 to 70 miles per day. The speed and endurance of cyclists qualified them for employment in all duties pertaining to messengers, orderlies and despatch bearers in peace and war. They could also act as scouts, a function which would be particularly important in any force weakly provided with or lacking cavalry. Other advantages were that the cycle needed neither forage nor water and little daily care or protection compared to animals, and that every cyclist could take his place in the firing line when action was joined whereas men were always needed to hold horses. Bicycles were also less conspicuous on the road and more silent on the march than any other form of transport.

The major disadvantage revealed by the manœuvres was the inevitable delay in pursuing an opponent who had been dislodged from a defensive position. This disadvantage might be removed, it was considered, if the cyclists were co-operating with cavalry, since the latter could take up the pursuit immediately, leaving the cyclists to retrieve their machines and follow as speedily as possible.

In November 1889 *A Manual of Cyclist Drill for the Use of The Cyclist Section of the Oxford University Rifle Volunteer Corps* was published by J Cook Wilson, a 2nd lieutenant in the corps, who had been entrusted with the formation of a cyclist section.[6] Wilson conceded that except in open country like the Downs many of his proposed evolutions would be of no use away from the parade ground, but he felt nonetheless that 'they are ornamental, they enliven the routine of drilling, they make the service more interesting to the individual soldier and encourage him to be smart'.

Section XIX, 'Formations to Resist Cavalry', certainly stimulates the imagination. If a party of cyclists was compelled to resist cavalry in the open without protection for the flanks or rear Wilson instructed them to form a square thus;

> 'At the command "Prepare for Cavalry" every file will turn to the left lifting
> his machine, take out rifle and bayonet, and lay them on the ground behind him
> (i.e. towards the centre of the square), then turn his machine quickly over, so
> that it rests upright on its saddle and the two handles. Bayonets should then be
> fixed. The wheels should be set spinning, as this both frightens horses and
> discomposes the aim of the carbines.

A second defence against mounted attack was to form a simple but formidable obstruction by grounding the machines in front of the lines. Apart from entanglement in the spokes the horses' legs would be badly cut by the hardened steel projections at the end of the pedals. It was unlikely that cavalrymen would try to 'jump' two rows of machines grounded in this way. It was, of course, doubtful what would happen to the machines themselves but, Wilson maintained, a cyclist could still ride, even with a great number of his spokes broken.

Five months later an official drill manual was published.[7] Cycle drill movements fell into two classes, dismounted and mounted. The former were calculated to ensure complete mobility in confined spaces or in conjunction with infantry, or where for any reason mounted movements could not be carried out. They were, as far as was possible, applications of the simpler movements of infantry drill to the requirements of men wheeling bicycles. The mounted movements were to be used only in the case of rapid movement over distances; they were inapplicable to confined spaces, or to drill movements in conjunction with infantry. The importance of practising route marches was stressed, since the special utility of cycles lay in the fact that they could traverse great distances along roads at high speed - a quality which was to be developed to the utmost. When they made contact with the enemy the cyclists were to act as infantry, with such slight changes of formation as were made necessary by the utilisation of cycles.

The role of bicyclists was a subject of much interest and debate for which the *United Service Magazine* provided a forum for discussion.[8] During 1890, four papers were given on the question of the most suitable mounted arm for Volunteers. To the usual arguments against the utility of cyclists Brigadier-General Viscount Melgund added an objection which, together with the problem of the retrieval of cycles was to provide the main ammunition for the anti-cyclist lobby for many years; cyclists, he maintained, were ineffective if they did not have good roads on which to ride. If for any reason they were forced to dismount and push or carry their machines, they lost their greatest asset - mobility. It was as orderlies in garrison towns and large camps and as despatch bearers that Melgund saw the destiny of cyclists, and he pointed out that it was in this capacity that they were employed on the Continent.

THE SOUTH AFRICAN WAR, 1899-1902

The outbreak of the War in 1899 gave the cyclists the opportunity to prove their mettle, not merely in the home defence role envisaged for them by the War Office, but also in the field in South Africa.

When hostilities began the City of London Imperial Volunteers were among several cycling corps that were ready for action. Several local regiments in South Africa, such as the Rand Rifles, and of course, the Cape Cycle Corps, also made use of bicyclists: at one stage they actually formed three per cent of the active British troops.

The main duty of the cyclist corps was despatch-riding, but they were used in a variety of additional tasks as the need arose. A commander usually had two cyclist orderlies to carry messages; cyclists would often ride ahead to forge a link between cavalry and infantry or to reconnoitre suitable roads for transport wagons, before returning to direct them. They were also used to reconnoitre camping grounds and sometimes stayed behind to attend the sick who were being transferred to hospital. Even during battle it was usual to find one or two cyclists up with the leading ranks to carry messages. Whenever a camp was established near a large town the cyclists were kept busy carrying mail, telegrams, despatches, money, and even groceries in their alpine rucksacks. A special eight-man 'war cycle' was introduced for use on railway lines. It had a detachable rim fitted to the pneumatic tyres enabling it to run on rails. When the rim was removed it would take to the roads in the usual way. These machines were also used for reconnaissance, carrying despatches, checking the line for demolition charges and also for removing the wounded from skirmishes which took place in the vicinity of a railway.

Volunteers at the Easter Manœuvres of 1898 preparing to defend themselves against an attack by cavalry. *Similar tactics had been advocated by Lieutenant J Cook Wilson of the Oxford University Rifle Volunteer Corps in 1889.*

Throughout the War, however, the horse remained the traditional mode of transport and the bicycle was employed only in an auxiliary role. An objective assessment of the utility of the cycle in South Africa was given by a member of the City Imperial Volunteers;

> 'The veldt itself is covered with thinly growing thorny scrub, just rideable for bicycles, but prevalent of punctures to all but the stoutest tyres. The roads and tracks are quite practicable, but very bumpy, and abounding in sandy patches where sideslips are the rule and riding is difficult, and are intersected with watercourses over which the wheels bump heavily. Nevertheless, with strong machines and careful riding, the bicycle is a most useful method of progression, though across country the horse had undoubtedly the advantage.[9]

At the conclusion of the war the performance of the bicycle was among the multitude of subjects examined by the Royal Commission on the War in South Africa.[10] One witness, Mr

Tandem bicycle, used for scouting along the railway during the South African War. A smaller version of the eight-man 'war cycle' it employed the same detachable rim fitted to the pneumatic tyre to enable it to run on rails. It could be ridden at speeds of between 25 and 30 miles per hour for short periods.

NAM. neg no 29429

J B Atkins, a reporter for the *Manchester Guardian*, had been astonished at the ease with which he and the cyclists of the City Imperial Volunteers could get about, even in the wet season. He felt that though the open nature of the country was an advantage to cyclists their task would be even easier in enclosed country where roads were numerous, and concluded that the bicycle would be more effectively employed in home defence than in expeditionary work.

The period between the establishment of the Territorial Force in 1908 and the outbreak of the Great War in 1914 saw the creation of fourteen cyclist battalions, in addition to which every territorial infantry battalion was authorised to form a cyclist section. The cyclist battalions were to be organised specifically for home defence and their field of operations was to be mainly in coastal districts. Their primary duty was to watch the coastline and in time of war to act as a substitute for cavalry in reconnaissance work.[11] The war establishment of a cyclist battalion was set out in a special *Army Order* of 30 September 1908.[12] It was to consist of a headquarters, a machine gun section, and eight companies with a total strength of 528 men and 504 cycles. Motor vehicles for the transportation of medical equipment, machine guns, ammunition, tools, signalling equipment, baggage and supplies were to be obtained from civilian sources.

Though the bicycle was to see service in both World Wars and was utilised to great effect by the Communist forces in Vietnam, as a means of transporting supplies[13] the bicycle has to all intents and purposes been displaced by motorised transport, which can travel much faster, carry heavier armaments or larger consignments of supplies and transport more troops than cycles could ever hope to do. It is an interesting paradox to note, however, that the bicycle has, since it was first employed in a military role in the last quarter of the nineteenth century, performed most effectively in the sort of terrain in which even its early and most earnest advocates would never have dreamed of employing it.

BRITISH INFANTRY FIELD SERVICE EQUIPMENT, 1855-1908

JOHN HARDING

A lthough prior to the Crimean War there had been some individuals interested in the efficiency and effect upon the soldier of the equipment or 'accoutrements' issued to the Army and to the infantry in particular, the authorities themselves had not paid any great attention to this matter. However, the critical reports about the conduct of this War and well publicized failures in administration and logistics, aroused considerable public interest in the state of the Army in general and, more particularly, in the health of the fighting man.

According to contemporary medical opinion, the soldier's equipment was the major cause of the prevalence of lung and heart complaints in the infantry;

> 'The knapsack straps cut under the arms and cause swelling and numbness of the hands and the weight of the pack is thrown upon the great nerve and arteries of the armpit, so as to produce these serious disasters to the soldier's health and effectiveness ... the crossbelt is not only tight against the chest but its pouch bumps and moves against the man when doubling.

In this climate of opinion it was no surprise therefore when, in 1865, a Committee was

Corporal, 5th (Northumberland Fusiliers) Regiment of Foot, showing the 1869 Valise Equipment.

NAM. neg no 34338

appointed to 'enquire into the effect on health of the present system of carrying the accoutrements, ammunition and kit of the infantry soldier'.[1] The Committee quickly established several criteria which they considered necessary for the efficient carriage of a soldier's belongings;

> '... To distribute the weight as far as possible over the whole body; to bring the weight as far as possible within the line of the centre of gravity; to allow no pressure on the principal muscles, nerves and arteries; to avoid most carefully all impediments to the fullest expansion of the lungs and the action of the heart.

Private, Royal Marine Light Infantry in marching order

c1885, showing the Valise Equipment 1882 Pattern.

Colour lithograph after Frank Dadd, c1885

NAM. 6503-44-62

During the Committee's investigations recent tactical developments were considered. The Austro-Prussian War of 1866 revealed that the new breech-loading firearms required a soldier to carry a larger amount of ammunition than before and yet remain capable of long, swift marches. Unfortunately, little effort was made to lighten his load since, in addition to the increased amount of ammunition, he still carried in his pack a full change of clothing, a greatcoat and spare pair of boots. Furthermore, the idea that his pack should be carried on carts was rejected as impracticable.

The Committee conducted lengthy trials, which included practical field manœuvres and live-firing, as well as questioning the NCOs and private soldiers taking part in the trials as to their personal views of the relative merits of the different equipments, thus obtaining practical information from the men most affected by the kit. The result was a set of equipment which fulfilled the criteria which both the Committee and the War Office had laid down.

A significant improvement on all previous equipments, its principle was that the load should be borne primarily by leather braces running from the waistbelt over the shoulders and back - in effect making a 'yoke', with the main weight of the pack or 'Valise' being borne on the strong hip girdle rather than on the man's shoulders and upper back muscles. To some extent both stability and good weight-distribution had been achieved.

Although accepted for service in 1869 as the 'Valise Equipment', the new kit was not without its critics. William Gordon Cameron, Colonel of the 4th Foot, complained; 'The

Guardsman, Coldstream Guards c1895

showing the 1888 Pattern, also known as the
Slade-Wallace Equipment.

valise or pack is not easily detached as may be desirable at a moment's notice should the man be required to make cover with them or to carry some important position with greater ease than if encumbered with it ...'. It was further found that the low position of the valise rendered it uncomfortable to wear, while the greatcoat, carried high on the shoulders, hindered firing when the soldier was in the prone position. Therefore, in 1879, a further Committee was appointed to examine various new equipments, as well as possible modifications to the existing pattern.[2]

During their deliberations the various criticisms of the existing pattern were studied, as were reports from officers recently returned from the Zulu War. These stated that it was rare for the valise to be carried by the soldier, except when transport was not available. Lieutenant-General George Erskine, a member of the Committee, put forward the view that the bulk of the soldiers kit in the valise should, as a rule, be transported from camp to camp by wheeled transport or pack animal and only carried by the soldier for short distances. These arguments notwithstanding, opinion remained divided, and the equipment ultimately accepted for service in 1882 was no more than a slight modification of the 1869 Pattern. The valise was positioned slightly higher on the back and enlarged to take the greatcoat, thus protecting the latter against the weather and freeing the man's shoulders from its load. The new design was not without its own faults however. It was still awkward for the soldier to detach the valise without assistance, and a strap from the valise now passed close under his armpit, the resulting pressure causing him discomfort.

In view of these faults and disagreements over the items to be carried on the man, the search for a satisfactory equipment continued, and over the next six years various minor alterations were mooted and some taken into service. Then, in 1888, after only very limited trials, a new set of equipment was adopted as the '1888 Pattern'. This was effectively based on that designed privately by Colonels Charles George Slade and Nesbit Willoughby Wallace, and which was intended to correct the faults of the earlier patterns. The principle was much simpler, in that the greatcoat was once more carried separately and strapped directly to the

Private, 5th Bn Royal Warwickshire Regiment in field service order, showing Bandolier Equipment, South Africa 1902.

NAM. neg no 29951

back of the waistbelt. The valise, which was not really intended to be carried on active operations, was smaller, more easily detachable and carried high on the man's back, fastened only to the braces in the front by straps running over the shoulders. Its weight was supposedly 'balanced' against that of the ammunition in the pouches on the front.

As might have been expected however, this 'solution', like its predecessors, was by no means ideal. In the peacetime training that was carried out using the new equipment, the valise was usually carried but little, if any, ammunition. As a result, the weight of the valise pulled the waistbelt up into the soldier's chest, restricting his breathing. This fault led to criticism, albeit somewhat unjustified in view of the designers' intention, that the equipment was primarily intended for active service. As a result, further trials were conducted throughout the 1890s on a wide variety of equipments, including some foreign designs. However, no solution had been found by 1899 and in that year the Army entered the South African War wearing the 1888 pattern equipment.

Another problem encountered in achieving a universally accepted design for both peacetime and war was the delay in substituting brown leather for buff. Previous enquiries, including the 1879 Committee, had found brown leather to be unquestionably superior as a material for accoutrements on a number of counts, including the fact that it was less conspicuous on the battlefield than white buff, a judgement confirmed by active service experience. However, in 1899, buff leather remained the main component; it could be pipe-clayed white, the appeal of its smartness on parade being considered more important than its battleworthiness.

The South African War subjected the Army and its equipment to a rigorous extensive active service trial. This quickly emphasised the contradictions inherent in the design of the 1888 pattern. As had been intended by the designers, troops in the field rarely carried the valise, but without it, the ammunition pouches on the front - now with their full load of live cartridges - had no adequate counter-balancing weight. In operations carried out against an elusive and fast moving enemy, the mobility of the individual soldier became a matter of great importance. The unsupported ammunition pouches dragged down on the man, making marching and rapid movement difficult. Rounds easily fell out of the pouches when the soldier was moving quickly over rough ground, yet it proved awkward to extract cartridges from them when the man was lying down, a firing position that became a prerequisite if troops were to avoid insupportable losses from the rifles of Boer marksmen. In addition, the extensive fire-fights that were a feature of some battles in South Africa, coupled with the difficulties in re-supplying troops in the forward firing line, meant that a greater quantity of ammunition was required to be carried on the man, even if this was only added just as he entered combat.

To meet this last need, a light, woven webbing emergency bandolier, holding 100 rounds, was introduced. These were packed, ready filled in boxes and issued just before going into action, the intention being that, when empty, they should be discarded. Owing to difficulties of supply in the field many soldiers used them as permanent carriers, with the result that their thin loops stretched, causing the loss of many rounds of ammunition. Nevertheless, the bandolier concept, already in use with the British cavalry, was adopted quite extensively, with newer, more robust designs being produced.

At the conclusion of the South African War a Royal Commission was set up to examine the shortcomings revealed and, amongst other things, the Commissioners took under consideration the equipment which had been supplied to the troops.[3] Both the webbing bandolier and the 1888 kit came in for criticism. Lord

Lance-Corporal, Royal Welsh Fusiliers, showing the 1903 Bandolier Equipment.

NAM. neg no 6099

Kitchener stated; 'Our losses in ammunition cannot be ascribed to want of care of the individual as much as to the peculiar suitability of the articles supplied to him'.

The War Office, keen to take account of recent operational experience, conducted experiments with new designs of equipment, manufactured in both leather and webbing. Efforts were concentrated on enabling the soldier to become as agile and self-sufficient as possible. The concept of a man carrying spare clothing and other items such as digging tools was finally abandoned, along with the valise. The preferred design was a bandolier equipment in brown leather. Designated the 1903 Pattern, this stowed the ammunition in small pouches on the waistbelt and in a pocketed chest bandolier. A greatcoat carried on the man's back, and a haversack and waterbottle completed his load. The major disadvantage with this set, was the re-introduction of a weight constricting the chest and the greatcoat was still carried unprotected against the elements.

Guardsman, Grenadier Guards, showing the 1908 Pattern Webbing Equipment.

This new equipment was to be only short-lived. By 1906 the British subsidiary of the American Mills Company, manufacturers of the webbing bandoliers and other webbing items used in the South African War, finally convinced the War Office of the superiority of webbing over leather as the basic material for infantry accoutrements. The Company then manufactured in webbing an equipment designed by Major Arnold Robinson Burrowes of the Royal Irish Fusiliers. In this equipment the soldier's basic battle load of ammunition and water would remain stable and balanced whether any load was carried on the soldier's back or not. In addition, his chest was kept free of straps and the back-pack which contained his greatcoat was both comfortable and easily detachable. The equipment was also very simple to don and doff.

After stringent trials in Britain and India, in which it proved a great success, the equipment was approved for issue early in 1908 and was retained, with minor alterations, as the infantry's basic equipment until 1937.

After some 40 years of experimentation the Army now had equipment that not only met its tactical and medical needs, but also became popular with the soldiers. Its merit was proved in the Great War. That the solution had taken so long to arrive at was due to some extent to continual improvements to firearms and changes in operational requirements and tactics. However, another important factor was the difficulty in reaching a consensus as to what constituted the best solution. The achievement of a universally acceptable solution was hindered by the, at times, intensely personal and emotive views on the subject of equipment, and the difficulty in obtaining general agreement meant that any design had inevitably to be a form of compromise. This, apart from the earnest desire to find the best solution, is perhaps the clearest lesson that can be derived from examination of the contemporary papers of Committees and the trials carried out during this period.

THE DAMNABLE CAVALRY
SKETCHING BOARD

JANE INSLEY

I n 1879 the Director of Military Education expressed the opinion that, as far as road-sketching was concerned, 'Any examination which does not include the adjustments of the theodolite and sextant must be considered unsatisfactory'.[1] Colonel W H Richards, appointed to the Staff College as Topographical Instructor from a similar position at the Royal Military College, did not agree, and as part of his efforts to improve the general standards of military map-making introduced the cavalry sketching case. This device appears to have been particularly useful, as it continued to be described in textbooks of field sketching and surveying for over 40 years, and several different kinds were patented or manufactured.

THE CAVALRY SKETCHING BOARD

A precursor can be found in A F Lendy's patent, No 84 of 1865,[2] which describes a surveying instrument applicable as a drawing board, a plane table, a prismatic compass, a level and a clinometer. A sheet of transparent paper was stretched over a board, which had a circular protractor, a prismatic compass and a sight vane on the upper surface, and a move-able metal clinometer and fixed semi-circle set underneath. The table could be carried by hand, or mounted on a tripod.

Colonel Richards' design was simpler, and was very much intended to be usable by a mounted soldier (plate 1).

The exact date of invention is difficult to pin down, but was probably about 1880. The details of Richards' career are not readily available. However, he arrived at the Staff College in the late 1870s and a demonstration of a collective survey by the students employing his tech-

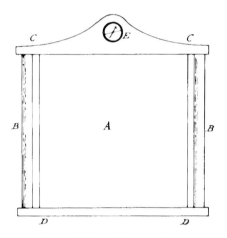

plate 1   *Colonel Richards' original case*, taken from *Verner's* Rapid Field Sketching and Reconnaissance *(1889) p5. A small drawing board (A) about 6 inches square, fitted with wooden rollers (BB) on either end, which revolve in sockets in a headpiece (CC) and a footpiece (DD) fixed on opposite sides. On these rollers a strip of paper of any required length, say 2ft, or more, is wound and thus stretched across the board (A). In the head-piece (CC) a small magnetic compass (E) is countersunk in a collar in which it can be revolved. On the glass of the compass a fine line is engraved, which is termed the 'working meridian'. In the centre of the back of the board there is a metal pivot to which a strap is attached, which latter is used to secure the board on the left wrist when working with it.*

nique (described below) in 1881, is the earliest recorded use known to the author. The instrument makers Negretti and Zambra published catalogues of their goods in 1880 and 1885; the earlier one does not mention the sketching board, and the later one does.

Until Richards' appointment to Camberley, six complicated treatises on surveying were in use. Richards substituted his own *Textbook of Military Topography*, published in 1888. It became the standard work, and the section on the cavalry sketching board appeared in subsequent editions in barely altered form until 1921, as discussed below.[3] Horseback sketching became a regular feature of the course, and Staff College students found that a universally high standard could be quickly reached, despite their exasperation with the board. In their second year, they were given the task of a collective survey of a large tract of country; each would be assigned to an area of about a square mile, and then Richards would paste the whole map together and reconcile the results.[4]

The Director General of the Staff College commended the excellence of the rapid sketches of the Senior Division of 1881 to the Commander-in-Chief, the Duke of Cambridge, who expressed astonishment at their neatness and accuracy when the conditions under which they were prepared were explained to him.[5]

A particularly voluble supporter of the board and its techniques was Captain Willoughby Verner of the Rifle Brigade (plate 2), who used it to great advantage during his tour of duty in the Sudan with the Nile Expeditionary Force between September 1884 and July 1885.

Verner published an album of watercolours entitled *Sketches in the Soudan* in 1885, which proved sufficiently popular for a second edition to be published the following year. In the caption to the last page, entitled 'Sketching and Surveying' - a sketch of the country about Metemneh [sic] (plate 3) - Verner commented;

'The main portion of this sketch, as well as of all the others I made in the Soudan, was done by the aid of a 'cavalry sketching board', the invention of Col. Richards of the Staff College. To those interested in the matter I may mention that this board is about six inches square and has a small magnetic compass fixed on it; the paper works on rollers and this admits of any length being carried. When in use the board is strapped to the wrist of the bridle arm. By this means, very rapid sketching can be done without the aid of any instruments beyond a straight-edged piece of

plate 2   **Colonel William Willoughby Cole Verner (1852-1922)**

NAM. neg no 71127

wood. Owing to this board I was enabled during the Desert March to sketch every mile of the way, the map opposite showing the last four miles of the 176 we traversed ... all the sketching whilst on the march was naturally done by "time".[6]

Despite his own enthusiasm and undoubted proficiency, Verner did admit that others could find the board difficult to use at first. In *Rapid Field Sketching and Reconnaissance* (1889), he related;

> 'Indeed I shall never forget my feelings on one memorable occasion when, after having equipped a friend with my own favourite sketching case, and, as I imagined, given him full instructions as to how to proceed, he returned it to me with thanks, and an intimation that he had found it so complicated that he had "fallen back on the simpler method" of carrying a large board, prismatic compass, protractor, etc.
>
> It is owing to similar experiences that I have been induced to write the following, as I am convinced that when once any man has mastered the extremely simple process of sketching with this board, he will never use anything else for rapid work in the field.[7]

Godwin-Austen's description of the Richards' cavalry sketching board as 'more practical (but damnable)' than surveying with theodolite and sextant was therefore perhaps justified.[8]

THE USE OF THE BOARD

A detailed description of the methods of use of the cavalry sketching board can be found in Verner's *Rapid Field Sketching and Reconnaissance*, from which the following brief outline has been paraphrased.

The first step was to turn the board so that the general direction of anticipated travel ran along the roll of paper. When the compass needle was at rest, the compass box would have been swivelled in its socket to a position where the working meridian lay directly above it.

Observations of direction were carried out by turning the horse in the required direction, and swivelling the board to align the needle with the working meridian. A ruler, held to the board by two elastic bands, would be directed at a distant object marking the direction to be travelled, and the line drawn with a pencil. This gave an approximate reading, but if the 'shots' were taken on objects as far away as possible, and back-sightings were used to check, this was sufficiently accurate for military purposes. As Verner remarked;

> 'There are however degrees of accuracy, and it is very plain that on the emergency of a reconnaissance sketch being required in a hurry, it would be far more preferable to be able to execute one that was approximately correct, and was ready when wanted, than to attempt a more accurate sketch which could not be finished in time.[9]

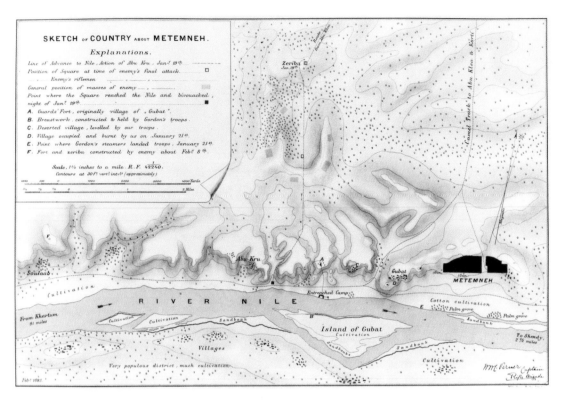

Distances were measured by counting the paces of one's horse and allowing for three yards of ground covered per rise in the saddle at a trot. Trots were more accurate than canters, and distances measured by horseback were more accurate than those measured on foot. In either case, it was best to estimate the working averages over undulating ground. If scales of hundreds of yards at the working map scale were marked on the ruler, features of interest could be drawn in immediately.

Roughly eight or nine miles on horseback, or three to four miles on foot, could be mapped in a day, but it was a rather solitary business as the soldier could not be interrupted in case he lost count of the paces. An alternative, used by Verner in the Sudan, was sketching by time, where distances were estimated by measurements representing the amount of ground covered in a given period. The daily output could be doubled or trebled by copying details in advance from an already existing map, and then concentrating on annotating this outline in the field.

OTHER DESIGNS

In his textbook, Richards added a footnote to the chapter on the cavalry sketching case to say that the cases were manufactured by Messrs Elliott, Instrument Makers, 101 St Martin's Lane. He continued;

'Since their introduction these cases have proved very suitable to active service. Many imitations of and deviations from the regulation pattern have been introduced. Care should be taken to procure none but those manufactured by the above-named maker, and stamped "Richards' Cavalry Case"; any others will prove disappointing.[10]

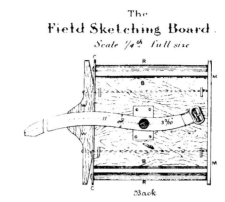

One of these variations was described in 1887 by Major H A Sawyer, writing in the *Journal of the United Service Institution of India*. He described and illustrated 'the ordinary pattern' of the Field Sketching Board, which weighed one pound, was strongly built, and could stand a good deal of knocking about (plate 4);

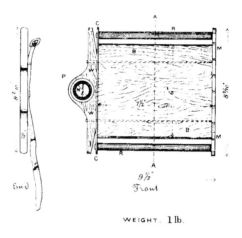

'Recently a lighter kind has been made with no metal about it except the spring copper strip. The compass is smaller, and the whole affair less than half a pound in weight. It is quite strong enough, and the difference in weight is of much more importance than generally supposed. I would strongly recommend the more modern and lighter kind for ordinary use; moreover it is half the price of the former. These are now made in Calcutta in the Mathematical Instrument Department.[11]

plate 4   *From the* **Journal of the United Service Institution of India,** *Vol XV (1887) No LXIX, p444*

After giving instructions and tips on its use and the best ways to present the sketch, Sawyer concluded;

'With a little practice, the "Field Sketching Board" can be a handy and valuable instrument in most officers' hands. It is now cheap, and can be obtained in India or made up in any regimental workshop. It can, moreover, be improvised without difficulty ... all I would point out is that, though with the above hints and his previous garrison training any fair draughtsman can learn how to use it by himself, some practice will be required before he can work rapidly. It is hard bodily work, and has the advantage over some other bodily exercises of being intelligent work as well.[12]

So by this stage the board was considered useful enough to be readily constructed by technicians, to be tricky to use, but to be worth the effort. Richards' concern over non-regulation designs expressed a year later may have been partly for maintenance of good quality manufacture, but he may also have been in a position to receive a royalty from the makers for each case sold that bore his name.

Verner's interest in the sketching board led him to patent two improvements. The first, in 1887,[13] consisted of mounting the roll of paper on spindles with a screw clamp, and also adding scales, measurements and angles to allow the board to be used as a clinometer as well. In *Rapid Field Sketching and Reconnaissance*, Verner commented;

'It is a great advantage to have the scales most commonly used in surveying engraved on the metal footpiece of the board, and for the reason that so long as the board itself is at hand, no other instruments are required. In a campaign in a civilised country, the loss of a protractor might be a matter of little moment, but to the British Officer who so frequently is called to serve in some savage and remote part of the world, it entails extreme inconvenience.[14]

Verner also noted that the board he used was manufactured by Elliott Bros., and the illustrations in his textbook showed the features covered by his 1887 patent. However he was more discreet than Richards, and did not mention that he had any hand in its invention, nor that there might have been a commercial connection with the company. The second patent, in 1891,[15] described the use of bent washers to help clamp the rollers, and added a ruler on a jointed arm which stayed in position without being clamped.

It is probable that Army officers were officially allowed to receive financial gain from their own inventions; records of the opticians J H Steward Ltd in the Science Museum Library include a ledger from 1911,[16] which shows that Verner received a royalty payment for other devices which the company manufactured. Verner retired in 1904, but his rapid sketching instrument and prismatic compass were both marketed by this company over many years, and his sketching board appeared in their catalogues between 1895 and 1929.

plate 5   *Cavalry Sketching Boards* advertised in the trade catalogue of J H Steward Ltd, London.
Courtesy the Trustees of the National Museum of Science and Industry

The year 1891 witnessed two other patents for sketching boards. Captain H Shute of the Coldstream Guards devised a new way of fixing the rollers, a combination of pivot and straight edge, and a new form of clinometer.[17] Captain J O Mennie of the 30th Regiment (3rd Belooch Battalion) of the Bombay Infantry invented a board comprising strips of wood joined together by canvas, and folding or rolling to bring the rollers to the centre of the pack.[18] In use, a strut swivelled across to hold the boards taut. The patent was applied for by H Steward of the opticians, J H Steward Ltd, and Mennie is also noted in their ledger as receiving a royalty. The following letter was printed in a Steward catalogue for 1895;

'Testimonial from Colonel Colville,
Uganda.

Headquarters, Uganda.

Dear Captain Mennie, - I must apologise for not having let you know before how your sketching board has worked here, but perhaps on the whole, it is more satisfactory that I should have waited, as it has given it a better trial. I have now had it in use for over a year in a hot and very damp climate, and often out in heavy rain, and you will be pleased to learn that it is practically as good as new, the wood has not warped in the least, nor (as I should have expected) has the cloth backing given way. The hinged sight rule is a very great convenience, the India-rubber bands of the old form of board was a great nuisance, and had a way (especially in the tropics) of breaking at inopportune moments. I hope the instrument will have the success it deserves.

Testimonials such as this were printed fairly frequently, and must also have received official sanction. Certainly it would appear that Mennie continued in active service, gaining promotion between taking out his patent and receiving his testimonial letter. The letter itself clearly indicates that it was written in the knowledge it would be used for publicity and publication. Commercial success was not frowned on by his senior officers.

Another improvement patented in 1899 was the earliest to originate with an instrument maker rather than a military man. S S Lawrence, an optician trading as Lawrence and Mayo of Chancery Lane, replaced the rubber bands normally used to hold a ruler to the board with strips of leather, which were kept tight by flat coiled springs, fitting into grooves cut for the purpose in the frame of the board.[19]

J W Mander, of the firm of Aston and Mander in Old Compton Street, London followed in 1901 with a patent for an alternative method of fixing the rollers, using concentric screws.[20] D V Smith, who categorised himself as 'Gentleman' in his patent of 1906, had the idea of incorporating a box underneath the board, to hold pencils and other instruments, and allowing vertical angles to be measured without unstrapping the whole thing from the arm.[21]

Two further patents were taken out, in 1908 and 1909, which were related to but not specifically for cavalry sketching case use. G S Smith of Washington DC, a topographical engineer, devised a method of incorporating a protractor in a plane table, where the length of the finished map was expected to be very much greater than the width.[22] The following year, G F Hodgson, the Assistant District Commissioner, Southern Nigeria, suggested mounting the compass under glass in the centre of the board, using semi-transparent paper, and mounting an alidade on a slotted bar at the side for drawing directions.[23]

Mention should also be made of two forms of board which were advertised in Steward catalogues but do not appear to have been successfully patented. One was the Bosworth Cavalry Sketching Board, first illustrated in 1904, and offered at one pound, twelve shillings and sixpence.[24] The engraving included the words BOSWORTH'S PATENT set at the left of the compass, but the board itself was very similar to the Verner type. The accompanying description implied the rollers had been specially designed, and had spring fasteners to hold the paper flat. Colonel W Bosworth intended it to be used on bicycles, with a tripod, or in motor vehicles as well as on horseback. Patented or not, this design appeared in Steward catalogues until 1916.

The other was the 'NCO' board, first mentioned in 1910, and having a larger working surface, but no rollers. This continued to be offered until 1934, and its price never changed from twelve shillings and sixpence[25] (plate 5).

WANING INTEREST

Richards devoted only a couple of pages to his board in his 1888 textbook, and Verner covered the topic quite comprehensively in 1889. Verner succeeded Richards as Professor of Military Topography, and in his 1898 revision of the textbook extended the two pages to seven. The 1904 *Manual of Field Sketching and Reconnaissance* published by HMSO without an attributed author, kept it to three pages. The 1912 *Manual of Map Reading and Sketching* had five, and the 1921 edition had three. However the 1929 *Manual of Map Reading, Photo Reading and Field Sketching* does not mention it at all, but includes large sections on aerial survey and photo-reconnaissance. So by the mid-1920s the Army appears to have moved away from the use of the cavalry sketching board.

A review of the patent literature shows a similar trend. *The Indexes of Abridgements for Philosophical Instruments - Sketching Boards and Plane Tables for Surveying and Military Purposes*, list only accessories from 1909 and 1920, and nothing at all between 1920 and 1945, when a patent was taken out for a board worn round the neck. The inventors themselves seemed to have lost interest from the end of the First World War. Presumably there was no longer

Cavalry Sketching Board.

P1145.

P1145 Cavalry Sketching Board, size 7¼ × 5 inches, with metal clinometer reading to single degrees, magnetic compass with bar needle, agate centre and revolving direction indicator, boxwood rule with rubber bands, and brass friction rollers for holding the paper. The edge of the board is divided with a scale of millimetres. The board is attached to the user's arm by means of a leather strap mounted on centre, which permits its being revolved to any bearing .. .. 3 0 0   £ s. d.

For Telegraphic Code see end of catalogue.

plate 6   A Cavalry Sketching Board

advertised in the 1931 trade catalogue of W F Stanley & Co Ltd, London.

Courtesy the Trustees of the National Museum of Science and Industry a perceived market, nor a chance of commercial success, and the device itself had been overtaken by other methods that did the required job in a better way.

This trend is not shown in the instrument makers' catalogues though. Steward continued to offer two types, the Verner Mark 1 and the NCO board until 1934 (the date of their last catalogue), (plate 5). W F Stanley and Co Ltd produced a catalogue in 1931 which included an engraving re-printed from *Surveying and Levelling Instruments* 4th edition, of 1914 (and reproduced in *The Field Manual* of 1920 by A Lovat Higgins) showing a Verner-like board, but with the Stanley name engraved on it, (plate 6). This illustration also showed the rubber bands for the ruler in a quite impossible position, so although the manufacturers may have known how to use the board, the artist certainly did not, and was probably working without an actual example in front of him. The other point that can be made here is that the boards were very easy to construct, and therefore may not have been kept in stock, but manufactured to order.

EXISTING EXAMPLES

There are examples of cavalry sketching boards in the collections of the National Army Museum, the Science Museum, the Imperial War Museum, and the Whipple Museum of the History of Science at Cambridge, the Ordnance Survey at Southampton, and a further three are known to be in private hands. They are listed overleaf in roughly date order. Some of the designs described in this paper may never have been manufactured, but some general observations can nonetheless be made.

Firstly, although the serial numbers on the boards cannot be taken as literal proof that that number was actually made, it is clear that many were. However they were cheap, constructed from combustible and perishable materials, with straps that might break, and removable compasses. The board was not a sophisticated piece of equipment, but rather an everyday tool which was effective and accurate enough for the job it was required to do.

plate 7   **Map case,** *owned by Lieutenant-Colonel C J B Jerrett 1914-18. It contained a compass and sketching board.*

NAM. 6602-74

Secondly, their use was widespread. Users are recorded from both artillery and infantry regiments, and the boards were official issue in Canada and India as well as Britain. Evidence exists of actual use in the Sudan and Uganda as well as in Europe.

Several makers are shown to have made many boards and over a considerable time, so during the period of active use there was obviously a profit to be made by both inventor and manufacturer. Individual inventors could still take their ideas to an instrument maker, and have the instrument manufactured and marketed, well into the twentieth century. The institutionalisation of instrument design was not yet complete.

plate 8   **A sketching board**, *Major Verner's patent.*

NAM. 5908-37

Date	Type where known	Maker	Serial No.	Institution	ID Number	Notes
1887	Capt Verner's patent	Elliott Bros	1149	ScM	1986-101	
1887	Sawyer type			IWM	44/81	formerly owned by Lt-Col Sir Henry Kerslake
1892	Sawyer type			-	-	Signed Welstesd Marh 1892
1891	Maj Verner's patent		740	NAM	5908-37	from Maj R Ferguson
1891	Maj Verner's patent		1122	-	-	
?		Elliott Bros	2141	NAM	6310-2-3	used by H Caffyn
1891	Maj Verner's patent		1150	IWM	205/77	from Maj D A B Williams
1901	Mander patent, 1901			NAM	7005-18	
1900-1905(?)	Elliott Bros			NAM	6602-74	owned by Lt-Col C J Jarrett. It has a detachable compass, and sprung leather straps similar to the Lawrence patent
		Fraser & Son	364	NAM	6310-2-3	
1908		Houghton's Ltd	751	IWM	31/75	used by Dent, Inneskilling Fusilliers
1908		Houghton's Ltd	908	OS		
1908		Houghton's Ltd		IWM	–	Dec 1909 issue, Canadian mark, owned by DA Thomas, 4th Canadian Field Artillery
1910		Houghton's Ltd	1967	ScM	1979-276	
1910		Aston & Mander	2252	–	–	
1910		Aston & Mander	2599	ScM	1972-427	presented by J H Steward
1912		Aston & Mander	4391	OS		
1913		Houghton's Ltd	5482	NAM	7709-32	
1914		Houghton's Ltd	5816	NAM	6410-18	
1914		Houghton's Ltd	6495	IWM	146/75	
1917		Houghton and Butcher		Whipple	2190	Catalogue number 199
1917		Houghton and Butcher		Whipple	2764	Catalogue number 200
1917	Maj Verner's patent		055	IWM	25/77	Indian issue, owned by Lt-Col J R Williamson RA, DSO
		Houghton and Butcher	10921	IWM	6273	Transferred from Woolwich
–	NCO Board	–		ScM	1986-574	in new condition, bought from Steward descendant, with other items

Key: **IWM** = Imperial War Museum   **NAM** = National Army Museum   **OS** = Ordnance Survey, Southampton   **ScM** = Science Museum   **Whipple** = Whipple Museum of the History of Science, Cambridge

A FORGOTTEN CAMPAIGN

SIERRA LEONE, 1898

MARION HARDING

In 1980 the National Army Museum purchased a collection of eighteen photographs relating to the little-known campaign in Sierra Leone in 1898 (NAM. 8001-7). The seeds of the conflict were sown in 1895 when, on 24 August, an Order in Council was passed to the effect that Her Majesty Queen Victoria had acquired jurisdiction in certain territories in West Africa adjacent to the colony of Sierra Leone, and it was ordained that it would be lawful for the Legislative Council of that colony to frame an ordinance to give effect to this jurisdiction.

Early in 1896 the Governor of Sierra Leone, Sir Frederic Cardew, held several assemblies throughout the country where the Protectorate Ordinance was explained to the tribal chiefs and a proposed scheme of taxation detailed. This took the form of a 'hut-tax' of five shillings on the owner of every habitable house and ten shillings on every house with four rooms or more. No village of less than twenty houses was liable to the tax, which could be paid in cash or in kind. Upon his departure from the various districts numerous petitions were received requesting the rescission of the hut-tax and the modification of several clauses of the ordinance which the chiefs believed deprived them of their ancient rights and powers. They stated that they thought 'the government would take their country from them ... that paying for our huts naturally means no right to our country'. The Ordinance itself was passed on 16 September 1896 to take effect immediately, with the exception of the sections relating to the hut-tax, which were not to come into force until 1 January 1898.

An insurrection began in the Karene district, where officials had been unsuccessfully attempting to obtain payment or part-payment of the hut-tax. A force composed of the Sierra Leone Frontier Police under Major A F Tarbet was despatched to arrest the chief Bai Bure, who immediately prepared to offer resistance. The force proceeded to Karene where it was virtually besieged, since the routes to Port Loko and Freetown lay through hostile country. At the end of two weeks, during which they were daily involved in defensive engage-

Left: Captain H G Warren, Limerick City Artillery, serving with the Sierra Leone Frontier Police, *Back: Surgeon O Horrocks*, *Right: Inspector Taylor, Front: Captain J E C Blakeney*, 4th Bn Essex Regiment serving with the Frontier Police. As a major, Blakeney was appointed to the command of the Sierra Leone Battalion, West African Frontier Force in 1902.

NAM. neg no 57144

ments, they were reinforced by a company of the 1st Battalion, West India Regiment under Major R J Norris, who had approached by a circuitous route from the south-east.

On 3 March 1898, the combined force of nearly 200 men of the West India Regiment and the Sierra Leone Frontier Police made another attempt to capture Bai Bure. From the moment they left Karene until they reached Port Loko they were subjected to continual harassment from an enemy who, fighting under dense cover afforded by the forest, inflicted many casualties. European officers were unfamiliar with this sort of fighting and numerous volleys were fired at the natives with no appreciable result. The casualties which the force sustained were considered to be the consequence of insufficient numbers and so, after forcing his way through enemy-held territory, Major Norris took up position at Port Loko to await further reinforcements from Freetown.

In the meantime Bai Bure began building stockades or sangars, usually circular stone enclosures large enough to conceal four or more men and pierced by several loopholes. Some were made from the thickest part of the banana tree, a tough, spongy substance which absorbed the force of bullets. They were normally located among giant trees, surrounded by almost impenetrable forest and were served by winding narrow tracks, almost invisible to the uninitiated, which allowed the defenders to escape before they could be surrounded.

While these measures were being put into effect a force of 94 officers and men of the 1st Battalion ,West India Regiment under Major W B Stansfield reached Port Loko on 6 March 1898, bringing the total number of troops there to 300.

The fighting now began to assume a more serious aspect. The superior weapons of the British forces gave them no advantage over an enemy which they could not see, a situation which threatened to undermine the morale of the men. The enemy, conscious of the disparity in numbers and the inability of the British to devise effective countermeasures, began to take the initiative.

Requests for reinforcements followed in quick succession. Valuable assistance to the land forces was rendered by HM vessels *Fox* and *Alecto*. In addition to the Marines and blue-jackets of these warships and the soldiers of 1st Battalion, West India Regiment already stationed in Sierra Leone, several companies of the 3rd Battalion were despatched from St Helena and an emergency detachment of Royal Artillery and others from England. Besides these, the Sierra Leone Royal Artillery, Royal Engineers, Frontier Police and armed Court messengers were employed. Some 2,500 men were mobilised just for the capture of Bai Bure.

The initial success on the part of Bai Bure and his followers encouraged other tribes, particularly the Mendis, to avenge themselves on those whom they considered to be interfering in their traditional way of life. An uprising was planned for about 27 April to end British rule, drive the Europeans out of their country and to murder any of their own people who could speak English or who wore English clothes. Starting in the Imperri district, bands of Mendis armed with cutlasses, clubs and a few ancient firearms overran all the seaports as far as the frontier with Liberia. Other parties advanced inland, while yet more attacked the Frontier Police in their several garrisons and even landed at Bonthe and entered Waterloo, towns next in importance to Freetown. Throughout the land towns and outposts were besieged and those who were unfortunate enough to be captured were usually tortured to death. At least 1,000 persons were killed. In a few instances, people were warned by friendly natives and managed to escape by hiding in the bush.

One of the besieged towns, Panguma, was now completely cut off. Orders were received from the Governor that it should be relieved at all costs, if possible from Bandajuma, four days good march away. Accordingly on 9 June a force consisting of 45 Frontier Police and a number

Captured Mendi tribesmen. *The majority of the insurgents who besieged Panguma were drawn from the Mendi tribes who had the reputation of being particularly savage. Armed with swords and sticks they took advantage of the unrest caused by the imposition of the hut-tax to initiate a massacre of Europeans and Europeanised natives.*

The camp at Panguma

Friendlies: *throughout the insurrection a number of chiefs remained loyal to the Government. Numbers of 'friendlies', as they were called, often accompanied Government forces and their knowledge of the country and the native method of warfare proved valuable.*

of friendly natives set off. No resistance was encountered until the second day, when the party was attacked by a large body of the enemy who were concealed in the bush. The relieving force pushed on to a town called Doja, where it again came under attack. The friendly natives and porters then refused to cross the Panguma border, despite all threats and inducements to do so. On 13 June, unable to proceed without the loads carried by the porters, which consisted of ammunition and provisions for the beleaguered garrison, the column was forced to retrace the 30 miles to Bandajuma.

On 12 June a second relieving force set out for Panguma from Kwalu under the command of Major E D H Fairtlough. It consisted of 75 picked Frontier Police and native gunners from the Sierra Leone Royal Artillery with a seven-pounder, fifteen armed Court messengers, and about 300 'friendlies'. When it was within three miles of Gagboro the enemy opened fire from an ambush. The contingent repelled them and, charging on, drove them out of the town, which was defended by three lines of stockades. Progress was very slow as the roads were frequently obstructed and the bush on either side was swarming with tribesmen who were doing their utmost to prevent the column reaching Panguma. At Dodo they launched a general attack, but were beaten back and the rescuers reached their objective at 1100hrs on 23 June. They found the defenders commanded by Captain J E C Blakeney in a bad way. They had held their position for two months during which time they had been surrounded by thousands of insurgents and attacked repeatedly. Their food supply had run short and everyone was living on half-rations, chiefly rice. The garrison was also short of ammunition. The barracks, in which the officers' quarters were situated, were stockaded, and this had probably saved them from destruction. There were a large number of casualties among the men and the medical officer, Dr O Horrocks, had attended them unceasingly.

The exertions of the relieving force were not yet at an end. After remaining at Panguma for five days it left on the return journey, but following a different route than that by which it had reached the town. During the course of the march it frequently encountered strongly defended stockades, which were held with great determination by the enemy, but which were all overrun. At Yomundu on 6 July an action took place which practically put an end to the fighting. Yomundu was really three large towns in one and was strongly stockaded by a triple row of fences. The action was opened by a bombardment from the seven-pounder and by volleys of musketry from the troops. Closing in, one section under Captain H de L Ferguson assaulted the right flank, a second under Major Fairtlough attacked on the left and the third, accompanied by a number of 'friendlies', cut their way through the centre. Here, a hand-to-hand struggle took place between the Frontier Police and the enemy in which three chiefs and 115 of their supporters were killed.

A number of chiefs now began to tender their submissions and although there were still war-camps and small marauding parties in the bush no further serious opposition was encountered. A great number of arrests were made and a judge was sent out from England to try the prisoners, the majority of whom were charged with murder. A general amnesty, with certain exceptions, was issued by the Governor on 17 January 1899.

REGIMENTAL RECORDS
OF THE BRITISH ARMY,
1850-1900

PETER BOYDEN

The regimental tradition in Britain is as old as its standing Army, and although a British soldier swears an oath of loyalty to the Sovereign his strongest affections are likely to be reserved for the regiment or corps to which he belongs. Since it was almost always the case that data on an individual's military career was compiled within the unit in which he served, regimental records are of considerable importance to genealogists and others seeking to reconstruct the lives of past generations of soldiers. This essay attempts to explain the background to the creation and preservation of regimental records in the second half of the nineteenth century, to indicate the types of document that were produced, to identify those that have been preserved, and to indicate where they may be found. The records of the regular Army, Militia, Volunteers, and Yeomanry will be treated *seriatim* after some general points on the compilation and preservation of records by public bodies.

The first and most important point about regimental (or any other officially-produced) records is that *it has never been a function of the British Government to create records and collect data for the benefit of future generations of historians*. What the Government does is to preserve for the researcher some of the material that has been created in the course of its normal business. This fact leads to a second related observation that records are created for a specific, immediate purpose and the data that they contain will be arranged in a way that meets the needs of the organization creating them. In use, and when non-current, these documents will be stored in a way that makes sense to those who use them - which may not be the same as that expected by the later researcher. It is also important to remember that in the short term the decision whether to destroy or preserve records is likely to be influenced more heavily by the likelihood of needing to refer to them again than their importance to historians. Not only may the documents be stored in a way that historians find incomprehensible, but they frequently find themselves using records for purposes for which they were not intended. The data they contain and the way in which they are arranged is not necessarily designed to yield the information desired by today's student, while the records probably contain information that is not required as well as omitting facts that are.

It is a good historian who can produce a creditable thesis from unpromising source material, but the researcher can often make his work easier if he approaches a collection of records having first studied the history of the documents themselves and considered the circumstances under which they were created. It is also helpful to note any instructions relating to their preservation, although these need to be handled with caution when considering records of the British Army. Although there were regulations specifying which records were to be kept and what was to become of them, it is a feature of the Army that its regulations are not always adhered to. This has introduced a rogue element into the preservation (and destruction) of its records in that things which should have been destroyed survive, documents that should have been kept have been lost, and others have been removed from their proper home and placed somewhere quite unexpected. This all adds to the interest of research in British regimental records.

THE REGULAR ARMY

The 1892 edition of *Queen's Regulations* distinguished between 'returns' and 'books and regimental records'.[1] The former, treated under the general heading of 'correspondence', were forms which had to be completed by units and submitted to the various departments at the Headquarters of the Army. The 'books and regimental records' were also compiled by units, but they generally remained with them. An officer commanding a unit would have submitted seventeen annual returns, a further four half-yearly, four more quarterly, nine monthly and two weekly, making a total of 253 forms to be completed each year, most of which were returned to the Adjutant-General. Examples are given on the illustrated extract from the regulations. Of the 36 series of returns specified, only three seem to be represented in the Public Record Office - muster books and pay lists (WO10-12, 14, 16), monthly returns (WO17) and casualty returns (WO25/1196-2755). There are in addition at least four other classes of document which contain information drawn from regimental returns - deserters' entry books (WO25/2906-2961), returns of Bibles and prayer books supplied (WO30/93), officers' records of service (WO25/744-870 and WO76) and lists of Long Service and Good Conduct Medal winners (WO102). The loss of the other 29 series does not necessarily mean that a great deal of information about an individual's service has been destroyed since some of it was recorded elsewhere - for example on the pay lists.

Four pages of the 1892 *Regulations* are taken up with tables of 'books and regimental records'[2] prefaced by general instructions on their compilation and care. Twenty-nine regimental books were specified, many of which had unique Army Book numbers as the illustrated extract shows. There were also thirteen quartermaster's books, four belonging to the veterinary officer; a register for civil employment (AB233), a register of recruits (AB303) and a canteen book. When the regiment was on active service overseas only certain books were to accompany it, and the remainder were to remain for safe keeping at the depot. One of the most sought-after of regimental documents is the record of a soldier's service, and the regulations give full instructions on how these forms were to be completed, including the 'Military History Sheet' (AF234).[3] A soldier's original attestation form was to remain at the depot and a duplicate accompanied him during his service around the world. The originals were to be destroyed after a year in the case of dead men, and five years for deserters and those who had been discharged. The duplicates, military history sheet and any other papers were

Correspondence, &c.

RETURNS—continued.

Description of Return.	Number of Army Form, &c.	To whom sent.	When to be sent.	
Return of Soldiers received from the Royal Hibernian Military School.	B. 222	Commandant of Royal Hibernian Military School.	1st January.	
Report on Military Bandmasters.	By letter	Commandant of Royal School of Music, Kneller Hall.	1st January.	
Return of Certificates of Education in possession.	B. 139	Adjutant-General	1st January.	
Annual requisition for Bibles, Prayer-Books, &c.	L. 1367	Under Secretary of State for War.	1st January.	
Return of Men desirous of transfer to Departmental Corps.	B. 242	Adjutant-General	See Sec. XIX., paragraph 30.	
Return of Swordsmanship (Cavalry only).	O. 1715, in duplicate	Inspector of Gymnasia, Aldershot.	On the termination of the annual competition for prizes.	
Nominal Return of Deaths and Invaliding.	B. 119	Adjutant-General	Home Stations 31st January. Stations abroad 31st March.	
Annual Report on Clothing supplied.	H. 1113	Adjutant-General through G. O. C.	1st April.	
Annual Requisition for Clothing.	H. 1107, H. 1171, H. 1130	Director of Clothing, ,, ,,		A.O. 149. 1890.
Return of New Clothing in Store.	H. 1114	,,		
Annual Musketry Return in duplicate.	B. 187	General Officer Commanding through District Inspector of Musketry.	31st December at Home, &c. 31st March in Tropical Climates.	A.O. 69. 1890.
Annual Report of Recreation Rooms.	N. 1510	General Officer Commanding.	1st January.	
Report of Instruction in Field Works undergone by Battalions (Infantry only).	M.S.	Adjutant-General through General Officer Commanding	31st March (Section VII., paragraph 266).	A.O. 2. 1890.
Report of Annual Instruction in Field Works (Royal Engineers only).	B. 2094	Adjutant-General through General Officer Commanding.	On completion of course (Section VII., paragraph 280).	A.O. 198. 1890.

Correspondence, &c.

RETURNS—continued.

(marginal notes: n. No. 2 2723.   O. 282 1890.)

Description of Return.	Number of Army Form, &c.	To whom sent.	When to be sent.
By Officers Commanding Troops quartered in Barracks, and Heads of Departments.			
Statement of new Works, Alterations, and Additions proposed for Barracks. Annual Estimates.	M. 1415	General Officer Commanding.	1st May.
By the Inspector of Gymnasia.			
Annual Return of Officers and Men under Instruction in Military Gymnasia.	Special Form	Adjutant-General	1st January.
Half-yearly.			
By General Officers Commanding.			
Index of General Orders issued in Ireland and at stations abroad.	A. 18	Adjutant-General	1st January and 1st July.
Return of Officers recommended to join Garrison Classes. (At home only.)	B. 2054	Adjutant-General	1st February and 1st August.
Lists of Candidates for Examination for 1st Class Certificates of Education.	C. 379	Adjutant-General	15th February and 15th September.
Return of Officers desirous of being examined for promotion.	B. 2053	Adjutant-General	1st April and 1st October.
Return of Officers of Militia and Volunteers desirous of being examined in Tactics.	E. 621 and E. 623	Adjutant-General	1st April and 1st October.
Report of Boards on Garrison Canteens. (Tenant system.)	A. 2 with F. 707	Adjutant-General	1st January and 1st July.
By Officers Commanding units.			
Report of progress made in Fencing (Cavalry only).	B. 157	Inspector of Gymnasia, Aldershot.	1st January and 1st July.
Certificate. Fitting Saddles. (Cavalry only.) (Sect. XII., para. 58.)	MS.	Inspector-General of Cavalry.	1st April and 1st October.

Books and Regimental Records.

GENERAL INSTRUCTIONS—continued.

No.	Book.	Army Book.
	REGIMENTAL BOOKS.	
1.	General Order Book	127
2.	Regimental Order Book	127
3.	Record of Officers' Services	83
4.	Portfolio of Attestations	234
5.	Casualty Book	156
6.	Letter Book	127 or 213
7.	Register of Letters Received	193
8.	Guard Book	22 & 23
9.	Register of Furloughs	86
10.	Register of Deserters	87
11.	Defaulter Book, prepared with Army Form B 120.	
12.	Officers' Court-martial Book.	129
13.	Court-martial Book, prepared with Army Form A 12	

Books and Regimental Records.

GENERAL INSTRUCTIONS—continued.

No.	Book.	Army Book.
14.	Digest of Services of the Regiment.	127
15.	Register of Marriages and Baptisms.	91
16.	Savings Bank Ledger	80
17.	Daily Register of Cooking.	162
18.	Description of Horses, Mounted Corps.	92
19.	Equitation Register, Mounted Corps.	93
20.	Weekly Report (Riding-Master).	94
21.	Register of Certificates of Education.	13
22.	Postage Book	97
23.	Register of Births at Stations Abroad.	112
24.	Register of Marriages at Stations Abroad.	113
25.	Register of Deaths at Stations Abroad.	114
26.	Nominal List of Men transferred to the Army Reserve (see Section XIX., paragraph 58).	249
27.	Drill, Battery Record of	A.F. B 85

* At War Office. † Kept by Royal Horse Artillery and Royal Artillery Depôts, Regimental Districts, Rifle and Cavalry Depôts.
‡ In territorial regiments, kept up at depôt.

From **The Queen's Regulations and Orders for the Army,** *1892*

then sent to the Secretary of State five years after discharge, and are now in the Public Record Office (WO97), the only class of regimental records preserved there.

Letter books were not to be kept for more than three years after they had been completed, although 'care was to be taken to keep copies of such letters as may be likely to be required for reference'.[4] Copies of monthly and other returns were to be kept in guard books and destroyed after three years 'with the exception of such as the O.C. may deem proper to retain'.[5] Indeed, 'with a view to obviate the inconvenience which is found to arise from the accumulation, in the military offices of districts or stations of records to which references are seldom made', arrangements were made for the periodical review of records, although that such a system was considered necessary at regimental level is surprising.[6] The practice of regiments carrying all their books, silver and possessions around the world had prevented many of them accumulating too much material since it was 'weeded' in the frequent shipwrecks and other disasters that befell them. The records of the 32nd Foot were presumably lost with the rest of the regimental property which was looted by the local inhabitants when the regiment was shipwrecked outside the Cove of Cork in December 1775,[7] while the 62nd Foot lost its possessions when the boat carrying the regiment up the Ganges in September 1842 overturned. When raised in May 1843 the Colours were found to be nearly destroyed, the records indecipherable and all the silver, with the exception of one piece, missing.[8]

For reasons such as this the preservation of regimental books and records of the regular Army is generally bad. Those that do survive are invariably to be found either in regimental museums or in record offices and other institutions where regiments have deposited them. These collections normally include a digest of services (AB127) and records of officers' services (AB83) but which (if any) of the other 47 types of book specified in 1892 have been preserved is totally unpredictable.

THE MILITIA

The 1853 *Militia Regulations* specified the returns to be made to the Secretary at War by commanders of Militia units.[9] Four of these related to their annual periods of training, but there were also pay lists and monthly returns to be submitted. In addition, the adjutant was to send to the Clerk of the General Meeting, for the information of the Lord Lieutenant, a half-monthly return of men who had joined and become casualties.[10] Of those returns only the pay lists (WO13/1-3393) and monthly returns (WO17/974-1002, 1041-1152) survive in the Public Record Office. There was no mention in these regulations of regimental books but some seventeen of them were detailed in the 1894 *Militia Regulations*.[11]

These included temporary and permanent regimental order books, records of officers' services, a letterbook, a digest of services, and a sub-cash ledger. Each company was also to have four books, although no regulations were laid down relating to the preservation or periodical destruction of these records. Alone among the British land forces, the regimental books and records of the Militia regiments were called into the War Office, probably between the two World Wars, and are now to be found in the Public Record Office as 'Militia Records' (WO68). Inevitably, not all of the extant records reached the War Office - those of the Royal Montgomeryshire Militia were kept by their last commanding officer Colonel E S St Barbe

Orderly Room, *c1850*

Watercolour, artist unknown, from a series entitled Life in an Infantry Regiment, *c1850*

It was here that the various regimental records and returns were compiled and stored including details of misdemeanours!

Sladen, and only got to Whitehall in 1937, after his death.[12] In other cases the records were kept by the regiments and are now to be found in regimental museums, county record offices, and occasionally in private hands. The early books of the Somerset Militia are preserved at Taunton, while the documents at Kew commence in 1836.[13] Similarly most of the regimental books of the Devon Militia regiments have been kept at Exeter, and the only item in the Public Record Office is a digest of service of the 2nd (South Devon) Militia.[14]

In general terms the range of books preserved by Militia regiments is much greater than that of regular regiments, a result of both their more 'static' history and the decision to collect up their records. Study of a sample of nineteen infantry Militia units' records at Kew revealed that thirteen each included digests of services and records of officers' services, ten order books, seven enrolment books, and four letter books. While not necessarily complete, and some units are poorly documented, in many cases enough survives to enable the history of a Militia regiment to be studied in detail back at least to the time of Napoleon.

A further class of regimental books, soldiers' attestations, which were to be preserved at the headquarters of the regiment according to the 1853 regulations,[15] are now to be found in the Public Record Office (WO96). They are arranged regimentally and filed alphabetically within the regimental grouping. They mostly date from the period 1870-1908, and have every appearance of having been collected from Militia headquarters, with rather more success than the regimental books.

The Volunteer Force came into being in 1859 in response to fears of a French invasion. The units were raised under the provisions of an Act of 1804, and were at first independent with little co-ordination between them. In 1860 they were brought together into Administrative Battalions, which in 1881 became Volunteer Battalions of line regiments. The Volunteer Force ceased to exist in 1908 and most of the battalions became part of the Territorial Army.

The 1881 *Regulations for the Volunteer Force* listed various returns that were to be made by Volunteer units,[16] a number of them at the time of their inspection by the local District GOC, although there were also quarterly returns and the regular submission of copies of the adjutant's diary of instruction given to the corps. Annual returns were to be made by the officer commanding on 1 November each year, and a nominal roll was to be submitted too. When the annual return had been checked at the War Office the nominal roll was sent to the Clerk of the Lieutenancy '... to be by him retained for the information of the Lord Lieutenant'. These regulations do not mention regimental books as such, only the three that were kept by the adjutant[17] - the muster book, record of attendance at drill, and his diary - which he was to transfer to his successor on leaving the corps. The adjutant also had financial responsibilities but no details are given of the account books that he was to make over with the 'balance in hand' to his successor.

These regulations contain no instructions for the future preservation of these books beyond the requirement that has been noted, and although they refer to regimental orders no obligation was placed on the units to keep copies of them.[18] These limited instructions, together with the early independent history of the Volunteer units, suggest that the commanding officers' preferences were important in determining how the unit was run, although they would have been loosely modelled on the practices employed in regular units. This vagueness is reflected in the fate of their regimental books which are to be found today in a variety of places. Some were carefully kept by the units and have come to rest in regimental museums, others were taken home and incorporated into officers' private papers, while some were sold or otherwise disposed of and have subsequently reached a variety of museums and archive repositories. It is clear however that the vast bulk of them have been lost. A few examples will illustrate the point. The 10th Cumberland Rifle Volunteers were formed at Egremont in July 1860, their Captain Commandant Henry Jefferson. The only extant record of this unit is its cash book for 1860-63 which is to be found among the records of Jeffersons the wine merchants, in which it was incorporated by its commanding officer.[19] What is less clear is how the record of drills of 'L' Company, 13th Middlesex Rifle Volunteers (Queen's Westminsters) 1886-87 became associated with records of the Thornbury detachment of the 1st (City of Bristol) Volunteer Battalion, the Gloucestershire Regiment.[20]

If the Volunteers' regimental books are poorly preserved, the fate of the returns which they regularly sent to the War Office has been even worse. The annual returns were to be passed to the Clerk of the Lieutenancy, so they should be in the county record offices of those counties that have lieutenancy records. Cheshire has a large collection of such material, but it does not include any of these returns,[21] and to date, none have been found elsewhere. The nominal rolls held by the War Office appear to have gone, as have the adjutants' diaries and the pay lists. There is an incomplete set of pay lists for Volunteer Permanent Staff 1873-78 at Kew (WO13/4622-4675) but the only other relevant material there are what are described in the booklet *Tracing your Ancestors in the Public Record Office*[22] as '... muster rolls of some London and Middlesex Volunteer and Territorial Units' (WO70/1-21). These items are actually the regimental books of the 10th Bn, the London Regiment, the 'Paddington Rifles'. This unit began life as the 36th Middlesex Rifle Volunteers, was renumbered as the 18th in

Pay parade, 10th Hussars, Aldershot 1886

Watercolour by T P Chapman, 1886

A great deal of information about an individual soldier's service can be derived from the pay lists.

NAM. 7003-7-2

1880, and became a battalion of the London Regiment in 1908. The battalion was disbanded in 1912 because of recruiting difficulties, and its records - muster and order books - were presumably passed to the War Office, being subsequently transferred to the Public Record Office where they remain as the only set of Volunteer records in official custody.

The failure to provide any instructions for the preservation of their books, and the destruction that most of the returns from Volunteer units have been subjected to, make research into their history difficult. Fortunately the Rifle Volunteers' activities were reported quite extensively in the contemporary local press, and from these reports it is usually possible to reconstruct the outlines of their history, even if information on specific individuals may be difficult to find.

THE YEOMANRY

In common with the Rifle Volunteers the Yeomanry existed under the provisions of the 1804 Volunteer Act (44 Geo III c.54). They were mounted Volunteers, usually formed into county-based units and, like the Rifle Volunteers, liable until the time of the Boer War only to serve at home.

The 1853 *Yeomanry Regulations*[23] lists a number of forms that were to be returned to the Home Office or War Office by the commanders of Yeomanry regiments, chiefly to facilitate payment of the men for their annual periods of training and to order supplies of arms and equipment. There were no references to regimental books then, although they duly appear with more forms and returns in the 1894 *Yeomanry Regulations*.[24] Yeomanry regiments were to be equipped with an adjutant's diary, musketry register, squadron return books, return of target practice and equipment ledger which were to be produced as required by inspecting officers, and copies of them were to be submitted regularly. The adjutant was also responsible for paying the unit's permanent staff, although there is no mention of his having any books for recording these transactions.

In common with the Rifle Volunteers there were no regulations for the preservation of these books, and a number of other volumes that probably existed such as regimental order books are not mentioned at all. Generally the preservation of Yeomanry records is bad. From a sample of sixteen counties it was found that there were good collections from only two, both of which have been carefully preserved in regimental custody. In addition there was one stray item from each of two other counties - one preserved in a drill hall, the other having been taken home by the commanding officer.[25] With the exception of muster rolls and pay lists of 1803-53 (WO13/3968-4159) no other returns from Yeomanry regiments have been found in either the Home Office or War Office papers in the Public Record Office.

CONCLUSION

The litany of the loss and dispersal of regimental books and returns that has occupied the preceding paragraphs might encourage a belief that precious little survives to document the history of Britain's land forces and the careers of the men who served in them. This view is somewhat pessimistic as the following table, which summarises the general practice of the preservation of regimental returns and books, reveals;

	RETURNS (All at PRO)	REGIMENTAL BOOKS
Regulars	Very few series kept, although some important ones well preserved	Badly preserved; scattered CRO, NAM, RM
Militia	Mostly destroyed	Preservation fairly good; some scattered, others centralised CRO NAM, PRO, RM
Volunteers and Yeomanry	Mostly destroyed	Very badly preserved; scattered CRO, NAM, RM. Some Yeomanry books still with serving regiments.

Key:	CRO: County Record Office	NAM: National Army Museum
	PRO: Public Record Office	RM: Regimental Museums

The survival rate of documents relating to Volunteer and Yeomanry units is poor, and it is frequently difficult or impossible to find references to individuals who served in them. However these Volunteers usually had other jobs and their military activities represented only a small percentage of their total lives. Militia-men of the second half of the nineteenth century also fell into this category, although here there is some chance of tracing details of an individual's service. For members of the regular Army though, their military career represented the whole of their working life (while they were serving) and a deliberate attempt was made to keep documentation relating to everyone who served as a regular soldier.[26] There is then an element of selection in the preservation of records of the different types of unit which reflects not only the importance of the military element in the lives of those serving in them, but also the significance of the unit itself as a military force.

THE RECONQUEST OF THE SUDAN, 1898

A PHOTOGRAPHIC RECORD

MARION HARDING

For the ten years after the death of General Gordon at the hands of the Dervish Army in January 1885 the situation in the Sudan was fairly peaceful. After the defeat of the Dervishes at the Battle of Ginnis in December 1885 the *Mahdi's* successor, the *Khalifa* Abdullah, abandoned the advance upon Egypt and concentrated on the pursuit of territorial ambitions in Abyssinia.

The British Government had hoped that this period of stability would eventually allow it to withdraw from the region, but it gradually came to accept the necessity for Britain not only to remain in Egypt but to extend its control to the Sudan in order to offset Italian ambitions in Abyssinia and the southern Sudan and French interest in the Upper Nile. Events were precipitated by the catastrophic defeat of an Italian army at the Battle of Adowa in Abyssinia in March 1896 which threatened to encourage co-operation between the Abyssinians and the *Khalifa* against the European presence in the area and thus strengthen the power of the *Khalifa*, which was assumed to be in decline.

In June 1896 the opportunity to recover lost territory presented itself in the guise of a diversion to take Dervish pressure off the Italian garrison at Kassala on the Atbara tributary of the Nile in southern Sudan; this demonstration of British support for Italy also had the effect of bolstering the Triple Alliance of Italy, Germany and Austria-Hungary, so that the political power of France and Russia should not be enhanced, thus tilting the European balance of power in their favour.

Major-General Sir Herbert Kitchener, the *Sirdar*, or Commander-in-Chief, of the Egyptian Army was therefore instructed to undertake a campaign for the re-occupation of Dongola and the main striking force of 15,000 British and Egyptian troops was assembled at Wadi Halfa preparatory to an advance up the Nile. This route was chosen because of the ease of water supply and the facilities for the transport

First Class sleeping car on the Sudan Military Railway.

NAM. neg no 21162

of supplies afforded by the Nile which was to be supplemented by the construction of a railway as the Army advanced. Preparations for the campaign were laborious and extensive and progress was slow. In June an enemy advanced detachment was surprised and driven back at Firket, but then an outbreak of cholera, bad weather, and a series of mishaps to the Nile flotilla accompanying the Army delayed the operation for three months. At last, early in September, all was ready for the decisive move and before the end of that month, Kitchener's forces were in secure possession of Dongola.

There then followed a long pause, during which the British Government seemed unable to make up its mind to push home the offensive, but a report that a French expedition to the Upper Nile was in contemplation seems to have finally put an end to its hesitation. The interval had meanwhile been put to good use in restoring order in the Dongola province, pushing the railway forward and many other preparations. For the advance to the Dervish capital at Khartoum Kitchener decided to adopt a different line of communications by driving a railway across the desert from Wadi Halfa to Abu Hamed, pending the completion of which the troops moved up river to this last location. The enemy forces, lulled into security by the lengthy pause after the taking of Dongola, remained quiescent around Khartoum, and the small detachment of Dervishes at Abu Hamed was easily surprised and overwhelmed in August 1897. As a result of this success, Berber was abandoned to the British, who pushed their advanced troops forward to the junction of the Nile and Atbara Rivers, less than 200 miles from Khartoum. Meanwhile the railway advanced rapidly, reaching Abu Hamed at the end of October.

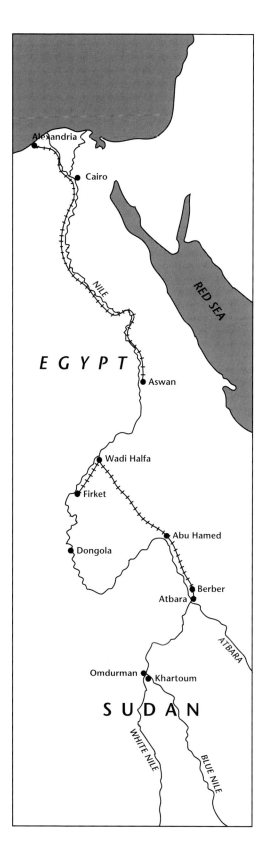

By this time the *Khalifa* had determined to make a last effort to ward off the danger which was advancing inexorably from the north, but his plans for effecting a powerful concentration of all available forces failed to materialise and his lieutenant, Mahmoud, was ordered to do his best with the 15,000 men at his disposal. He decided to move against Berber via the Lower

Mahmoud in his bloodstained jibba, or tunic, just after his capture at the Battle of the Atbara, 8 April 1898. His escort is provided by men of the 10th Sudanese Battalion.

NAM. neg no 21017

Atbara, hoping to turn Kitchener's left flank, but the latter's concentration was too rapid and Mahmoud's entrenched camp was stormed, his army dispersed and he himself made prisoner at the Battle of Atbara on 8 April 1898. Four months later the *Sirdar's* Army, now reinforced to 26,000 men of whom one-third were British troops, set out on its final march to Khartoum. At the end of August Kitchener reached Omdurman, on the left bank of the Nile opposite Khartoum. Here, on 2 September, the Dervishes attacked the British *zariba* (an entrenched camp surrounded by a thick thorn fence) and were repulsed with heavy loss. Kitchener then advanced to drive the enemy before him into Omdurman and capture the place, but in the course of the operation the Egyptian Brigade on the British right became isolated and was attacked in front by the centre of the Dervish Army, while its flank and rear were threatened by the Dervish left, which had not previously been engaged. The position was critical, but, thanks to the steadiness of the Sudanese troops, the attack was repulsed.

The *Khalifa* escaped into Kordofan Province where he was hunted down and killed the following year. A key Mahdist lieutenant, Osman Digna, was captured on 19 January 1900. The battle of Omdurman completed the reconquest of the Sudan: on 19 January 1899 Britain and Egypt established a ruling condominium, later called the Anglo-Egyptian Sudan.

The *raison d'être* behind the Kodak camera, introduced by George Eastman in 1888, was

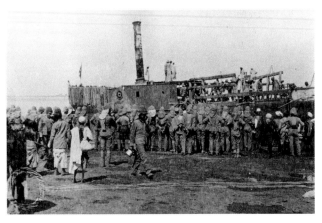

1st Battalion, the Grenadier Guards embarking on a river steamer.

NAM. neg no 13195

the reduction of photography to a simple mechanical process which relieved the 'photographer' of all responsibility for its chemistry. This small camera, the name of which was formed from a purely arbitrary combination of letters chosen by Eastman because it was short and vigorous, was the first to incorporate a roll-film, and provided the greatest single stimulus to amateur photography. By 1891 over 90,000 had been sold. During the next decade several innovations were made so that by 1898 cameras were being produced which were so compact that they could fit into the pocket, which utilised daylight-loading film

Men of the Grenadier Guards during a field day at Atbara Camp, 15 August 1897. The commanding officer, Lieutenant-Colonel V Hatton, is mounted on the donkey.

NAM. neg no 41948

and which gave an average of twelve exposures varying in size between one-and-a-half by two inches and four by five inches.

Speaking of the results to be obtained from the Kodak, Eastman said, 'A collection of these pictures may be made to furnish a pictorial history of life as it is lived by the owner that will grow more valuable every day that passes'. This pronouncement was calculated to appeal to a nostalgically inclined public, among them an officer of the Grenadier Guards who was present during the later stages of the reconquest of the Sudan.

Edward Douglas Loch was the only son of Henry Brougham Loch, whom he succeeded as second Baron Loch of Drylaw in 1900. He joined the 1st Battalion, the Grenadier Guards in 1893 and was with them in Gibraltar in 1897 when they were posted to the Sudan. At this time

Captain A C McLean and 'G' Company 1st Battalion, the Queen's Own Cameron Highlanders leaving Wad Hamed.

NAM. neg no 21020

1st Battalion, the Grenadier Guards awaiting the Dervish attack, Omdurman, 1500hrs, 1 September 1898.

NAM. neg No 21164

he was Battalion Signalling Officer and during the advance to Omdurman was made Brigade Signalling Officer to the 2nd Brigade under the command of Sir Neville Lyttleton.

For his services in the Sudan Loch was mentioned in Despatches, received the Queen's Sudan Medal, the Khedive's Medal with clasp and the Distinguished Service Order, with which he was decorated by Queen Victoria in person.

Of the two collections of Loch's photographs in the Archives of the National Army Museum the 131 arranged in more or less chronological sequence with printed titles in an album[1] most clearly reflect the progress of the reconquest. Loch may have obtained a few of his photographs from another source for scenes early in the album record the aftermath of the Atbara battle in April 1898, whereas the 1st Battalion, the Grenadier Guards did not reach Alexandria until the end of July. Thereafter the photographs follow the progress of the Battalion, together with that of some of the other regiments in the two British infantry brigades[2] and that of the 21st Lancers which is chronicled in a series of 'despatches' from an anonymous 'Very Own Extra Special Soudanese Correspondent' with the Grenadier Guards published in *The Household Brigade Magazine* in 1898. Not all the photographs in the album are dated, but the 'despatches' reveal that the Grenadiers disembarked at Alexandria on 27 July, setting out for Cairo by train at 0620hrs the following day. The Headquarters and half the Battalion left for the front on 30 July, the remainder entraining for Luxor on 2 August, arriving at 1300hrs on the following afternoon and bivouacking there for the night. On 4 August the journey by train was resumed as far as Aswan where they transferred to the

The first batch of Dervish prisoners leaving the battlefield of Omdurman, 2 September 1898.

NAM. neg No 13215

steamboats which carried them to Wadi Halfa, which they reached on the 8th. Here they returned to the railway which transported them to Atbara camp, arriving on 9 August;

'The rest of our week here was most pleasantly passed with field days, practising the new attack advancing and firing in line, trying to unlearn the old familiar one associated so happily with Hyde Park and Wimbledon Common, forming squares, 5.45 a.m. to 8.30 p.m.; bivouac and zereba making parades 5 p.m. to 6.30 p.m., the interval of every day being most agreeably spent by the whole battalion in instructive fatigue

Three cheers for the Queen - *raising the British and Egyptian flags above the ruins of General Gordon's Palace, Khartoum, 4 September 1898.*

The Mahdi's tomb, Omdurman, showing the effects of shelling.

parties. A cheery dinner, quartettes at each table outside the mess tent, with an occasional concert aided by the band and vocalists of the Rifle Brigade, on an impromptu stage, under the able direction of Sergeant-Major Fowles.[3]

On 18 and 19 August the Battalion resumed its journey in barges towed by gunboats to Wad Hamed camp where it bivouacked at 1700hrs on Sunday 22 August. After three days of 'fatigues' - adjusting camel loads, practising loading them and so on, all the while combating terrific dust storms and dirt and sleeping out every night fully equipped under arms - the Grenadiers and other units rose at 0330hrs on 25 August, packed up and at 0530hrs left Wad Hamed on their march towards Khartoum.

On 1 September, the column halted at 1230hrs, five miles from Omdurman, where scarcely had they had time for a meal than they were warned of the advance of a large enemy force, and ordered to construct a *zariba*. Though no attack materialised, half the troops remained under arms all night. At 0330hrs the column was once again ordered to stand to arms, which they did until well after daybreak, when they were dismissed for breakfast;

'The Hon. E. D. Loch and signallers had meantime re-occupied the hill, and

Men of the 1st Battalion, the Queen's Own Cameron Highlanders, washing and shaving whilst their train was stopped at Abu Hamed.

NAM. neg no 21027

word came thence that an immense body of Dervishes formed in three wings were advancing rapidly straight on us. All camels, &c., were promptly sent to the rear of the zereba, and at 6.30 a.m. the host of Dervishes appeared with countless banners, singing and yelling- a most magnificent sight which one can never see again. You know all about the battle, or at least you ought to. It has been fully described by abler pens than mine.[4]

At 1630hrs the column started for Omdurman; the 1st Battalion, Grenadier Guards were the first British troops to enter. On Sunday 4 September eighteen officers and 48 men from every battalion proceeded in steamers to Khartoum;

'... where all had the satisfaction of seeing the British and Egyptian flags hoisted on Gordon's Palace, and took part in that most impressive and never-to-be-forgotten service...

The Queen's Company, 1st Battalion, the Grenadier Guards, coming down from Omdurman to the Atbara in a gyassa. The regimental red and blue cockades on the men's helmets, and the protective neck curtains and spine pads are clearly visible.

NAM. neg no 13191

September 5th, both British Brigades marched through the streets, great mosque enclosure etc... of Omdurman, halting to see the Mahdi's tomb, Khalifa's house etc ...[5]

On 10 September the Grenadier Battalion started back in sixteen *gyassas* (native sailing boats), three of them, including one with '... all our battalion loot, the Sirdar's presents, brass gun from battlefield, standards, drums, coats of mail, swords, spears ...'[6] foundering in a storm.

By 14 September the Battalion was back at Atbara ready to retrace its footsteps to the Delta;

'In due course we reached Wadi Halfa, and Assouan, and then came that awful train journey again to Luxor and Cairo, where we arrived smothered in dust. Only stopped for breakfast at the station and came straight on to our camp at Sidi Gabr, close to Alexandria.[7]

It is with scenes taken in this camp beside the sea that the album closes. The series of 160 loose photographs[8] taken by Loch are, when duplicates of those in the album are set aside, found to focus on the river journeys undertaken by the Battalion, and contain much interesting detail, the overwhelming impression being of cramped conditions.

On 1 October 1898 the 1st Battalion, Grenadier Guards marched through huge crowds from Waterloo Station to Wellington Barracks. The Commanding Officer, Lieutenant-Colonel Villiers Hatton, was made a CB: five officers won the DSO and five NCOs the DCM. Before the end of the year some 29 men died of enteric contracted in Egypt. The following June the regiment was awarded KHARTOUM as a battle honour.

The Queen's Own Cameron Highlanders, breakfasting at Luxor station.

NAM. neg no 21040

Guard-mounting at the Grenadiers' camp, Sidi Gabr, near Alexandria.

NAM. neg no 21174

'CHARIOTS OF WAR'

STEAM ROAD TRANSPORT IN SOUTH AFRICA, 1899-1902

MARION HARDING

The uses to which steam-driven vehicles were put during wartime were far from being as spectacular as that envisaged in the following extract from a letter to the editor of Colburn's *United Service Magazine* in 1832;

> '... in former times chariots of war were highly esteemed for their destructive operation yet ... were ultimately disused on one account viz the great difficulty of managing horses when frightened or wounded and the impossibility of impelling them on the pikes of a formidable phalanx. This objection would have a double weight with the modern use of fire arms ... the great forte of steam is its passiveness. Secure the boiler and the machinery from the stroke of a cannonball, and you might drive a steam chariot triumphantly through a regiment. Imagine three or four of these machines driven at a galloping speed through a square of infantry ... a body of cavalry about fifty yards in the rear would enter the furrows ploughed by these formidable chariots, and give the coup de grâce ... the chariots might be armed with scythes both in front and flank; and if the first shock were avoided by the men opening their ranks, they might easily be made sufficiently manageable to wheel round and return on any part of the square which stood firm.'[1]

Road locomotives were first used in the Crimea a quarter of a century later. They were employed in the transport of heavy artillery and of wagon-loads of ammunition from the magazines at Balaclava to the front across tracts of country impassable by other vehicles.

In the period following the Crimean War steam traction engines were used for the transport of camp material, for filling the water tanks, and in pumping water. The report of the Commander-in-Chief, Lord Wolseley, on the manœuvres at Salisbury in 1898, contained only one reference to them; 'The manœuvres show clearly that mechanical traction by means of traction engines is an efficient supplement to animal traction, especially in carrying supplies in the rear of an army'.[2]

The war in South Africa opened up new prospects for the traction engine. Mechanical transport was especially valuable in a country where the conditions necessitated the use of draught oxen and supply columns became of almost unmanageable length, requiring the troops detached for convoy duty to be proportionately numerous. Rinderpest (a virulent, infectious disease affecting ruminant animals, especially oxen, characterised by fever, dysentery and inflammation of the mucous membranes) and horse fever, made it impossible to rely only on animals.

A special traction engine detachment of 100 men, the 45th Company, Royal Engineers, together with three civilian engineers and a few civilian drivers was formed under the command of Colonel J L B Templer, who had been instrumental in persuading the War Office to recognise the value of the engines. In November 1899 fifteen engines had been sent to South Africa. Those used at the outset of the campaign were not altogether suited to the demands of that Continent and Messrs Fowler of Leeds received an order from the War Office to manufacture traction engines more suitable for use there. Fortunately the firm had already supplied the Boer Republics of the Transvaal and Orange Free State with engines for use in mining and agriculture and were therefore well acquainted with the problems involved.

A steam traction engine and train crossing a river in South Africa, c1900.

Steam traction had the advantage of speed over animal traction. On a fairly good road oxen could accomplish about two miles per hour. Traction engines could keep up an average of four miles per hour unless the roads were very bad, and under favourable conditions could reach eight. They could ascend inclines which animals could not attempt and could even cross soft ground. If the going was very bad, the engine would proceed alone, and having made some progress would let out a rope, winding the wagons up behind it. If the ground was so soft that even the engine alone could make no headway it was sometimes possible to fix an anchor some distance ahead, the engine winding itself along and afterwards sending back the rope for the

Armoured steam transport, c1898.

wagons. Bennet Burleigh, war correspondent of *The Daily Telegraph*, described traction engines in use during the passage of the Tugela;

> 'The much-laughed-at score of Aldershot traction engines did not stick or flounder in the mud, but lumbered about doing duty with comparative ease and considerable regularity. An ox-wagon stuck in the middle of Blaauw Krans Drift. Eighty oxen were tried but were unable to move the wagon an inch. A traction engine was requisitioned ... and walked away with the wagon, conveying it some distance to a high and dry part of the roadway.[3]

The usefulness of the engines extended beyond simply towing wagons. Most of the engines which were sent to South Africa were fitted so that they could drive a crane, dynamo or pump from the fly-wheel. When the engine reached camp, it was not rested for several hours as animals had of necessity to be, but was used to load or unload wagons, generate electricity for military searchlights, or pump water for the whole camp.

Some traction engines and wagons were armoured with steel sufficiently thick to protect them from rifle fire and shrapnel. It was proposed to employ 'trains' of these armoured engines to bring up heavy guns against fortified Boer positions. All working parts were brought within the protection of armour plates which could be easily removed when it was unnecessary to burden the engines with the extra weight.

The wagons were designed to War Office specifications. The sides could be opened upwards or closed inwards, according to the purpose for which the wagon was being used. If they were to be occupied by men the sides were fixed in a vertical position, the top open to the sky. They incorporated loopholes which could be opened partially or completely, or entirely closed. When the wagons carried ammunition, the sides were inclined inwards to form a complete bullet- and waterproof cover.

The first of the armoured engines, with four bullet-proof trucks, arrived in South Africa in July 1900, to be followed by a second two weeks later. A total of four Fowler B5s, as they were called, were armoured. The first two armoured road trains were sent to Bloemfontein, where the plate was removed from both engines and trucks to make armoured railway trains. Towards the end of 1901 the general officer commanding the Kimberley District asked for further trucks to be fitted with armour so that the troops needed for road convoy escort duties could be reduced, and the War Office was requested to supply two armoured trucks. Recalling the fate of the first two sent, the War Office chose not to meet the request.

The gun-carrying truck inspired a prominent German military writer, Lieutenant-Colonel Otfried Layriz,[4] to suggest that quick-firing guns should be mounted on the wagons to act as a sort of mobile fort to protect bridges and other strategic points against flying columns of Boers. The idea, which anticipated by many years some elements of the tank, was not adopted.

Traction engines were far from popular in some quarters. An article in one Cape Town newspaper complained that;

> '... the employment of traction engines with their heavy trains ... has had the effect of well-nigh ruining the main arteries of traffic in town and district. The huge fluted wheels of the cumbrous machines bite into the roads, pick up road metalling by the square yard, carry it for a distance and then deposit it in a heap. The process is repeated with every revolution of the wheels, and the soft bits of the road soon become deep holes, veritable pitfalls to other species of pedestrian and vehicular traffic.[5]

Even apart from this incidental damage it was the great weight of the engines which diminished their usefulness. Bigger and more powerful engines required larger quantities of coal and water to power them, with the result that the useful load which could be carried was relatively small. This consideration was reflected in the *Report of the Royal Commission on the War in South Africa* published in 1903. It stated that;

> '... traction engines with trains of trucks were used to carry supplies across the Veldt with a considerable degree of success. Their employment is limited by circumstances of weather, ground, fuel and water, and they can, in Lord Kitchener's opinion, only be regarded as supplementary to animal transport.[6]

The demise of the steam traction engine as a means of wartime transport was hastened by the invention of the internal combustion engine by Gottlieb Daimler in 1886. This engine was adopted for transport and fighting vehicles almost to the exclusion of steam by about 1910.

THE DEVELOPMENT OF SOLDIERS' WEAPONS, 1816-1914

MICHAEL BALDWIN & KEITH MILLER

Between the conclusion of the Napoleonic Wars and the outbreak of the First World War in 1914 the British soldier progressed from a battlefield which had been dominated by short-range, muzzle-loading weapons for more than two centuries to one in which the products of the Industrial Revolution were in full and devastating sway - the machine-gun and quick-firing artillery. During this period the British Army was a deeply conservative organisation, responding mainly to technological advances made by its potential rivals and enemies in Europe.

THE SOLDIER'S FIREARM

The basic firearm of the infantry in 1816 was the .75 inch India Pattern flintlock musket, a cheaper version of the Long Land Pattern and its variants which had served the Army for nearly a century. As the Army contracted after the Napoleonic Wars the India Pattern was replaced in the Foot Guards and some senior line regiments by the New Land Pattern musket, introduced in 1802, which was still a flintlock muzzle-loader with a maximum effective range of 150 yards. An increase of range for the common musket was not a prerequisite at the time,

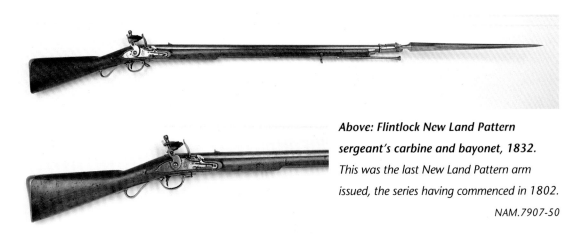

Above: Flintlock New Land Pattern sergeant's carbine and bayonet, 1832. This was the last New Land Pattern arm issued, the series having commenced in 1802.

NAM.7907-50

Flintlock New Land Pattern sergeant's carbine, 12 bore, 1832. Close-up, showing the flintlock mechanism.

NAM. 7907-50

Flintlock Baker rifle, calibre .625 inch, c1805. First introduced in 1800, the Baker remained in service until 1840.

NAM. 7704-47

as most formal infantry engagements opened at 50 yards or less. The cavalry were armed with flintlock carbines - the heavy cavalry with a 26-inch barrel weapon and the light cavalry with the sixteen-inch Paget carbine. However, as the lance was re-introduced in 1816, the cavalry regarded the sword and the lance as their principal weapons.

One section of the Army, the Rifle Corps, had a more accurate arm. The Baker Rifle, introduced in 1800, had a rifled barrel with a reduced calibre of .625 inches which was accurate up to 300 yards. Other than that it was not significantly different in operation to the other firearms.

However, civilian manufacturers and marksmen were already embracing technological change. The percussion lock, in which the charge was ignited by a detonating cap containing mercuric fulminate, promised much more reliable shooting. Patented in 1818, the new system rapidly gained ground with sporting shooters but little was done in military circles dominated by the Duke of Wellington, then Commander-in-Chief. By 1830, it appeared that the French were experimenting

Percussion Pattern 1853 Enfield rifle, calibre .577 inch, 1854. This was the British Army's first universally adopted rifled weapon.

NAM. 7907-60

with the percussion system and this galvanised the Army to experiment with the new method. Percussion showed itself overwhelmingly superior to flintlock ignition and new percussion muskets and carbines, based on locks developed by George Lovell, Inspector of Small Arms at the Royal Small Arms Factory, Enfield, were introduced in 1838, together with conversions of flintlock weapons. Stocks of a later series were destroyed in a disastrous fire at the Tower of London in 1841 and the new type was re-issued as the Pattern 1842. Produced in three barrel lengths and

two calibres, this pattern equipped the infantry, sergeants of infantry and the Royal Artillery, while the Victoria carbine, actually introduced in 1837, became the arm for all cavalry. The Baker rifle was replaced by the two-groove Brunswick rifle, which was widely criticised because of the difficulty of loading a ball into the tightly rifled bore when fouled by firing. It was clear that a new system was required to make the rifle more effective and less tiring to use.

Breech-loading Snider rifle Mk1, calibre .577inch, 1867. Close-up, showing Snider's breech-loading conversion of the Enfield Rifle.

NAM. 7709-125

Breech-Loading Martini-Henry rifle Mk II, calibre .45 inch, 1875. Close-up, showing the breech. This was the Army's first purpose-built breech-loader using reduced calibre ammunition.

Short Magazine Lee-Enfield rifle Mk III, calibre .303 inch, 1913. Close-up of the breech mechanism. Loaded by five-round chargers, the SMLE remained in service from 1903 to 1955.

Experiments in France with expanding bullets had begun in the 1820s and culminated in the Minié system perfected in 1849. This system allowed cylindro-conoidal bullets to be easily loaded and also improved accuracy, as the hollow-based projectiles expanded on firing to grip the grooves of the rifling. The success of this method led to the possibility of issuing rifled arms to all troops. The British Government quickly moved to utilise the Minié system, incorporating its principles into the Pattern 1851 Rifled Musket. This was quickly superseded by the .577 inch Enfield Rifle-Musket of 1853, later manufactured at the new Royal Small Arms Factory at Enfield Lock. Although only a small proportion of troops were armed with the Enfield Rifle during the Crimean War its long-range accuracy swiftly persuaded the War Department to make it the standard weapon throughout the Army. In

Views of the Royal Small Arms Factory Enfield, *1861*.

Wood engraving from The Illustrated London News, *21 September 1861, p298*

SMLE Mk III and 1907 pattern bayonet.

colonial wars marksmen could hit targets over 1,000 yards away, while the penetrative power of the bullet diminished but little over these ranges. Used as a 'long' rifle by the infantry and in a shortened form by other branches of the Army its only drawback was a slow rate of fire.

These new developments in infantry weapons highlighted the relatively ineffective weapons still on issue to the cavalry. Firearms were rarely used in action because of the difficulty of re-loading them on horseback. Experiments carried out with breech-loading rifles in Germany and France pointed the way to easier and faster loading and in 1857 the Army began testing breech-loading carbines for the cavalry. After many competitive trials, in which American carbines were also tested, the Westley Richards capping breech-loader was adopted by the British cavalry in 1861. Although a significant improvement, these weapons were handicapped by a poor cartridge; further technological change was to make these new carbines redundant within a few years.

Flintlock New Land Pattern cavalry pistol, calibre .65 inch; Oxfordshire Yeomanry Cavalry, c1820. The standard pistol, with a 9-inch barrel incorporating a swivel rammer.

The Prussian Army had defeated both Denmark and Austria between 1864 and 1866. Part of its success was attributed to the breech-loading needle-gun with its centre-fire cartridge. Although the British Army rejected the German system on account of gas leakage and corrosion, it was clear that some form of breech-loading firearm was to be the weapon of the future. In 1866 the British Army adopted the Snider rifle, which was a conversion of the Enfield Rifle-Musket. By 1867, an improved metal-bodied cartridge developed by Colonel Edward M Boxer, Superintendent of the Royal Laboratory at Woolwich, made the Snider an efficient and fast-firing weapon, devastating in the colonial wars of the period. However, at the same time the Army was testing a much more radical type of weapon; a purpose-built breech-loading rifle with a reduced calibre of .45 inch.

Percussion Pattern 1842 pistol for lancers, calibre .75 inch; 12th Lancers, c1845. This was basically a flintlock pistol, converted to percussion. After 1838, when the pistol was abolished as a cavalry weapon, these weapons were only issued to sergeant-majors and trumpeters.

199

Double-action Beaumont-Adams percussion revolver, 54 bore, c1860. Along with the Colt, these commercially manufactured pistols were the first revolvers issued to the Army.

NAM. 6312-251-205

Breech-loading Enfield revolver Mk I, calibre .476 inch, 1880. Developed at the Enfield Small Arms Factory, the pistol was not a notable success.

NAM. 6312-251-277

Breech-loading Webley revolver Mk IV, calibre .455 inch, 1900; Imperial Yeomanry. First introduced in 1887, the Webley remained basically unchanged until the First World War.

NAM. 8902-165

The result was the Martini-Henry, introduced in 1871 and destined to remain the standard rifle and carbine of the British Army for nearly two decades.

Experiments with explosive compounds in France in the late nineteenth century brought into use smokeless powder for cartridges, thus removing the clouds of white smoke which had hitherto obscured the battlefield. This improved propellant also led to an increase in projectile velocity and enabled even smaller calibres to be considered - at first .298 inch and finally .303 inch. The combination of a simple and efficient bolt-action and box-magazine resulted in the development of the Lee-action rifle, adopted in 1888. At first with Metford seven-groove rifling and, later, with the Enfield five-groove system to counteract the corrosive effects of the new powder, Cordite, this rifle was to be the British soldier's personal weapon for 70 years. Even here, the conservatism of the Army caused problems; the magazine was seen as a last resort and officially the rifles were to be used as single-shot weapons to save ammunition. During the South African War, the clip-fed Mauser rifles and carbines of the Boers proved superior to the Lee-Enfields both in rate of fire and accuracy. Charger-loading, by which five rounds could be loaded at a time, combined with improvements to the sights, solved this problem. However, during the South African War, the Lee-Enfield cavalry carbine was severely criticised and development was concentrated on the concept of a universal rifle for all arms of the Service. Introduced in 1902, the Rifle, .303 inch, Short Magazine Lee-Enfield Mk I, had several teething problems before being re-sealed as a pattern in 1903. Charger-loaded, with a ten-shot magazine, accurate up to 1,000 yards with a maximum range of 2,800 yards, the SMLE in the hands of trained troops was a potent weapon. During initial engagements of the First World War, in 1914, German troops thought they faced machine-guns rather than rifle fire.

Pistols were considered to be of little importance during the nineteenth century. Carried mostly by cavalry they were fired once, if at all, with the trooper resorting to sword or lance for the charge. Apart from the change from flintlock to percussion ignition in the 1840's the Army's pistols remained basically similar to those of the eighteenth century, normally with a nine-inch barrel and hinged rammer. In 1838 the pistol was abolished as a cavalry arm and only retained, at thirteen to a regiment, for use by sergeant-majors and trumpeters. The Crimean War and Indian Mutiny changed the Army's views on pistols. The new revolvers had been displayed at the Great Exhibition of 1851 and many had been privately purchased by officers in the cavalry and foot regiments. In the hand-to-hand fighting that occurred in both conflicts revolvers, the majority made by Colt or Adams, came into their own. Initial purchases by the Royal Navy were followed by further consignments for the Army which had set aside its earlier reservations. The Army eventually chose the Adams revolver in .45 inch calibre as having better stopping power than the .36 inch Colt. In fact .45 inch remained the nominal calibre throughout virtually the whole of this period.

Both the Colt and Adams revolvers were muzzle-loaders but, during the 1860s in parallel with longarms, the Army turned to breech-loading weapons firing metallic cartridges. However, the commercial weapons bought were disappointing and many were rejected as defective by inspectors. In 1880 the War Department decided to design and produce a revolver at Enfield; this became the official pattern for Army and Navy and was issued to cavalry rank-and-file for the first time. The Enfield self-extracting revolver was not a success and, after trials, the Webley revolver Mk I was approved in 1887. With, normally, a four-inch barrel this robust pistol remained virtually unchanged until 1914. Various small changes resulted in five separate Marks by that date.

EDGED WEAPONS

During the nineteenth century the principal weapon of the cavalry was the sword. The whole period was one of controversy between those experts who advocated the efficacy of a cutting

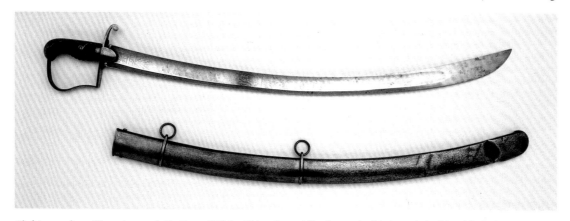

Light cavalry officers' sword, Pattern 1796. This stirrup-hilted sword with broad slashing blade has been regarded as one of the British Army's finest swords.

NAM. 7502-2

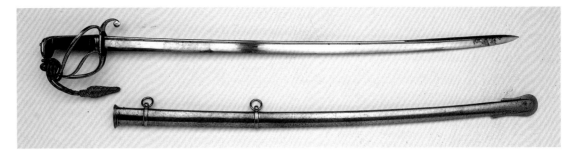

Light cavalry officers' sword, Pattern 1822. *The 'three-bar hilt' had a compromise blade, which was intended for cutting and thrusting. In action, it was found to be ineffective in both modes.*

NAM. 6509 15.

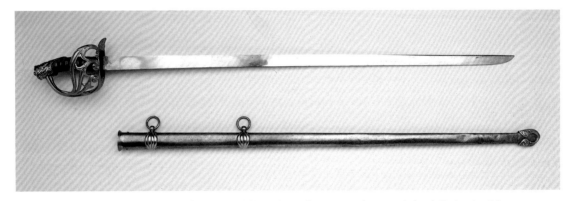

Royal Horse Guards officers' sword, Pattern 1834. *Some heavy cavalry swords had distinctive hilts, notably the brass variants made for the Royal Horse Guards.*

NAM. 6602-24-3

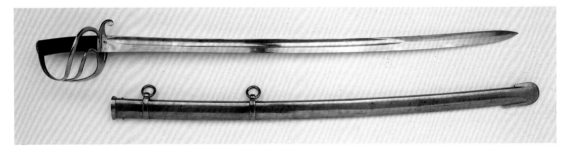

Universal cavalry troopers' sword, Pattern 1853. *Intended to be the standard sword for all cavalry, the Pattern 1853 was severely criticised after the Crimean War.*

NAM. 8704-33

or thrusting blade, or a combination of both. In addition, 'sword scandals' erupted at every major conflict as each successive pattern of sword was denounced as faulty, imperfectly made, incorrectly designed or improperly procured.

In 1816 the heavy cavalry regiments were equipped with a rather clumsy sword, but the light cavalry had one of the best swords ever issued, with a curved blade ideal for a slashing cut. Both these swords were replaced in 1821, the heavy cavalry with a similar blade but better hand protection, while the light cavalry lost their slashing blade and stirrup hilt, being provided with a 'cut-and-thrust' sword with a three-bar hilt. During the long peace, various modifications were suggested for these swords but little was done.

However, in 1853 a 'universal pattern' sword, designed at Enfield, was introduced for all cavalry. Once again it was a compromise 'cut-and-thrust' weapon and it was soon criticised for its poor grip and defective blade. This criticism mounted to a crescendo during the Crimean War, when the point was reported to be incapable of penetrating Russian greatcoats. In 1864 it was replaced with a sword with an identical blade but with a more extensive bowl guard. This pattern lasted until the Afghan War of 1878 when it was, in turn, criticised for being too heavy and clumsy. After much experimentation, a much lighter and handier sword was introduced in 1882, but this very advantage made the weapons less durable on active service. So commenced a period when swords were introduced at regular intervals, i.e. 1885, 1890 and 1899, but which were no better received. The War Office at last decided to design

Cavalry troopers' sword, Pattern 1908. *Introduced after lengthy consultation and testing, the Pattern 1908 has been considered to be the finest sword ever issued to the British cavalry.*

NAM. 5905-107

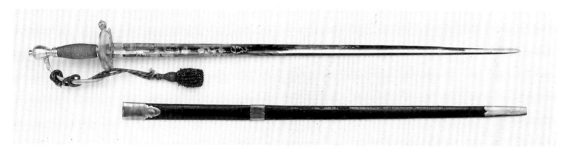

Infantry officers' sword, Pattern 1796. *With its flimsy guard and poor blade, the sword was never regarded as a serious hand-to-hand weapon.*

NAM. 7706-56

Infantry officers' sword, Pattern 1822. *The 'Gothic' hilt in its steel-mounted version is still in use today. As with the Pattern 1796, it was regarded as more decorative than useful.*

NAM. 6209-27

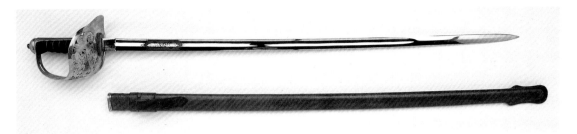

Infantry officers' sword, Pattern 1897. *A larger-hilted version of the Pattern l892 sword, this was regarded as an excellent fighting sword. A leather scabbard was introduced in 1899.*

NAM. 9208-151

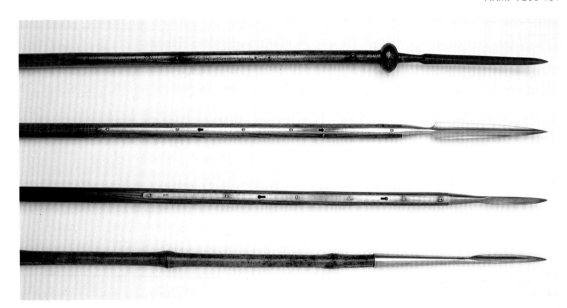

Lances (from top to bottom), Patterns 1820, 1846, 1860, 1868. *The lance, reintroduced in 1816, was tried in several patterns throughout the century. Lance shafts could be made from ash or bamboo.*

NAM. 9309-101, 6310-164-2, 6706-40-21, 6310-165-2

Bayonets *(from top to bottom), New Land Pattern, 1802; Enfield Pattern, 1856; Martini-Henry, Pattern 1876; SMLE, Pattern 1907. Throughout the century bayonets were seen as an integral part of the soldier's longarm. Generally speaking, they progressed from socket to sword types, although the Pattern 1876 was a temporary reversion to the socket.*

NAM. 7205-8-31, 6309-380-14, 6312-251-150, 9207-210

a sword scientifically, conducting exhaustive trials and taking account of suggestions from the cavalry regiments. While these tests were being conducted the engagements during the South African War proved that the cavalry charge was already obsolete against an enemy armed with modern weapons. It is therefore ironic that, when the thrusting sword was finally approved in 1908, it was arguably the best sword ever produced for cavalry which would soon find itself on a battlefield where the machine-gun was the dominant weapon.

For infantry officers the sword had become a less essential weapon and the Pattern 1822 sword, with the so-called 'Gothic' hilt, remained in service with some regiments throughout the whole period. A new thrusting blade was introduced in 1892, which together with a better and more comprehensive guard introduced in 1895, resulted in an excellent fighting sword. But, as with the cavalry, the use of personal firearms and automatic weapons rendered the sword obsolete. Infantry privates no longer carried swords but during this period all infantry and artillery firearms were fitted with their appropriate bayonets.

1816 marked the re-introduction of the lance as the secondary weapon of the cavalry. As related earlier in this book, the British had been impressed with the performance of Napoleon's Polish lancers and there was lively debate during the nineteenth century as to whether the sword or lance was the more effective weapon for cavalry. The lance was little used on the European battlefields but was employed extensively in Indian conflicts. However, the South African War dealt the *coup de grace* to the lance and it was abolished in 1903. Perversely, it was re-introduced in 1909 and was carried into battle in 1914, a medieval anachronism on the modern battlefield.

MACHINE-GUNS

The continuing acceleration of technology during the nineteenth century eventually produced a weapon that radically changed battlefield tactics - the machine-gun. By 1871 the hand-cranked Gatling gun, capable of firing heavy .45 and .65 inch calibre bullets at 600 rounds a minute, was available for the British Army. These guns, used in colonial wars of the period, terrified the native armies of the Ashantis and Zulus and broke up their massed

Maxim Machine-Gun, calibre .303, c1900. With the introduction of the fully-automatic Maxim gun in 1889, earlier hand-cranked machine-guns were rendered obsolete. By 1890 the Maxim was the only machine-gun on issue to the Army.

NAM. 6605-1

Vickers Class C Machine-Gun, calibre .303, c1910. Privately developed, this weapon was quickly adopted by the Army as the Vickers Mk 1 in 1912. The Vickers remained in service with the British Army until the middle 1960s.

NAM. 6710-47.

Hand-cranked, Nordenfelt three-barrelled machine-gun, calibre .45inch. Used initially by the Royal Navy, the Nordenfelt was available in three, five and even ten-barrelled variants. The first field carriages were too heavy for active service and the lightweight three-barrelled version was introduced in 1887.
Taken from T Nordenfelt, The Nordenfelt Machine Guns, *Portsmouth & London (1884)*

NAM. neg no 78094

charges. Other machine-guns in use were the Gardner and Nordenfelt types but these were also manually operated. The appearance of a truly automatic gun, the Maxim, in 1889, later allied to the smokeless .303 inch cartridge, gave the machine-gunner a dominant role on the battlefield. Experience against such weapons in the South African War gave the British Army the best-trained men in modern warfare but conservatism and misunderstanding initially resulted in machine-guns being considered as an adjunct to artillery and, later, to be issued only in small quantities per battalion. The Maxim, after development by Vickers-Maxim, finally became the Vickers Mk 1 in 1912 and remained in service for a further six decades.

ARTILLERY

Throughout the period 1816-91, although gunnery was a remarkably exact science within the limitations of range and the tactical principles of the time, artillery in its various forms of fortress, siege, field, mountain and horse had changed less than any other arm. The main improvements, up to the late 1870s, were to ammunition - particularly to the form and fuzing of shells for specific purposes. These innovations were, in general, at the instigation of Edward Boxer, (then a Captain), of the Royal Laboratory. The middle decades of the century saw the tentative introduction of breech-loading for the lighter guns, based on the experiments of William Armstrong and Joseph Whitworth but, due to problems with breech-sealing and operation, these were discarded in 1865. The British artillery reverted to the muzzle-loading principle, albeit with rifled ordnance, until the successful re-introduction in 1881 of breech-loading 'quick-firing' field-pieces firing self-sealing metallic ammunition. Advances in metallurgy allowed

Muzzle-loading 9-pounder brass field gun and carriage, c1855. By the middle of the century muzzle-loading smooth-bore cannon were approaching the end of their useful lives.

NAM. 8404-153-59

Rifled, breech-loading Armstrong 12-pounder field gun, c1861. Sir William Armstrong's artillery experiments resulted in a viable breech-loading field gun by 1860, but problems with breech-sealing and difficulties encountered on active service led to the gun's withdrawal from service in 1865.

breech-loading principles to be applied to the heavier equipments firing separate charges and projectiles - up to the monstrous 80- and 100-ton coastal and siege guns in fashion with all nations at that time.

Experience during the South African War, where German innovations were much in evidence, led to the introduction in 1903 of the eighteen-pounder quick-firing field-gun which became the mainstay of British mobile artillery. Firing a variety of explosive and shrapnel shells these guns, together with the machine-gun, would dominate the industrialised battlefield of the First World War.

Breech-loading 18-pounder field gun, c1914. Introduced in 1904, the 18-pounder was a steel, quick-firing field gun. It was one of the most widely used artillery types of the First World War, firing over 100 million rounds.

From Text-book of Gun Carriages and Gun Mountings, *London (1924)*

THE KING'S AFRICAN RIFLES AND THE EXPEDITION AGAINST THE NANDI, 1905-1906

MARION HARDING

During the last decade of the nineteenth century Britain consolidated the interests she had acquired in eastern and central Africa by the declaration of Protectorates over East Africa, Jubaland and Uganda.

The military needs of the new territories were at first met by the formation of Volunteer Contingents in India, but the Government of India was reluctant to establish a precedent whereby that country became a recruiting ground for the support of British interests in Africa. The fact that the arrangement was an expensive one gave an added incentive to the enlistment and training of indigenous tribesmen as soldiers although the Indian contingents continued to form part of the regular military forces of the territories until the growth of confidence in the reliability of locally raised regiments enabled them to be withdrawn. The first Indian contingent was raised for service in central Africa in 1891; the last left Uganda in 1913.

THE ORIGINS OF THE KING'S AFRICAN RIFLES

The local regiments which superseded the Indian contingents had been allowed to develop on an *ad hoc* basis and were often led by regular Army officers on leave in Africa. In 1895 they were formally embodied in three colonial regiments. In Nyasaland the native levies which had been formed around the nucleus of the Indian contingent were re-organized as the Central Africa Rifles, re-named the Central Africa Regiment in 1900. In January 1899, when the South African War was imposing a severe strain on Britain's military resources, a second battalion was raised for employment under the War Office outside the Protectorate. In Uganda, Sudanese troops formerly of the army of the Khedive of Egypt provided the basis of the Uganda Rifles and in East Africa the private armed forces raised by the Imperial British East Africa Company to protect its trading interests were amalgamated into the East Africa Rifles when in 1895 the East Africa Protectorate was formed and the administration of the territories passed from the Company to the Foreign Office. During the seven years of their existence the regiments were staffed by officers on secondment from the regular Army.

By the turn of the century, it had become apparent from the experience gained in a number of operations that none of the territories could be self-sufficient in a military sense. In West Africa the local forces had been centralised to form the West African Frontier Force and early in 1901 the War Office pointed out the advantages of adopting a similar system in East Africa.

The main object of the re organization was the fusion of existing forces into a single regiment with a common policy in organization, training and equipment whose battalions were allocated to each territory. Also under consideration was the formation of a reserve battalion which could be sent wherever it was required at short notice.

On 1 January 1902 the King's African Rifles came into being, with the original forces of the Protectorates incorporated as follows;

- 1st (Central Africa) Battalion, eight companies (formerly 1st Central Africa Rifles)
- 2nd (Central Africa) Battalion, six companies (formerly 2nd Central Africa Rifles)
- 3rd (East Africa) Battalion, seven companies and one camel company (formerly East Africa Rifles)
- 4th (Uganda) Battalion, nine companies (formerly the African companies of the Uganda Rifles)
- 5th (Uganda) Battalion, four companies (formerly the Indian Contingent of the Uganda Rifles)
- 6th (Somaliland) Battalion, formed later from local levies in British Somaliland

One of the two Central Africa battalions was always employed in operations or garrison duty outside the Protectorate. The two companies of the Indian contingent in central Africa were to be attached to whichever battalion was on internal garrison duty. The camel company of the 3rd Battalion was intended for service in Jubaland only. In the ordinances of the King's African Rifles (1902) Commissioners were empowered, at the direction of the Secretary of State, to order the employment of a battalion or any part thereof outside its own protectorate. The total strength of the regiment soon after formation was returned as 104 officers and 4,579 native officers and men.

THE NANDI

During the first few years of its existence the new regiment had to contend with a number of tribal disturbances, some of which involved operations on a considerable scale. One tribe which proved particularly troublesome was the Nandi, inhabitants of the country along and beyond the mountainous escarpments west of the Rift Valley. When the boundaries of the Uganda Protectorate were expanded to include the Nandi country it fell to the Uganda Rifles to undertake

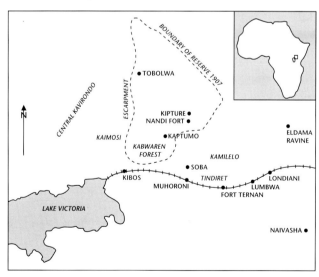

punitive expeditions in search of murderers or to exact fines of cattle. Both the nature of the country and the organization of the tribe made such operations difficult. The Nandi lived in scattered

'E' Company, 1st Bn, King's African Rifles, *which formed part of No 1 Column. Lieutenant-Colonel Harrison stated; 'The marching powers displayed by the rank and file, burdened with blankets, ammunition, accoutrements, and - at times - seven days' rations on the person, were often remarkable'.*

NAM. neg no 66610

homesteads rather than villages and had evolved their own military system. The tribe was divided into a number of *pororiet* comprising a deliberative council concerned with the affairs of war and a fighting unit of young men of military age. Such an organization enabled the tribesmen to plan a concerted resistance well suited to the nature of the country, with the result that expeditions against them generally met with only qualified success.

A telegram received on 26 September 1905 by Alfred Lyttleton, Secretary of State for Colonies, from the Acting Commissioner for the British East Africa Protectorate, Frederick (later Sir Frederick) Jackson, describes the circumstances which precipitated the largest punitive expedition to be mounted in the Protectorate with the exception of the Jubaland Expedition of 1901;

> 'During the last six months the Nandi have repeatedly committed murders and highway robberies on the railway and on the main roads near the lake; among those killed being soldiers of the 3rd battalion, policemen, coolies, and traders. This has caused cessation of work and deadlock on railway besides loss of prestige. All white settlers have had to leave their farms owing to fear of attack. In July Commissioner, Harrison, Bagge, and I held a meeting with Nandi Chiefs, and it was arranged that the actual murderers should be given up and blood money paid. Later on, owing to the chiefs making representations that the murderers had fled, it was agreed that they should be pardoned on the condition of payment of blood money. Nothing, however, has been done towards reparation and murders and thefts continue. Commissioner, on his return from tour of inspection, arranged, as the Nandi were still truculent and defiant, for expedition to visit their country, and decided to mobilise field force of King's African Rifles, assisted by levies ... Expedition leaves shortly under Harrison.[1]

THE OPERATIONS

The arrangements for the mobilisation and the composition of the field force were determined at a meeting held in Nairobi on 26 September 1905. It was to consist of six companies, 1st King's African Rifles, six companies, 3rd King's African Rifles, 200 police and 1,000 native levies. It was proposed that operations should commence about the third week in October.

On 28 September, after careful consideration of the available intelligence and consultation with those of the local authorities who possessed knowledge and experience of the Nandi tribe, the Officer Commanding Nandi Field Force, Lieutenant-Colonel E G Harrison DSO, published his mobilisation orders. He planned to divide his force into four columns which would strike north and west from the railway, whilst holding Kaimosi Mission with a detachment and the Kibos-Londiani section with line of communication troops. The aim of this first stage in the operations was to drive the Nandi away from Lumbwa and to clear the Nandi country proper of fighting men and livestock, pushing a large number into the Kabwaren Forest where they could be dealt with by a subsequent concentration of the columns upon that area.

On 18 October No 1 Column comprising A, E and F Companies 1st King's African Rifles under Lieutenant-Colonel E H Gorges DSO marched north from Londiani and traversed Sirikiu and the Ravine: its operations were independent of those of the other three columns. No 2 Column, formed from B, C and D Companies 1st King's African Rifles under Major H A Walker, left Lumbwa on 20 October and advanced via Tindiret and the Kamilelo country to Kaptumo. On the same date No 3 Column of V and VI Companies 3rd King's African Rifles, led by Captain F W O Maycock, left Muhoroni for Kaptumo via the Soba Hills afterwards continuing along the escarpment to the west. No 4 Column comprising III and VII Companies 3rd King's African Rifles under Captain W E H Barrett concentrated at Nandi Fort and marched north to Tobolwa returning to Kaimosi along the escarpment that formed the boundary between the Nandi country and Kavirondo. Each column was accompanied by porters and supported by native levies.

A further two companies of 3rd King's African Rifles were detailed to two armoured patrol trains, whose steel trucks were proof against the enemy's arrows and bullets. They were to be used as mobile bases to attack parties of Nandi seen near the line. Operation orders, issued on 15 October, laid down that from the 21st of that month the trains were to patrol their respective sections of line daily. The orders also stated; 'Commanders of Columns and units on the Line will do their utmost to get into signalling communication with one another and with Nandi Fort whence messages will be transmitted to Headquarters'. The latter was established at Muhoroni.

The following entry from the Field Force Diary does little to convey the hardship of an operation carried out in a country broken up by hillsides and ravines, or the dangers of skirmishes with an enemy who, though possessed of few firearms, was not to be underestimated;

> 'Officer commanding No II Column reported by wire from Lumbwa that his total captures on the 21st are 411 cattle, 3,000 goats and sheep, while the enemy's casualties amounted to 81 killed. Further, that on the night of 21st some 200 of the enemy collected on hills round No II column zareba and during the night sniped camp with arrows.[2]

Captain Richard Meinertzhagen, who commanded a detachment of 3rd King's African

Major (temporary Lieutenant-Colonel) E H Gorges DSO was appointed a lieutenant-colonel by brevet in recognition of his services as commander of No 1 Column. In a despatch printed in The London Gazette *he was described by Lieutenant-Colonel Harrison as showing conspicuous ability in command of troops in the field.*

NAM. neg no 66612

Rifles at Nandi Fort and who acted as Staff Officer No 4 Column, records such a night attack in his *Kenya Diary (1902-1906)*;

'Last night at 9.15pm a considerable body of Nandi warriors crept unobserved to within arrow-shot of our camp and delivered a hail of poisoned arrows for about a minute. The alarm was at once sounded and the camp stood to arms. We blazed away with rifles and machine guns for about two minutes. One of the men at a machine gun was hit and fell over, so I took the gun and was at once hit in the hand by an arrow. When all the excitement was over we found that one porter and 7 goats had been killed, 7 men wounded and most of the porters severely frightened. Over 270 arrows were picked up in camp this morning.[3]

Occasionally the Field Force Diary itself reveals more than just statistics;

'... at noon yesterday (26th instant) a raiding party from No III Column, strength 12 rifles No 6 Company, 3rd King's African Rifles, and 21 spearmen, were cut to pieces at Kibturi (?Kipturi) by a strong body of Nandi under Arab Samboi, while driving looted cattle back to their column.

Rifles and ammunition lost.

Report brought in by two Masai levies who state that they are the two survivors of the party. They stated that the soldiers were unable to get off more than one round apiece before they were rushed. They themselves escaped (one wounded) by lying in a stream till dark.[4]

By 31 October, Harrison was able to report that according to intelligence received from various sources Nandi proper had been cleared of the enemy and his herds, and that a concentration of scattered bands with the remnants of their stock had taken place in the Kabwaren Forest. On that same day Harrison announced his intention to attack these by a concentric movement of Nos 2, 3 and 4 Columns, together with the detachments which had been detailed to the armoured trains, and on 2 November Headquarters moved from Muhoroni to Nandi in order that the operation could be better supervised.

By 7 November the principal chiefs were suing for peace and professing their readiness to settle in any reserve which the Government should decide upon. As there was no longer any objective for the Field Force to be directed against, Harrison planned to occupy the Nandi country with a network of company-strong detachments, well entrenched, in signal communication with one another. These detachments were to work through the districts in which they were posted and harry any Nandi who remained until the whole tribe had moved into the reserve selected for them. The country was further divided into two military districts, the eastern under Lieutenant-Colonel Gorges who had led No 1 Column and the western under Captain Barrett who had been in charge of No 4 Column.

Six days later, when the sites for the posts had been decided upon, orders were issued dissolving the flying column and distributing the detachments to their various bases. Arrangements were made for demobilising all Masai levies who on 14 November were to march towards Naivasha where they were to be paid off. On 14 November also, HQ moved

Men of 1st Bn, King's African Rifles fording a stream. The expedition, carried on as it was at high altitude and in difficult forest and hilly country, was 'trying to all concerned' and the officer commanding spoke highly of the conduct of the troops throughout the operations.

NAM. neg no 66613

to Kipture where the Chief Political Officer and Officer Commanding Troops were to meet a representative gathering of the Nandi chiefs to discuss the future settlement of the country.

Hostilities were suspended pending the results of the conference. On 1 December, the maintenance gangs were allowed to resume work on the railway and the local settlers, who had gathered at Lumbwa while operations were in progress were returned under guard to their farms.

As Officer Commanding Military District, Gorges was instructed to impress upon the Nandi that those who moved of their own accord before 15 January 1906 would get their stock returned in full; others would be moved by force.

The Kamelilo division of the tribe, who with the Kapchepkendi had been largely

A conference with chiefs of the Nyangori tribe. *The hostile attitude of the tribe, which was related to the Nandi, resulted in an attack against them on 10 December in which some 150 were killed.*

NAM. neg no 66611

responsible for the misdemeanours which had provoked the expedition, had already shown signs of restlessness and it was evident that the Field Force would be fully employed in supervising the move to the reserve. Further assistance in guarding the railway was therefore sought from Uganda and three British and two native officers and 98 Sikhs of the Indian Contingent were despatched to Muhoroni, while No 4 Company, 4th Battalion, King's African Rifles having handed over its duties at Jinja to the police, were sent to Fort Ternan.

On 14 January 1906 Captain Meinertzhagen wrote in his diary;

> 'As it now seems certain that the Nandi will not move into the reserve without force being used, we are to take part in a huge drive in a north-westerly direction, starting operations on the 19th. All crops are to be destroyed, all huts burned, and the country generally laid waste ... The driving line is divided into two wings, Gorges commanding the right wing and Hookey [Major H A] Walker the left ... The whole line is some 40 miles long and some 1100 men are employed, split up into 11 small columns.[5]

On 8 February the entry reads;

> 'Since this second phase of the expedition began my company has burned 917 huts, 239 granaries, and 46 stock enclosures, captured 8 prisoners, killed 51 of the enemy and captured 54 head of cattle and 399 sheep and goats. We have also destroyed 145 acres of standing crops, mostly millet. I doubt if a single hut or square yard of cultivation has been left behind the driving line ...[6]

Masai Levies. *They were usually armed with shields, spears, swords and knobkerries. Fifty Masai who had been discharged as time-expired from the police and 3rd Bn King's African Rifles were armed with rifles and attached as irregulars to No 3 Column.*

NAM. neg no 66614

On the following day, part of the driving line was reformed into a subsidiary or second line to catch any of the enemy who broke through the first line.

By 21 February Meinertzhagen was able to record;

> 'I arrived in Nandi Fort soon after breakfast ... I learn that the Nandi are moving fast into the reserve and that pressure is to be slightly relaxed. But a ring of posts is being established round the reserve, and Nandi found outside it are to be shot on sight.[7]

On 27 February the Field Force was disbanded, though five companies remained to garrison the district. In June those troops, 800 men with 100 armed police under Major Walker's command, carried out a drive of the whole area lasting three weeks, to ensure that no Nandi remained outside the reserve. The troops were withdrawn on 1 August: the Nandi had lost 1,117 killed, and the Government forces 121 killed and wounded.

This little known expedition against the Nandi is the subject of one of three albums of photographs taken by Oswald Gamble, which were donated to the National Army Museum in 1984.[8] Gamble, who was Paymaster of 1st King's African Rifles, was appointed Staff Officer (Finance Branch) in the mobilisation orders.[9] In a manuscript draft of the assembly timetables, prepared for the expedition by the Chief Staff Officer Major L H R Pope-Hennessy, Gamble is listed among those entraining at Nairobi for Muhoroni at 5.45pm on 19 October.[10] He and his travelling companions were assigned to No 3 Column and Headquarters. A number of photographs show detachments leaving Nairobi, the starting point for most of the regular troops involved in the campaign. Masai levies are recorded at Nakuru, where Gamble's train stopped for over eight hours on its journey to Muhoroni to pick up 200 of them together with a British Officer and 'two followers'. The officers who appear in groups and portraits were attached to No 1 Column but were probably photographed at Muhoroni. There are also views of the civil *boma* or enclosure at Nandi where Headquarters arrived on 2 November, Soba Fort which was on the route of No 3 Column, the paying off of Masai levies, Nandi prisoners, captured cattle, 'peace' talks and troops on the march.

THE
GOVERNOR-GENERAL'S
GOLD MEDAL

WILLIAM REID

Battalion Sergeant-Major S F C Sweeny, *winner of the Governor-General's Gold Medal and the Sword of Honour at The Royal Military College, Kingston, Ontario, June 1912.*

NAM. neg no 54098

When in 1980 the National Army Museum purchased the Governor-General's Gold Medal of the Royal Military College, Kingston, Ontario[1] it acquired one of the rarest of all military distinctions, for a single award was made each year and the design varied according to who was then Governor-General of Canada.

In October 1911, Arthur William Patrick Albert, Duke of Connaught and Strathearn, Queen Victoria's third son, moved into Government House, Ottawa.[2] It is his portrait in profile, alongside that of his Duchess, which appears on the Kingston medal. The Duke entered the Royal Military Academy Woolwich in 1866 to undergo the military training common to all cadets. Two years later he received a commission in the Royal Engineers. After the School of Military Engineering at Chatham he transferred to the Royal Artillery and then, in 1869, to the 1st Battalion, the Rifle Brigade in Montreal. He told his mother, 'The more I visit Canada the more I like and admire the people. They are a state of fine, honest, free-thinking but loyal Englishmen'. Loyal they undoubtedly were, but Canada was restless and exasperated with the home Government, and the Duke was to see action against the Fenians before returning to Woolwich after 'a very happy and interesting year'.

The Governor-General's Gold Medal, signed F. BOWCHER F 1911, Reverse, showing the arms of the Duke of Connaught viz The Royal Arms differenced by a label of three points, the centre point charged with St George's Cross, the other points with a fleur de lys. The rim is engraved: B.S. MAJ S.F.C. SWEENEY (sic) ROYAL MILITARY COLLEGE 1912.

Diameter 51mm, Weight 110.63 grams

NAM. 8006-61

His progression through the higher ranks of the Army was steady. He became a lieutenant-general in 1889 while serving in India and in 1893 was promoted general and appointed to the Aldershot Command. He became a Field Marshal in 1903. As Governor-General of Canada from 1911 to 1916 he renewed the affection he had felt for the Canadians ever since he had been quartered among them as a subaltern. It was this appointment that led to his distinguished features appearing on the medal awarded to Kingston's outstanding cadet for 1912, Battalion Sergeant-Major Sedley Fleming Campbell Sweeny.

Sweeny, 'Ben' to his friends and family, was from boyhood a scholar and an outstanding sportsman. Born in Vancouver on 9 January 1891, he played in the Haileybury 1st XV in the 1907-08 season. He also shot in the school VIII and held the rank of cadet lieutenant in the Corps. He joined the Royal Military College as cadet number 832 on 26 August 1909 at the age of eighteen years seven months, sixth in his entry and quite some way behind the first man in his marks. Just over six foot tall with light brown hair, fair complexion and grey eyes, the photograph taken at the end of his course shows him as a thoughtful young man. The June following his entry saw him promoted to lance-corporal, and a year later he was Battalion Sergeant-Major, the senior cadet. His sporting ability was recognised when he played for the college Canadian football team, Dominion champions in 1910 and 1911. After graduating with honours from Kingston on 20 June 1912, to be commissioned into the Royal Engineers a month later, he won British Army Rugby caps in 1912 and 1913. After the war he played for a Vancouver club without missing a season from 1920 to 1939. His son, Major Sedley Sweeny informed me that he and his father played together in a club match in 1935. Sweeny Snr was fit enough to go on playing rugby football until 1940 when, at the age of forty-nine, he captained a Canadian Army XV. He was also a fine oarsman and a first class shot.

Sporting prowess can help a man considerably, but Sweeny would not have won the Governor-General's Gold Medal had he not also been capable of achieving the highest standards in all he did at Kingston. The terms of his award are mentioned on a record board in Currie Building;

> 'Awarded to the Cadet who was 1st in general proficiency, i.e. conduct, discipline and intellectual and physical qualities combined as determined from the date of joining to that of graduation.

His all-round abilities were confirmed by the award of the College Sword of Honour as the cadet who best combined high standards in the academic, military and sporting aspects of his training. It is no surprise to learn that the Commandant, Colonel J H V Crowe, considered his character exemplary. Sweeny was fortunate to receive his prizes from the hands of the Governor-General himself on one of the Duke's visits to Kingston, an institution he was to inspect more than once during his term of office.

Sweeny began the First World War as a lieutenant in the Royal Engineers, and served with the BEF in 1914. He was promoted captain and acting major in 1917 when he commanded 219 Field Company, in which, incidentally, the writer's father served as a pioneer and then as a sapper. In the middle of 1918 he was posted to Murmansk, chosen perhaps on the supposition that a Canadian would understand the hazards of real winter.[3] A citation in *The London Gazette* of 3 June 1919 records that he was appointed an Officer of the Military Division of the Most Excellent Order of the British Empire 'for valuable services rendered in connection with Military Operations in *North Russia (Murmansk Command)*'. He was then a captain.

In the following year Sweeny was out of the regular Army, taking his family back to Vancouver, where his wife and he had been among the first native white children. He then held a reserve commission in the Seaforth Highlanders of Canada. The difficult, depressed years between the wars were not kind and attempts to establish himself as a civil engineer failed. In the words of his son, 'His trials ... would have broken lesser men'. At various times he held responsible positions including Safety Engineer to the Port of Vancouver, Development Engineer with Consolidated Mining in the North, and Chief Engineer of the British Columbia Highways Department, but he also suffered long periods of unemployment and was forced to take unskilled jobs to keep his family. But by 1933 he was on the staff of St George's School, Point Grey, BC, where he taught most subjects and, one suspects, derived great pleasure from training the school's oarsmen and Rugby footballers.

It would not be cynical to suggest that Sweeny may almost have welcomed the outbreak of the Second World War, for he had been a good soldier. Two years earlier, in 1937, he transferred to the Corps Reserve of Officers, and on 1 December 1939 he was placed on active service and promoted to major. The pay of his new rank may have eased his financial difficulties and allowed him to apply himself to those things he did best, which included the leadership of men. His new unit, where he served as relief battery commander, was the 56th

Heavy Battery, 5th (British Columbia) Coastal Brigade, Royal Canadian Artillery. Six months later he transferred to the 6th Field Company, Royal Canadian Engineers. It was while in command of that company that he was killed in an accident at Debert Camp, Nova Scotia on 22 November 1940.

It is difficult to imagine how a cadet of such potential, courageous, determined, and extremely fit, did not reach the highest ranks of the army, but his fault, if it can be called one, seems to have been a lack of personal ambition. Perhaps a desire to help others may have intruded upon the more immediate need to devote his energies to furthering his own advance. Even in the years between the two World Wars, when he faced acute personal hardship, he struggled to set up an adventure training college on an island in Vancouver Harbour. Had he succeeded, he may well have been remembered as the originator of a movement that led to the formation of Atlantic College, but the Depression was hardly the time to raise money for altruistic causes. In a letter written on his son's 22nd birthday, 29 November 1939, he included two definitions which seem to underline the manner of man Sweeny was: 'Physical courage is the ability to think clearly under abnormal circumstances, and moral courage is the ability to act decently under the same circumstances'.

Sweeny's gold medal was designed and made by one of England's better-known medallists. Close to the double-portrait of the Duke and his Duchess on the obverse appears the inscription 'F. BOWCHER.F 1911'. Frank Bowcher (1864-1938) was a talented artist. He was a National Scholar at the National Art Training School, now the Royal College of Art, after which he spent six years in the studio of the sculptor E Onslow Ford RA. His interest in modern medallic art led him to seek the counsel of the best French practitioners, among them artists of the calibre of Chaplain and Roty.[4]

Bowcher was a creative and prolific medallist, if hardly an innovator. Linked to a genuine feeling for his medium was an outstanding technical competence that gave his portraits a reputation for realism. His more famous subjects included, among many others, Queen Victoria, for the Jubilee medal issued by Messrs Spink and Son of London, Robert Burns, Baden-Powell, and Lord Roberts. His *Absent-minded Beggar Medal* may have been the most popular representation of a poet's imaginary character ever sold. It has been implied that Frank Bowcher was employed as Engraver at the Royal Mint after the death of G W de Saulles in 1903,[5] but although he did undertake work for the Mint from time to time, Bowcher was never officially appointed to its staff. His most important official commission was the completion of de Saulles's unfinished designs for the Great Seal of Edward VII. Although no evidence has survived to confirm that the Governor-General's gold medals were made at the Royal Mint the dies used to strike them are preserved in the Royal Mint Museum.

NOTES
AND
FURTHER READING

CHAPTER 1
NOTES

1. M Girouard, *Life in the English Country House, a social and architectural history*, New Haven & London (1978), p9
2. J C Risk, *The History of the Order of the Bath and its insignia*, London (1972), pp18-20
3. *Morning Post* (12 March 1812)

CHAPTER 2
NOTES

1. National Army Museum 8707-48-1, Adlercron's Journal 1754-58
2. *Dictionary of National Biography*, Vol XIV, p496
3. National Army Museum 8711-116-2, Gomm Papers
4. P Napier, *Raven Castle, Charles Napier in India 1844-1851*, Salisbury (1991), pp208-11
5. National Army Museum 8711-116-50, Dalhousie to Gomm, 10 April 1852
6. National Army Museum 7101-23-27-69, Roberts Papers, Dufferin to Roberts 17 Feb 1882
7. B Robson, 'The Eden Commission and the reform of the Indian Army 1879-1895', *Journal of the Society for Army Historical Research*, Vol 60, 1982, pp4-13

FURTHER READING

The Army of India and its Evolution, Calcutta (1924)
T A Heathcote, *The Indian Army. The Garrison of British Imperial India, 1822-1922*, Newton Abbot (1974)
P Moon, *The British Conquest and Dominion of India*, London (1990)

CHAPTER 3
NOTES

1. James Andrew Broun Ramsay, tenth Earl and first Marquess of Dalhousie, Governor-General of India 1848-56.
2. J G Baird (ed.), *Private letters of the Marquess of Dalhousie*, Edinburgh (1910) in 'The Uniform of European and Native Troops in the British Service in India 1760-1860' by Captain Russell V Steele, *Journal of the Society for Army Historical Research* Vol XIII, 1934, pp 189-94

3.   National Army Museum 7707-32, 71st Highland Light Infantry c1864.

4.   National Army Museum 8403-38, 70th Foot c1839.

5.   National Army Museum 7905-24, 13th Foot, other ranks c1848.

6.   National Army Museum 5909-11-2, Royal Marine Light Infantry c1855.

7.   National Army Museum 9104-203-4, 2nd Madras Light Cavalry c1855.

8.   Horse Guards Circular 1 Sep 1856.

9.   Horse Guards Circular 2 Jan 1857.

10. National Army Museum 9111-35-2, 20th Madras Native Infantry 1857-59; National Army Museum 6612-36-8, 30th Bengal Native Infantry c1860; National Army Museum 6610-24-20, Army Medical Department c1881.

11. *Dress Regulations, India* 1891, Sec 1, p6.

12. National Army Museum 7402-52, Universal sealed pattern 1865-91.

13. General Order 65 1873.

14. National Army Museum 7403-96, Rifle Regiments, sealed pattern 1886.

15. National Army Museum 8006-115, Universal sealed pattern 1896.

16. National Army Museum 9009-66, Frock Serge B, Duke of Cambridge's Own (Middlesex Regiment), 8th (Territorial) Bn c1916.

17. National Army Museum 9111-35-1

18. General Order 71 1872

19. General Order 57 1874

20. General Order 94 1876

21. National Army Museum 8906-5, 17th Foot 1872-1881.

22. National Army Museum 7402-61, Infantry, sealed pattern 1896.

23. Army Order 260 Dec 1891

24. National Army Museum 7802-59, 17th Bengal Native Infantry 1884.

25. Sir Harry Burnett Lumsden 1821-96.

26. Major A C Whitehorne 'Khaki and Service Dress', *Journal of the Society for Army Historical Research* Vol XV, 1936, p181

27. Major William S R Hodson (1821-58), Commandant Corps of Guides 1853; raised Hodson's Horse 1857.

28. G H Hodson, *Twelve Years of a Soldier's Life in India*; Being Extracts from the letters of the late Major W S R Hodson, London (1859) in Capt R V Steele 'The Uniform of European and Native Troops in the British Service in India 1760-1860' *Journal of the Society for Army Historical Research* Vol XIII, 1934, pp189-94

29. Sir Patrick Cadell 'Beginnings of Khaki' *Journal of the Society for Army Historical Research* Vol XXXI, 1953, pp132-33

30. See note 28.

31. R J T Hills Note 397 *Journal of the Society for Army Historical Research* Vol XV, 1936, pp250-51

32. Major A C Whitehorne 'Khaki and Service Dress' *Journal of the Society for Army Historical Research* Vol XV, 1936, p181

33. Rev Percy Sumner 'Indian Mutiny Recollections of Bugler Johnson, 52nd Light Infantry' *Journal of the Society for Army Historical Research* Vol XX, 1941, p172

34. Proceedings of the Government of India, Military Department, May 1885, Consultation No 1517 in Major N P Dawnay 'The Origin and Development of the Gorget Patch' by *Journal of the Society for Army Historical Research* Vol XXIV, 1946, p74

35. National Army Museum 6208-6, 5th Regiment, Hyderabad Contingent c1885. Worn by General T T Turton.

36. R J T Hills Note 397, *Journal of the Society for Army Historical Research* Vol XV,1936, pp250-51

37. Memorandum 18 April 1868 'British Infantry on the day of the advance on Magdalawill wear khaki clothing' in Major A C Whitehorne 'Khaki and Service Dress', *Journal of the Society for Army Historical Research* Vol XV, 1936, p182

38. National Army Museum 8604-109, 1st Somersetshire Rifle Volunteers.

39. Field Marshal Sir Garnet Joseph Wolseley (1833-1913)

40. G B Keester 'British Naval and Military Operations in Egypt 1882' from reports of Ensign Charles C Rogers USN and Lieutenant-Commander Casper F Goodrich USN, *Journal of the Society for Army Historical Research* Vol XXXIX, 1961, pp44-48

41. E Fraser and L C Carr-Laughton, *The Royal Marine Artillery, 1804-1923*, London (1930)

42. Lieutenant-Commander C G Goodrich, *Report of the British Naval and Military Operations in Egypt, 1882*, Washington (1883). See note 40

43. 'Operations of the British Navy and Transport Service during the Egyptian Campaign 1882', *Proceedings of the United States Naval Institute* Vol VIII, No 4 Jan 1883. See note 40

44. National Army Museum 7402-62, Universal pattern invisible grey sealed pattern 1888-1904.

45. National Army Museum 7402-63

46. H P E Pereira, 'Early Khaki Uniform for Home and Foreign Service, *Journal of the Society for Army Historical Research* Vol XXXV, 1957, pp37-38

47. National Army Museum 9111-39

48. National Army Museum 7403-85, Waistcoat, khaki serge, Infantry Experimental issue approved 30 January 1884. Obsolete 21 June 1920.

49. Army Order no 83 1896

50. Army Order no 10 1902

51. Army Order no 1033 15 Dec 1902

CHAPTER 5
NOTES

1. Most of the biographical detail in this article comes from *The Life of the late General F R Chesney Colonel Commandant Royal Artillery D.C.L., F.R.S., F.R.G.S., ETC*, by his Wife and Daughter, edited by S Lane-Poole, London (1885)

2. *Reports on the Navigation of the Euphrates.* Submitted to Government by Captain Chesney, of the Royal Artillery, London (1833)

3. *The Expedition for the survey of the Rivers Euphrates and Tigris.* Carried on by order of the British Government in the years 1835, 1836, 1837. By Lt-Col Chesney, RA FRS FRGS, Colonel in Asia, Commander of the Expedition. Vols I and II, London (1850)

4. *Narrative of the Euphrates Expedition.* Carried on by Order of the British Government during the years

1835, 1836 and 1837. By General Francis Rawdon Chesney, Colonel Commandant, 14th Brigade Royal Artillery, DCL FRS FRGS, Commander of the Expedition, London (1868)

5.   *Observations on the Past and Present State of Firearms and on the Probable Effects in War of the New Musket.* With a proposition for Reorganizing the Royal Regiment of Artillery by a Subdivision into Battalions in each special arm of Garrison, Field and Horse Artillery, with Suggestions for Promoting its Efficiency. By Colonel Chesney, DCL FRS, Royal Artillery. London (1852)

6.   *The Russo-Turkish Campaigns of 1828 and 1829.* With a View of the Present State of Affairs in the East. By Colonel Chesney, RA DCL FRS, London & New York (1854)

7.   The archives of the Athenæum, 107 Pall Mall, London, SW1.

8.   National Army Museum 7903-74, 75

9.   *Military Reminiscences of the latter end of the 18th and the beginning of the 19th Centuries, by General A C Mercer*, manuscript in the Royal Artillery Institution: quoted by D Alastair Campbell, *The Dress of the Royal Artillery*, London (1971)

10. *Ibid.*

11. National Army Museum 9307-21-1 to -6. Uniform worn by Gen F R Chesney, Royal Regiment of Artillery, 1822-41.

CHAPTER 6
FURTHER READING

The Army Lists, London (various dates)

J B M Frederick, *Lineage Book of the British Army*, New York (revised edn. 1984)

Colonel Lloyd-Verney, *Records of the Infantry Militia Battalions of the County of Southampton*, London (1894)

Ernest J Martin 'The Cyclists Battalions and their Badges, 1888-1921', *Journal of the Society for Army Historical Research* Vol 22, 1943-1944, pp277-78

R Westlake, *The Rifle Volunteers*, Chippenham (1982)

R Westlake, *The Territorial Battalions; a Pictorial History 1859-1985*, New York and Tunbridge Wells (1986)

CHAPTER 7
NOTES

1.   Richard Caton Woodville *Random Recollections*, London (1914) p79; in 1927, suffering from depression, he committed suicide. Whether or not the latter part of his statement remains exactly true, it is hard to say, since there has been, at least up until the recent regimental re-organization in accordance with 'Options for Change', a small but flourishing practice in the depiction of recent and historic actions commissioned by regiments for their messes.

2.   Allan Ramsey Skelley, *The Victorian Army at Home*, Montreal & London (1977), *passim.*

3.   J M W Hichberger, *Images of the army. The Military in British Art 1815-1914*, Manchester (1988), pp1-3

4.   Oliver Millar, *The Queen's Pictures*, London (1977), p173 *et seq.*.

5.   Matthew Paul Lalumia, *Realism and Politics in Victorian Art of the Crimean War*, Michigan (1984), pp2-6, & 26

6.	The significance of these paintings has been widely discussed since the 1940's, most recently in David H Solkin, *Painting for Money, the Visual Arts and th Public Sphere in Eighteenth-Century England*, New Haven & London (1993). A succinct summary is to be found in in Lalumia, *op. cit.*, pp16-23. The death of Admiral Lord Nelson at the Battle of Trafalger in 1805 created the perfect subject for the translation of this treatment into a naval idiom, and it was tackled by many artists, including Benjamin West, Arthur William Devis and Mather Brown. The 'battle-cum-group portrait' was also a new departure in naval painting, which had been developing in Britain under the aegis of maritime painting with the work of artists such as Dominic Serres, Nicholas Pocock, Thomas Whitcock and Thomas Luny, and owed its ancestry to the genre of seascape developed by Dutch painters of the seventeenth century.

7.	For example, Robert Home's *Death of Col Moorehouse at the Siege of Bangalore, 1791* (NAM.7107-5). The composition of such works had direct antecedent in painting in the subject of the Deposition of Christ, which would have been obvious to contemporary spectators, and additionally imbued these pictures with reverential overtones.

8.	The most famous exposition of these ideas is to be found in Sir Joshua Reynolds' *Discourses on Art*, for which, among various editions available, see that edited by Robert R Wark, New Haven & London (1975). Contemporary and subsequent discussion of these theories are explored in John Barrell, *The Political Theory of Painting from Reynolds to Hazlitt*, New Haven & London (1986)

9.	*The Times* 3 February 1816 p3, quoted in Lalumia, *op. cit.*, pp27-28

10.	A list of paintings and Jones's career as a military artist is described in Peter Harrington, 'The Battle Paintings of George Jones RA (1786- 1869)', *Journal of the Society for Army Historical Research*, Vol LXVII, 1989 pp239-52

11.	Hichberger, *op. cit.*, pp42-47

12.	J M W Hichberger 'Democratising Glory? The Victoria Cross Paintings of Louis Desanges', *The Oxford Art Journal*, 7:2, 1985 pp42-51

13.	It has been suggested that Elizabeth Thompson's marriage to William Butler in 1877 was a significant factor in her decline in popularity; see Paul Usherwood, 'Elizabeth Thompson Butler: The Consequences of Marriage' *Women's Art Journal*, 9, 1 (1988)

14.	Pat Hodgson, *The War Illustrators*, London (1977); R J Wilkinson-Latham, *From our special correspondent. Victorian war correspondents and their campaigns*, London (1979)

15.	Field Marshal Lord Wolseley, *The Story of a Soldier's Life*, London (1903)

CHAPTER 8
NOTES

1.	The Duke's lack of interest in his food caused his chef Felix to tender his resignation: 'I serve him a dinner which would make Ude or Francatelli burst with envy, and he says - nothing; I go out and leave him a dinner badly dressed by the cookmaid, and he says - nothing'; H Morris, *Portrait of a Chef*, Cambridge (1938), p7

2.	G R St Aubyn, 'Wellington: The Man' in M Howard (ed.), *Wellington Studies*, Aldershot (1959), p14

3.	C Firth, *Cromwell's Army*, London (1902); C Carlton, *Going to the Wars: The Experience of the British Civil Wars, 1638-1651*, London (1992); J Childs, *The Army of Charles II*, London (1976); R E Scouller,

The Armies of Queen Anne, Oxford (1966).

4.   E Mole, *A King's Hussar*, London (1893), p155

5.   A Schaumann, *On the Road with Wellington*, London (1924), p38

6.   *Standing Orders*, 45th Regt (1841), p74

7.   Mole, *op. cit.*, p29

8.   E Blaze, quoted in Sir C J Napier, *Lights and Shades of Military Life*, London (1850), p257

9.   *Report from the Select Committee on Military Organisation*, London (1860), p2866

10.   *Report from the Select Committee on the Army before Sebastopol*, London (1855), p3429

11.   Nicholas Bentley (ed.), *Russell's Despatches from the Crimea*, London (1966), p157

12.   Soyer's recipe for cooking salt meat for 50 men:

      1.   Put 50lbs of meat in the boiler

      2.   Fill with water, and let it soak all night

      3.   Next morning wash the meat well

      4.   Fill with fresh water, and boil gently three hours

      PS.   Skim off the fat, which, when cold, is an excellent substitute for butter.

      A Soyer, *Soyer's Culinary Campaign*, London (1857), p405

13.   *Ibid.*, p585

14.   Later Sir Robert (1797-1882). In his career at Edinburgh Christison held the chairs of medical jurisprudence, *materia medica* and therapeutics, and clinical medicine. At the age of eighty he still held a captaincy in the University Rifle Volunteers.

15.   *Report of the Army Sanitary Commission*, London (1857-58), ppxxii-xxiii.

16.   (1810-1861) Secretary at War 1845, 1852-55, Secretary for War 1859-60.

17.   *Report from the Select Committee on Military Organisation*, London (1860) 28/3, 2878

18.   *Ibid.*, 2965

19.   *Ibid.*, 2886

20.   W H Sykes 'Comparison of the Organisation and Cost in detail of the English and French Armies', *Journal of the Statistical Society*, Vol. 27 March 1864, p13

21.   Colonel Sir G J Wolseley, *The Soldier's Pocket-Book for Field Service*, London (1871), p45

22.   National Army Museum, 7906-138 War Office Memorandum 1891

23.   *Report on the Account of Army Expenditure*, London (1888-89), p79

24.   *Journal of the Royal United Service Institution*, Vol. xxxv, 1891, p239

25.   *JRUSI*, Vol xxxv, 1891, p241

26.   *Committee ... on the Terms and Conditions of Service in the Army*, London (1892) 10171

27.   *The Queen's Regulations and Orders for the Army*, London (1892), p190

28.   *Terms and Conditions of Service in the Army*, London (1892), p3569

29.   *Op. cit.*, p253

CHAPTER 9

NOTES

1.   Maj-Gen Sir Henry Havelock KCB (1795-1857) died while commanding the garrison at Lucknow.

2.   Gen Lord William Henry Cavendish Bentinck GCB GCH MP (1774-1839), second son of the

3rd Duke of Portland. Governor-General of Bengal 1827-33, first Governor-General of India 1833-35. Colonel, 11th Regiment of (Light) Dragoons 1813-39. Details of the influence which Bentinck exerted to have Havelock appointed to the adjutancy of the 13th are contained in J C Pollock, *Way to Glory: The Life of Havelock of Lucknow*, London (1957), pp43-44

3. That of the 26th (or the Cameronian) Regiment had 159 members out of an average regimental strength of 736 in 1838 and 185 out of 728 in 1839 (figures from a manuscript appendix in an annotated copy of the anonymous *Some Account of the Twenty-Sixth or Cameronian Regiment*, London (1828))

4. Anonymous (Staff Sergeant Percival), *Camp and Barrack-Room: or, The British Army as it is*, London (1846)

5. Capt John Buckley, an officer in the 92nd (Highland) Regiment of Foot 1819-40. Barrack-Master at Devonport 1855-56 and at Chatham 1856-70.

6. Public Record Office WO32/6212, Buckley to the Brigade Major, Chatham, 4 Apr 1856

7. PRO.WO32/7207. All references to the Report are from this original source.

8. Capt Pilkington Jackson, Royal Artillery 1854-68.

9. Public Houses were licensed to sell spirits, beer houses licensed only to sell beer.

10. Lt-Gen Sir John Pennefather KCB (1800-72); later General and GCB.

11. The information contained in these two paragraphs concerning temperance and total abstinence in the rifle volunteer movement has been largely drawn from articles on the subject written by Mr W J Steeple and published in the *Bulletin of the Military Historical Society*, Vols XVI (1965) and XVIII (1967)

12. India Office Library and Records L/MIL/7/9982 The Rev R A Norman to Sir James Outram Bt. GCB

13. Field Marshal Lord Strathnairn GCB GCSI (1801-85). As Gen Sir Hugh Rose he was Commander-in-Chief, India, from 1860 until 1865.

14. J C Marshman, *Memoirs of Major-General Sir Henry Havelock KCB*, London (1860) pp368-70

15. IOR. L/MIL/7/9983. All references to the growth of the Soldiers' Total Abstinence Association are derived from documents under this reference.

16. The Rev. J G Gregson, *Through the Khyber Pass to Sherpore Camp, Cabul. An account of Temperance Work among our Soldiers in the Cabul Field Force*, London (1883)

17. Gen the Lord Wolseley of Cairo GCB GCMG; later Field Marshal The Viscount Wolseley KP GCB OM GCMG (1833-1913)

18. Maj-Gen Sir Frederick Roberts Bt VC GCB CIE; later Field Marshal The Earl Roberts of Kandahar, Pretoria and Waterford VC KG KP GCB OM GCSI GCIE VD (1832-1914)

19. Gen Sir F Roberts *Correspondence with India while Commander-in-Chief in Madras 1881-85*, Simla (1890), pp136-37

20. Gen Sir F Roberts *Speeches 1878 to 1893* (1895) No 59 (1884)

21. Roberts, *op. cit.*, No 76 (1888)

22. Gen Sir F Roberts *Correspondence with the Viceroy of India (Marquess of Lansdowne) 1888-1893*, Calcutta (1893), p52

23. Field Marshal Sir George White VC (1835-1912), Commander-in-Chief, India, 1893-98.

CHAPTER 10

NOTES

1. India Office Records: L/MIL/17/2/433, Bengal Regulations 1812, p262, quoting 'GOCF 4th May 1810'. Unpublished Crown-copyright material in the India Office Records reproduced/ transcribed in this publication appears by permission of the Controller of Her Majesty's Stationery Office.

2. The Court of Directors of the East India Company had announced its intention to adopt percussion ignition in a despatch dated 2 September 1840 (IOR: L/MIL/3/2081, Mil Letter to Bengal/India No.58) which would have arrived at Calcutta in early 1841.

3. IOR. L/MIL/17/2/433, Bengal Regulations 1812, pp262, 266, confirmed by references in *Reports* below.

4. H L Blackmore, *British Military Firearms 1650-1850*, London (1961) p213, quoting also *Queen's Regulations 1844*.

5. IOR. L/MIL/17/2/412, p152, GOGG 13 Dec 1828

6. Sir Jasper Nicolls (1778-1849); Ensign HM 45th Regt 1793; Lt-Gen 1839; C-in-C India 1839-43.

7. Sir Joseph Thackwell (1781-1859); Cornet (Worcestershire Fencible Cavalry) 1798; 15th Light Dragoons 1800; served in the Peninsula and lost his left arm at Waterloo; commanded 3rd (King's Own) Light Dragoons from 1837; Maj-Gen 9 Nov 1846 (see D*ictionary of National Biography*, 'Thackwell, Joseph').

8. IOR. P/37/15, India Military Proceedings 23 Sep 1840, Nos. 23-24

9. George Eden GCB, Earl of Auckland (1784-1849); Governor-General of India 1836-42.

10. IOR. P/37/15, IMP 23 Sep 1840 No. 25

11. Sir William Casement KCB (1778-1844); Cadet 1795; Maj-Gen 10 Jan 1837; Military Secretary to the Government of India and Member of the Supreme Council, 17 Jun 1839.

12. IOR. L/MIL/3/319, Encls to No. 63 from Bengal/India 6 May 1841

13. IOR. L/MIL/3/326, Encls to Mil Letter from Bengal/India No. 135 dated 11/13 Oct 1841, referred to hereafter as *Reports*. There are two copies of the reports in this volume; the second set has been used, as it is paginated.

14. James MacKenzie (1804-59); Cadet 1820; Capt 5 Oct 1836; Bt-Col 28 Nov 1854; Commandant 6th Bengal Irregular Cavalry 1840 to 1846.

15. *Reports*, p402

16. Sir James Rutherford Lumley KCB (1773-1846); Cadet 1794; Maj-Gen 10 Jan 1837; Adjutant-General of the Army from 28 Nov 1833 to 28 Feb 1846; served continuously for 50 years in India.

17. John Sutherland (1792-1848); Bombay Army; Cornet 1810; Lt-Col 28 Feb 1838. Author of *Sketches of the relations subsisting between the British Government in India and the different Native States* (1833); *Memoir on the Kaffirs, Hottentots and Bosjimans of South Africa* (1847)

18. *Reports*, p268

19. Robert Ewbank Chambers (1790-1842); Cadet 1804; Lt-Col 10 Oct 1836; killed in action, Jagdalak Pass, during retreat from Kabul, 12 Jan 1842.

20. *Reports*, p209

21. James Blair (1792-1847); Cadet 1809; Commandant 3rd (or Blair's) Local Horse, 1823; Lt-Col 2 Dec 1838; served with the Nizam's Army from 1835, later commanding the Nizam's Cavalry Division with rank of Brigadier.

22. *Reports*, pp185-86

23. IOR. L/MIL/17/2/412, Index to Bengal Standing Orders etc. 1816-30, p61

24. *Reports*, p129

25. *Ibid*, pp185-86

26. *Ibid*, p401

27. Charles Newbery (1805-43); Cadet 1820; Maj 23 Dec 1839.

28. *Reports*, p384

29. IOR. L/MIL/3/2081, Military Despatch to Bengal and India No. 49 dated 16 Jun 1841

30. IOR. L/MIL/3/422, No. 22 of 21 Mar 1848, referring to GOCC dated 27 Sep 1847

31. IOR. L/MIL/3/523, Encls to Mil Letter from Bengal/India No. 144 of 3 Aug 1852

32. IOR. Letter to Bengal/India No. 157 of 1 Dec 1854

33. IOR. P/49/37 paras 567-72

CHAPTER 11

NOTES

1. Previously a Mention in Despatches was the only form of recognition for gallantry extended to officers and other ranks alike, and this carried no medal, or visible proof until the introduction of bronze oakleaf emblems in the First World War.

2. Further awards were gazetted during 1857, making the total number for the Crimea 111.

3. Public Record Office WO 98/1

4. The Warrant instituting the Cross actually described it as a 'Maltese Cross'. M J Crook, *The Evolution of the Victoria Cross*, Tunbridge Wells (1975), p309 further discusses the heraldic terms used to describe the shape of the Cross.

5. *Ibid.*, p29

6. PRO.WO 32/7345

7. PRO.WO 32/7370

8. PRO.WO 32/7397

9. PRO.WO 32/3443

10. Crook, *op. cit.*, pp289-90

11. Figures given by P E Abbott and J M A Tamplin, *British Gallantry Awards*, London (1981), p293

FURTHER READING

GENERAL

P E Abbott and J M A Tamplin, *British Gallantry Awards*, London (1981)

The Register of the Victoria Cross, Cheltenham (1988)

O'Moore Creagh and E M Humphris, *The VC and DSO* Vol 1, London (1924)

Brig Sir John Smyth, *The Story of the Victoria Cross*, London (1924)

M J Crook, *The Evolution of the Victoria Cross*, Tonbridge Wells (1975)

James W Bancroft, *The VC Roll of Honour*, Manchester (1989)

C E Lucas Phillips, *Victoria Cross Battles of the 2nd World War*, London (1973)

D Pillinger and A Staunton, *Victoria Cross Locator*, Maidenhead (1991)

Ian Robertson, ' "The Merit of Conspicuous Bravery"- Essex-born Victoria Cross Winners 1856-1914', in
K Neale (ed.) *Essex Heritage: Essays presented to Sir William Addison as a tribute to his life and work for Essex history and literature*, Oxford (1992), pp303-24

CHAPTER 12
NOTES

1. Anonymous, *Inside Sebastopol and Experiences in Camp being the narrative of a journey to the Ruins of Sebastopol by way of Gibraltar, Malta and Constantinople, and back by way of Turkey, Italy and France; accomplished in the Autumn and Winter of 1855*, London (1856), p196.
2. Col F Campbell, *Letters from Camp to his Relatives during the Siege of Sebastopol*, London (1894), p357
3. *Ibid.*, pp357-58
4. The photographs illustrated are drawn from National Army Museum 8011-27 but other examples of Robertson's work are to be found in the Museum's Collections.
5. National Army Museum 8604-101
6. *Dictionary of National Biography 1922-1930*, London (1953), pp765-67
7. Sir E Colebrook, *Journal of Two Visits to the Crimea in the Autumns of 1854 and 1855*, London (1856), pp100, 116

CHAPTER 13
NOTES

1. E T Evans, *Records of the 3rd Middlesex Rifle Volunteers and of the various Corps which formed the Second and Sixth Middlesex Administrative Battalions to which it is prefixed a general account of the Volunteer Forces of the United Kingdom compiled from official and private sources from 1794 to 1884*, London (1885)
2. The book by Ian F W Beckett, *Riflemen Form: A Study of the Rifle Volunteer Movement 1859-1908*, Aldershot (1982), is essential reading and should be supplemented by Chapter 6 (The Volunteer Triumphant) in the same author's *The Amateur Military Tradition 1558-1945*, Manchester (1991). Beckett's research is indispensable to any student of the Volunteer Movement. As it does not appear either that Evans' book is widely known or that the former Middlesex Regiment Archives have hitherto been drawn upon, it is hoped that this paper will supplement, rather than duplicate, what is at present easily accessible in print.
3. The organizational changes are of considerable complexity and the most helpful guide is Ray Westlake, *The Rifle Volunteers: The History of the Rifle Volunteers 1859-1908*, Chippenham (1982)

CHAPTER 14
NOTES

1. James Belich, *The New Zealand Wars and the Victorian Interpretation of Racial Conflict*, Auckland (1986), *passim.*
2. Extract from Despatch from the Rt Hon Earl Granville KG to Governor Sir G F Bowen KCMG, dated 2 Oct 1869. Appendix to the *Journals of the House of Representatives of New Zealand*, 1870; A No. 1A, p8

3. See J Roberts, The New Zealand Cross, *Orders and Medals Research Society Journal*, (December 1966), pp57-61

4. J Cowan, *The New Zealand Wars*, Wellington (1922) Vol. II, pp411-12, 426

CHAPTER 15
NOTES

1. *Journal of the Society for Army Historical Research*, Vol XXXVIII, 1960, p43

2. A R Savile, 'Military Cycling' *Journal of the Royal United Service Institution*, Vol 32, 1888-89, pp731-55

3. *Reports of Volunteer Cycling Committee*, PRO. WO 33 49 A160, 12 Mar, 29 May 1888

4. *London Gazette*, 24 Feb 1888, p1228

5. A R Savile, *art. cit. passim*

6. J Cook Wilson, *A Manual of Cyclist Drill for the Use of the Cyclist Section of the Oxford University Rifle Volunteer Corps*, Oxford (1889) *passim*

7. *The Drill of a Cyclist - Infantry Section*, London (1890)

8. Brig-Gen Viscount Melgund, Capt Eustace Balfour, 'The Best Mounted Arm for the Volunteers', *The United Service Magazine*, Vol 1 (New Series), 1890, pp305-40

9. J B Lloyd, *One Thousand Miles with the CIV*, London (1901), p50

10. *Royal Commission on the War in South Africa*, Vol II, London (1903), p483

11. H Baker, *The Territorial Force. A Manual of its Law, Organisation and Administration*, London (1909), p76

12. *Territorial Force. War Establishments (Provisional) for 1908-1909*, London (1908), pp68-71

13. M Caidin & J Barbree, *Bicycles in War*, New York (1974), pp127-136

CHAPTER 16
NOTES

1. 'Committee to Inquire into the Effects on the health of the Present System of carrying the Accoutrements, Ammunition and Kit of the Infantry Soldier and the Drill &etc of Recruits' (later also called the 'Knapsack Committee'). Four Reports plus a Supplement produced as Confidential Papers between 1865 and 1869.

2. 'Committee on Infantry Equipment'. Two Reports issued as Confidential Paper in 1880.

3. 'Royal Commission on the War in South Africa'. Published as a Command Paper (Cd 1791) in 1903.

CHAPTER 17
NOTES

1. A R Godwin-Austen, *The Staff and the Staff College*, London (1927), p198

2. A F Lendy, Patent No 84, 1865. See Abridgement Class Philosophical Instruments, entered under the indexes of surveying instruments; angle-measuring instruments; compasses, magnetic; and levels.

3. W H Richards, *Textbook of Military Topography*, London (1888), pp159-60. Compare *Textbook of Military Topography, Part I*, London (1898), pp170-76; *Manual of Field Sketching & Reconnaissance*, London (1904), pp70-72; and *Manual of Mapreading & Field Sketching*, London (1921), pp128-30. The *Manual of Mapreading, Photo Reading and Field Sketching* of 1929 does not mention sketching boards.

4.   Godwin-Austen, *op. cit.*, p199

5.   *Ibid*, pp210-11

6.   W W C Verner, *Sketches in the Soudan*, London, 1st Edition (1885) 2nd Edition (1886); the latter included a four-page list of subscribers.

7.   W W C Verner, *Rapid Field Sketching and Reconnaissance*, London (1889), p3

8.   Godwin-Austen, *op. cit.*, p199

9.   Verner, *op. cit.*, p43

10.   Richards, *op. cit.*, p159

11.   H A Sawyer, 'The "Field-Sketching" Board: How to Use It', *Journal of the United Service Institution of India* Vol 15 No 69 (1887), pp442-49

12.   Sawyer, *op. cit.*, pp448-49

13.   W W C Verner, Patent No 4198, 1887. Abridgement Class Philosophical Instruments, entered under the indexes for scales and protractors; clinometers; compasses, magnetic.

14.   Verner, *op. cit.*, 1889, pp9-10

15.   W W C Verner, Patent No 22, 128, 1891. Abridgement Class Philosophical Instruments, indexed under Sketching Boards

16.   Science Museum Inventory No 1986-607.

17.   H Shute, Patent No 2937, 1891. Abridgement Class Philosophical Instruments, indexed under Sketching Boards

18.   J O Mennie, Patent No 6609, 1891. Abridgement Class Philosophical Instruments, indexed under Sketching Boards

19.   S S Lawrence, Patent No 20495, 1899. Abridgement Class Philosophical Instruments, indexed under Sketching Boards, Military

20.   J W Mander, Patent No 13508, 1901. Indexed under Philosophical Instruments, sketching boards

21.   D V Smith, Patent No 3710, 1906. Indexed under Philosophical Instruments, sketching boards

22.   G S Smith, Patent No 18481, 1908. Indexed under Philosophical Instruments, sketching boards

23.   G F Hodgson, Patent No 17738, 1909. Indexed under Philosophical Instruments, sketching boards and plane tables

24.   *Catalogue*, K Edition, J H Steward Ltd, 1904, p25

25.   *Catalogue*, P Edition, 1910, p52

CHAPTER 18
FURTHER READING

The Last Military Expedition in Sierra Leone: or British soldiers and West African Native Warriors by 'an Africanised Englishman', Manchester (nd)

C Braithwaite Wallis, *The Advance of our West African Empire*, London (1903)

Col A Haywood, *The History of the Royal West African Frontier Force*, Part 1, Aldershot (1964)

Correspondence relating to the disturbances in the Sierra Leone Protectorate, 1898, Colonial Office: African (West) No 533, July 1899 and No 587, June 1901

CHAPTER 19

NOTES

1.   *The Queen's Regulations and Orders for the Army 1892*, London (1892), pp568-82 (returns) 583-619 (books)

2.   *Ibid.*, pp584-87

3.   *Ibid.*, pp590-601

4.   *Ibid.*, pp603-04

5.   *Ibid.*, p604

6.   *Ibid.*, pp588-89

7.   G C Swiney, *Historical Records of the 32nd (Cornwall) Light Infantry, now the 1st Battalion Duke of Cornwall's L.I.*, London & Devonport (1893), pp46-47

8.   N C E Kenrick, *The Story of the Wiltshire Regiment (Duke of Edinburgh's). The 62nd and 99th Foot (1756-1959)*, Aldershot (1963), p54

9.   *Militia Regulations Made by the Secretary-at-War in pursuance of The Act 15 & 16 Vict. Cap 50; Dated, War Office, 15th July 1853.* Presented to Parliament and ordered to be printed 29 July 1853, pp52-53, 57-63

10.   *Ibid.*, p5

11.   *Regulations for the Militia 1894*, London (1894), pp69-70

12.   Public Record Office WO68/450-55

13.   PRO.WO68/158-72, 441-44. Information on the material held at the Light Infantry Office, Taunton, derived from an unpublished list at the National Army Museum.

14.   PRO.WO68/139. Information on material in the Devon Regiment Museum derived from an unpublished list at the National Army Museum.

15.   *Op. cit.*, p5

16.   *Regulations for the Volunteer Force. War Office, 1881*, London (1881), pp168-72

17.   *Ibid.*, p23

18.   *Ibid.*, p72

19.   Cumbria Record Office, Carlisle, DB/69/47

20.   Gloucestershire Record Office, deposited by Crossman and Thurstons, Solicitors - Royal Commission on Historical Manuscripts, National Register of Archives Report 24231

21.   *Cheshire Record Office and Chester Diocesan Record Office*, Chester, nd, 1986, p11

22.   J Cox & T Padfield, *Tracing your Ancestors in the Public Record Office*, London (1981), p30

23.   *Yeomanry Regulations: being an abridgement of the Regulations for the Formations and Movements of the Cavalry, adopted to the use of Yeomanry Corps; ...1851*, London (1853), pp214-18

24.   *Regulations for the Yeomanry Cavalry, War Office, 1894*, London (1894), pp31, 67-68, 71, 85, 92-94

25.   These observations are based on data in the National Register of Archives early in 1987.

26.   This issue is discussed in a memorandum to the Deputy Accountant General of Feb 1889, PRO.WO32/6171 which also contains other papers of relevance to this study on the 'Weeding of Official Papers'.

CHAPTER 20
NOTES

1. National Army Museum 7305-42. Album of photographs compiled by Lt Hon E D Loch

2. The British component of Kitchener's force was as follows:

    INFANTRY

    1st Brigade - 1st Royal Warwickshire Regiment; 1st Lincolnshire Regiment; 1st Seaforth Highlanders; 1st Q.O. Cameron Highlanders; six maxims with detachment 16th Co., Eastern Division, Garrison Artillery. 2nd Brigade - 1st Grenadier Guards; 1st Northumberland Fusiliers; 2nd Lancashire Fusiliers; 2nd Rifle Brigade; four maxims with detachment 1st Royal Irish Fusiliers.

    CAVALRY

    21st Lancers

    ARTILLERY

    32nd Field Battery, R.A.; 37th Field Battery, R.A., with 5in. howitzers; detachment 16 Co. Eastern Division, Garrison Artillery, with two x 40-pounders; Detachment Royal Engineers; detachment R.A.M.C..

3. *The Household Brigade Magazine*, Vol. 1, 1898, p702
4. *Ibid.*, p746
5. *Ibid.*, p747
6. *Ibid.*, p749
7. *Ibid.*, p751
8. National Army Museum 7009-11; photographs collected by Lt Hon E D Loch.

CHAPTER 21
NOTES

1. 'Steam Chariots of War', *The United Service Journal and Naval and Military Magazine*, 1832
2. *Report on the Manœuvres held in the Neighbourhood of Salisbury, August and September 1898*, London (1899)
3. Bennet Burleigh, *The Natal Campaign*, London (1900), p281
4. Lt-Col Otfried Layriz, translated by R B Marston, *Mechanical Traction in War for Road Transport*, London (1900)
5. National Army Museum 7405-58-1, p25; scrapbook of newspaper cuttings relating to the activities of Col J L B Templer as Director of Steam and Road Transport during the South African War, 1899-1902.
6. *Report of His Majesty's Commissioners appointed to inquire into the military preparations and other matters connected with the War in South Africa*, London (1903), pp115-16

CHAPTER 22
FURTHER READING

GENERAL

Maj-Gen B P Hughes *Firepower: Weapons effectiveness on the battlefield, 1630-1850,* London (1974)

H Strachan, *From Waterloo to Balaclava: Tactics, Technology and the British Army 1815-54*, Cambridge (1985)

D Featherstone, *Weapons & Equipment of the Victorian Soldier*, Poole (1978)

SMALL ARMS

D W Bailey, *British Military Longarms 1715-1865*, London (1986)

H L Blackmore, *British Military Firearms 1650-1850*, London (1969)

C H Rhodes, *The British Soldiers Firearm 1850-1864*, London (1964)

I D Skennerton, *A Treatise on the Snider*, Margate, Australia (1977)

I D Skennerton, & B D Temple, *A Treatise on the British Military Martini*, Burbank, Australia (1983-89)

I D Skennerton, *The Lee Enfield Story*, London (1993)

D L Goldsmith, *The Devil's Paintbrush: Sir Hiram Maxim's Gun*, Toronto (1989)

AMMUNITION

I V Hogg, *The Illustrated Encyclopædia of Ammunition*, London (1985)

SWORDS

B Robson, *Swords of the British Army*, London (1975)

BAYONETS

I D Skennerton, & R Richardson, B*ritish & Commonwealth Bayonets*, Margate, Australia (1984)

ARTILLERY

O F G Hogg, *Artillery: its Origin, Heyday & Decline*, London (1970)

CHAPTER 23
NOTES

1.   Ministry of Defence Library, Colonial Office, African No 771. Correspondence 7 April 1905 to 8 June 1906 relating to Affairs in the East Africa Protectorate. 34514 No 40 Acting Commissioner Jackson to Mr Lyttleton.

2.   MOD Lib. Colonial Office, African No 771, Staff Diary, Nandi Field Force, p126

3.   Richard Meinertzhagen *Kenya Diary (1902-1906)*, London (1983), p241

4.   MOD Lib, Staff Diary, Nandi Field Force, p128

5.   Meinertzhagen *op. cit.*, p276

6.   *Loc. cit.*.

7.   *Ibid.*, p285

8.   National Army Museum 8407-1 to 3. Photograph albums compiled by Capt O Gamble.

9.   Public Record Office WO106/5992 East Africa Protectorate. King's African Rifles.

10.   *Ibid.*.

FURTHER READING

Lt-Col H Moyse-Bartlett, *The King's African Rifles. A Study in the Military History of East and Central Africa, 1890-1945*, Aldershot (1956)

'Bugle with Strings', *Army Quarterly* Vol 97, Jan 1969, pp223-34

M Cocker, *Richard Meinertzhagen; Soldier, Scientist and Spy*, London (1989)

National Army Museum 8007-31. Typescript of memorandum of the affair of 19th October at Ket Parak Hill and incidents arising from it, by Maj L H R Pope-Hennessy, 3rd King's African Rifles.

CHAPTER 24
NOTES

1.   National Army Museum 8002-62

2.   Maj-Gen Sir George Aston, *His Royal Highness the Duke of Connaught and Strathearn*, London (1929)

3.   Public Archives, Canada: Particulars of *Service, Canadian Armed Forces, Maj S F C Sweeny*.

4.   L Forrer, Biographical Dictionary of Medallists, London, revised edition of 1904. I, pp252-58

5.   Ibid. I, p253

CONTRIBUTORS

Michael Baldwin started his working life in the English Gun Trade, served with the Royal Air Force as an Armourer and, in 1955, joined the Kenya Police as Inspector of Smallarms. After the Colony became independent he joined the Weapons Department of the National Army Museum in 1969, where he was responsible for the development of the Firearms and Artillery Collections. In 1985 he was recruited by Sotheby's to head their British and European Arms and Armour Department. In 1991 he returned to the National Army Museum as Head of the Department of Weapons, Equipment and Vehicles. In 1991, with Keith Miller, he organized the Museum's Special Exhibition 'The Gunners' Favourite: The 25 Pounder Gun' and co-authored the accompanying publication.

Dr Peter Boyden is Head of the Museum's Department of Archives, Photographs, Film and Sound, and an historian of his native county of Essex. He is co-organizer with Sylvia Hopkins of the Permanent Exhibition 'The Victorian Soldier' and the author of *Tommy Atkins' Letters: The History of the British Army Postal Service from 1795*, National Army Museum, London (1990), which accompanied the Special Exhibition of the same name. He is also Honorary Secretary of the Society for Army Historical Research.

Aubrey Bowden studied military uniforms, equipment and related material from an early age. He later worked in the National Army Museum's Department of Uniform for eleven years before becoming the Militaria Consultant at Christie's, for whom he works in this country and sometimes abroad. His other interests include Dreadnought battleships and Court Dress.

David Harding served in the 10th Princess Mary's Own Gurkha Rifles, 1974-77 and the 2nd Battalion The Yorkshire Volunteers, 1977-78. He is Regimental Archivist of 10 GR and has been a contributor to the National Army Museum's annual publication *Army Museum*. He is currently completing a major study, *Firearms of the East India Company: Smallarms of the British Indian Armies, 1600-1856*.

John Harding is an Historian with the Ministry of Defence, carrying out in-house writing and research. He has previously worked at both the National Army Museum and the Imperial War Museum.

Marion Harding is a member of staff of the Museum's Department of Archives, Photographs, Film and Sound and has a particular knowledge of the Collection of Photographs. She has contributed a number of articles to the Museum's published *Annual Reports* and its successor annual publication *Army Museum*. She organized, and was co-author of the Special

Exhibition publication *Butterflies and Bayonets: The Soldier as Collector*, National Army Museum, London (1989).

Sylvia Hopkins is Head of the Department of Uniform, Badges and Medals and is based at the Museum's Out-station at Sandhurst. A member of the Museum staff for 30 years, in 1989-90 she was co-ordinator of the Permanent Exhibition 'The Road to Waterloo'. Together with Dr Peter Boyden she is co-organizer of the Permanent Exhibition 'The Victorian Soldier'. She is a member of the Army Dress Committee.

Jane Insley is Curator of Environmental Sciences at the Science Museum, London, where she has worked since 1974. Her interest in scientific instruments was consolidated by a five year spell cataloguing the microscope collections at the Science Museum and after a further period of general exhibition work she has written on topics as diverse as Sir George Everest's theodolites in India, audio-visual aids in museum displays, European instrument collections in several countries, and the representation of environmental topics in museums. Her most recent exhibition was on stratospheric ozone. She serves on the History Group Committee of the Royal Meteorological Society.

Ian Maine studied Economic History at Portsmouth Polytechnic. After graduating in 1988 he worked for the Royal Armouries and the National Army Museum in the Department of Weapons, Equipment and Vehicles. He is now a Curator in the Department of Uniform, Badges and Medals, National Army Museum.

Keith Miller is a Curator in the Department of Weapons, Equipment and Vehicles, National Army Museum. He was a major contributor to the publication *Touch and Go: The Battle for Crete 1941*, National Army Museum (1991), which accompanied the Special Exhibition of the same name. With Michael Baldwin he co-authored *The Gunners' Favourite: The 25-Pounder Gun, A Brief History* to accompany the Special Exhibition of the same name, which opened in December 1991.

William Reid CBE who began his distinguished museum career as Assistant Keeper of the Armouries, HM Tower of London, 1956-70, was Director of the National Army Museum, 1970-87. A Fellow of the Society of Antiquaries of London and Honorary Life President of the International Association of Museums of Arms and Military History, he has written widely on arms and armour, and other military subjects. His book *The Lore of Arms*, London (1976), has been published in seven languages. In retirement he is a trustee of a number of civil and military museums.

Ian Robertson attended The Queen's College, Oxford, where he read Modern History. He holds the Museums Diploma (Archaeology Option) and is a Fellow of the Museums Association. He served two terms as President of the Museums Association in 1986-87, and 1987-88. A past President of the Society for Post Medieval Archaeology, he served on the statutory Ancient Monuments Advisory Committee of English Heritage from 1984 until 1990. Coming from a family with strong regular Army connections, (the Victoria Cross of his late uncle, Brigadier Alfred Maurice Toye, is on display in the National Army Museum), Ian Robertson served in the 7th Bn Middlesex Regiment (DCO) TA, Oxford University OTC and 4th/5th Bn Essex Regiment TA as well as RARO. He has been Director of the National Army Museum since January 1988. He regards assisting Regimental and Corps Museums as an important part of his work and became a Trustee of the Royal Artillery Historical Trust on 4 April 1991.

David Smurthwaite is Assistant Director (Museum Services) at the National Army Museum and a member of the Council of the Society for Army Historical Research. He is the author of *The Ordnance Survey Complete Guide to the Battlefields of Britain* (1984 and later editions). He was co-author of *Project Korea: The British Soldier in Korea 1950-53*, National Army Museum (1988), which accompanied the Special Exhibition of the same name. He co-authored and edited the publication accompanying the Special Exhibition 'Touch and Go: The Battle For Crete 1941', National Army Museum (1991) and, most recently edited the publication accompanying the Permanent Exhibition 'The Forgotten War: The British Army in the Far East 1941-1945' (1992).

Lesley Smurthwaite is a senior Curator in the Department of Uniform, Badges and Medals at the National Army Museum, and an Associate of the Museums Association. She is the author of numerous articles on badges and medals which have appeared in the Museum's published *Annual Reports* and their successor publications *Army Museum* and *The National Army Museum Year Book*.

Jenny Spencer-Smith is Head of the Department of Fine and Decorative Art at the National Army Museum. An Associate of the Museum's Association, she organized the Special Exhibition, 'Lady Butler, Battle Artist' in 1987 and was co-author of the catalogue which is the standard work on the artist. Since then, she has been responsible for several Special Exhibitions at the Museum and their accompanying publications, including *Portraits for a King: The British Military Paintings of A-J Dubois Drahonet* (1990). She is currently working on a Special Exhibition devoted to the wartime work of the English artist Rex Whistler, who was killed in Normandy in 1944, and the accompanying publication, to be entitled *Rex Whistler's War*.

Stephen Wood has been keeper of the Scottish United Services Museum since 1983 and worked in the Department of Uniform, Badges and Medals at the National Army Museum from 1971 until 1983. The subject of his MA thesis (University of London, 1984) was the history of the Temperance Movement in the British Army. He is the author of *The Scottish Soldier*, Manchester (1987); *In the Finest Tradition*, Edinburgh (1988), and *The Auld Alliance*, Edinburgh (1989), as well as numerous articles on military history and military museums in a variety of journals.

INDEX

ILLUSTRATIONS ARE INDEXED IN BOLD TYPE